Horror in the Modernist Block

2
Introduction
Melanie Pocock

28
Horrid Objectivity
Joshua Comaroff

34
Laëtitia Badaut Haussmann

36
Simon & Tom Bloor

38
Ruth Claxton

40
Shezad Dawood

42
Ola Hassanain

44
Ho Tzu Nyen

46
Richard Hughes

50
Karim Kal

54
Kihlberg & Henry

56
Firenze Lai

60
Diego Marcon

62
Ismael Monticelli

64
NT

66
Amba Sayal-Bennett

70
Seher Shah

74
Monika Sosnowska

76
Maria Taniguchi

78
Abbas Zahedi

Texts by Lucy Mounfield and Melanie Pocock

81
Plum Pudding: Boot House
Stuart Whipps

94
Contributors

95
List of Works

Introduction

Melanie Pocock

Horror in the Modernist Block is an exhibition that explores the relationship between architectural modernism and horror. It takes Birmingham, a city renowned for its brutalist architecture, as a starting point, bringing together work by contemporary artists which unpacks the troubled legacy of modernist buildings around the world. Spanning film, photography, sculpture, installation, painting, drawing and printmaking, the exhibition connects motifs of horror with qualities of modernism, evoking the brutality and fear often associated with its design and materials. Horror tropes such as darkness, illusions in reflective glass, and feelings of being watched often surface in the history and identity of modernist architecture. The roots of these fears run deep, reinforced by the perceived failure of modernism to fulfil the utopian visions of architects,[1] and its links to social violence and authoritarian regimes.

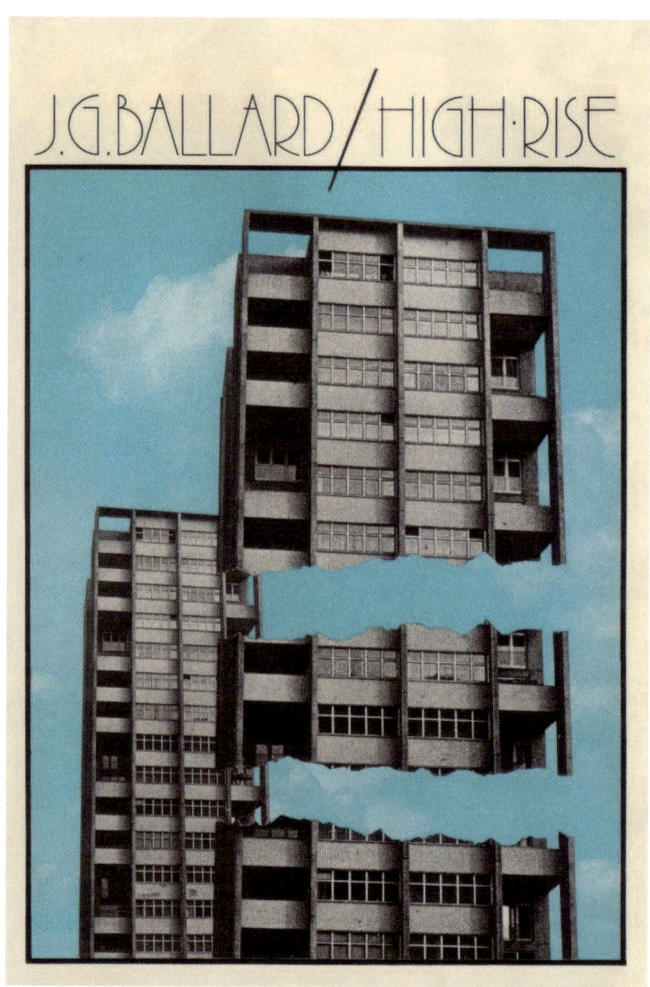

Fig. 1. Cover taken from *High-Rise* by J.G. Ballard, 1975, published by Jonathan Cape

1. Nathaniel Coleman, 'The Problematic of Architecture and Utopia', *Utopian Studies* 25, no.1 (2014): 3-4.

The focus of the exhibition on contemporary art reflects the critical role of the artistic imaginary in forming modernism's brutal image. Since the 1950s, high-rise towers, modernist buildings and estates have formed the backdrop to terrifying representations of dystopias. In J.G. Ballard's novel *High-Rise* (1975) (fig.1), the social hierarchy and compartmentalised topography of a modernist tower foster apathy and resentment among residents, who, emboldened by their isolation from wider society, spiral into anarchy.[2] In 1971, Thamesmead – an estate built in south-east London in the 1960s – became famous as the set to Stanley Kubrick's film adaptation of Anthony Burgess' book *A Clockwork Orange* (1962), which follows protagonist Alex and his gang of 'droogs' as they engage in wanton violence under the watch of a totalitarian state.[3] Such chilling tales are not limited to British culture: in Italy, Bernardo Bertolucci's film *The Conformist* (1970) situates the beginning of Alberto Moravia's original story of a repressed bureaucrat in buildings of the EUR, a district in Rome built in the 1930s as a homage to Benito Mussolini's fascist regime.[4] In Brazil, architect Oscar Niemeyer turned to painting to express his horror at the military coup in 1964, through compositions that depict the modernist buildings he designed for the city of Brasília as dismembered ruins (fig.2).

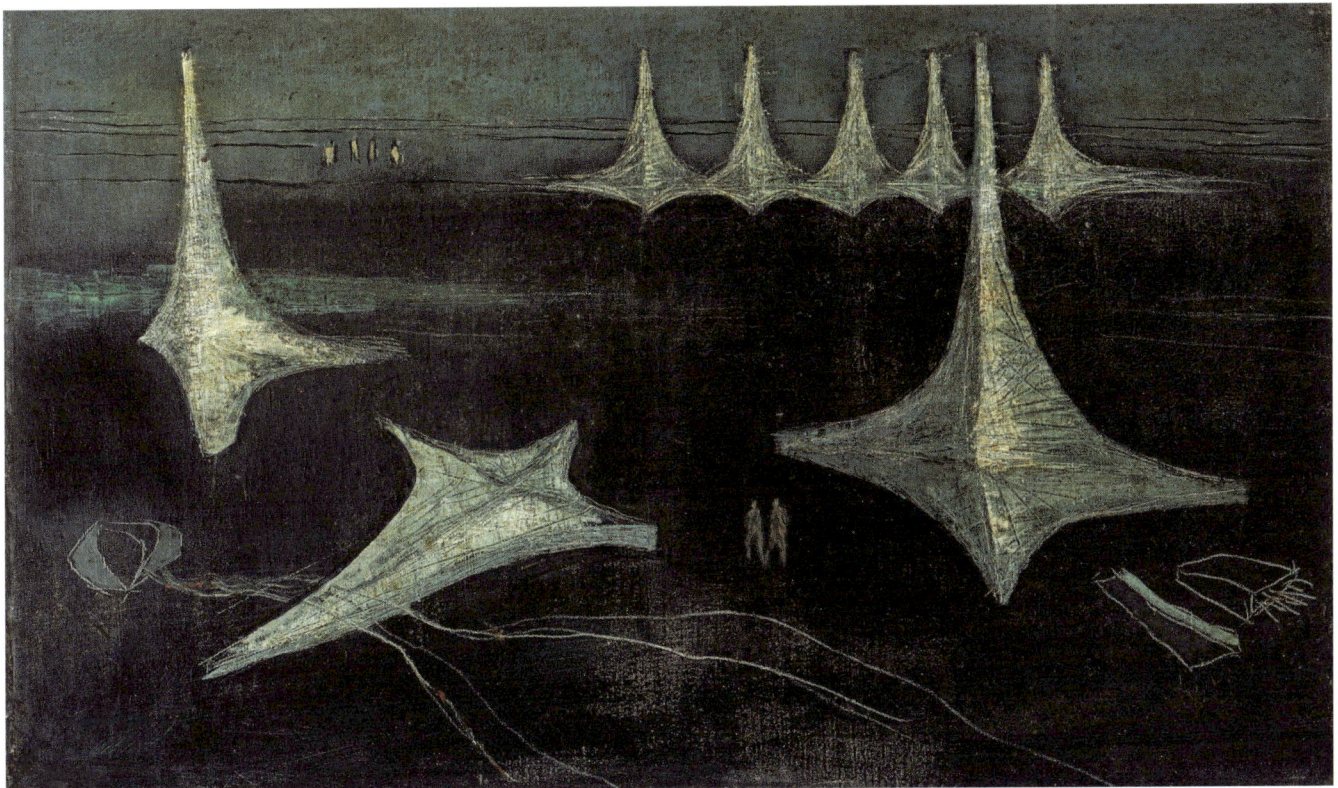

Fig. 2. Oscar Niemeyer, *Ruínas de Brasília* (Brasília ruins), 1964, oil on canvas, 46 × 77 cm

2. J.G. Ballard, *High Rise*, (Plymouth: Firebird Distributing, 1975).

3. *A Clockwork Orange*, directed by Stanley Kubrick (Warner Bros, 1971).

4. *The Conformist*, directed by Bernardo Bertolucci (Mars Films, 1970).

The military's seizure of Brasília just four years after its inauguration as the country's new federal capital only increases the pathos of Niemeyer's paintings. Their date, like these films and novels, is significant, indicating the relatively quick demise of post-war modernist architecture at the hands of shifting politics and architectural culture. A development from the concrete pavilions of early modernism such as Le Corbusier's Villa Savoye (1931), post-war modernist architecture was characterised by large, imposing structures constructed with swathes of concrete, steel and sheet glass.[5] Though often built by the same architects (or others trained in their schools of thought), its large scale, robust design, and repetitive forms were distinct, and symptomatic of the immense imperative to re-construct cities that were bombed during the Second World War. The principles of modernism – that the function of a building should be reflected in its forms, and the materials used in its construction transparent – captured for many architects and post-war governments the values of the progressive societies they hoped to rebuild.[6]

However, for writers like Ballard, the hard-edged geometry and industrial materials of modernist architecture created harsh environments that were difficult for residents and users to navigate.[7] Almost as soon as they were erected, the appeal of modernist buildings amongst architectural critics, the media and public faded. Cold interiors, their ubiquitous, dull, grey concrete, and – in modernist homes – the voyeurism encouraged by floor-to-ceiling glass were just some of the criticisms levelled at its architecture.[8] For many, the concept of the self-sufficient modernist estate was equivalent to a hermetic enclave, sealed from the outside world and its laws. The social isolation and crime which have become a feature of modern estates invariably stem from these architectural and design elements; a violence that has in turn led to the stigmatisation of residents.[9] The casualties caused by the partial collapse of the Ronan Point residential block in London in 1968, for example, forms one such case; a disaster which contributed to the British public's loss of confidence in high-rise towers.[10] In the *banlieues* of French cities such as Paris and Lyon – captured in nocturnal photographs by Karim Kal in *Horror in the Modernist Block* – dilapidated concrete passageways mark the divide between these cities' affluent centres and maligned suburbs; a racial and socio-economic cleavage so significant that it has been equated to a form of apartheid (p. 50).[11]

5. In his book *Theory and Design in the First Machine Age*, 2nd ed. (Cambridge: MIT Press, 1980), English architectural critic Reyner Banham identified the difference between architecture (as well as design and visual art) of the 'first machine age' and the 'second machine age'. In the former – centred on the 1920s and 1930s – Banham argued that architecture was characterised by industrial production and motorised transportation, as opposed to the consumer technologies and images that defined the latter. J.G. Ballard also identified what he saw as the distinction between 'the heroic period of modernism from 1920 to 1939' and its post-war iterations, embodied in '... motorways and autobahns, stone dreams that will never awake, and in the Turbine Hall at that middle-class disco, Tate Modern – a vast totalitarian space ... so authoritarian that it overwhelms any work of art inside it'. J.G. Ballard, 'A Handful of Dust', *The Guardian*, 20 March 2006, www.theguardian.com/artanddesign/2006/mar/20/architecture.communities.

6. Brent Brolin, *The Failure of Modern Architecture* (New York: Van Nostrad Reinhold Co, 1976).

7. Ballard was a vocal critic of post-war modernist architecture. His novels *The Atrocity Exhibition* (1970), *Concrete Island* (1974), and *Crash* (1973) led to the coining of the term 'Ballardian', which refers to 'dystopian modernity, bleak manmade landscapes and the psychological effects of technological, social or environmental developments'. See Chris Hall, 'J.G. Ballard: 1930–2009', *Architects' Journal*, 6 May 2009, www.architectsjournal.co.uk/archive/j-g-ballard-1930-2009.

8. See Reyner Banham, 'The New Brutalism', first published in *The Architectural Review* in December 1955. Regarding the Hunstanton School in Norfolk, England, designed by Alison and Peter Smithson, Banham describes how 'it [was] the ruthless logic more than anything else which most hostile critics [found] distressing'. See *The Architectural Review*, online edition, www.architectural-review.com/archive/the-new-brutalism-by-reyner-banham. Beatriz Preciado also describes how floor-to-ceiling glass in architect Mies van der Rohe's Farmsworth House transformed the domestic interior into '... an intensive surveillance post that obliges the eye living in the house to stay open 24 hours a day'. 'MIES-CONCEPTION: The Farmsworth House and the Mystery of the Transparent Closet', *Multitudes 1*, no. 20 (2005): 53.

9. Paul Watt, 'Territorial Stigmatisation and Poor Housing at a London 'Sink Estate'', *Social Inclusion* 8, no. 1 (2020): 20–33.

10. Richard Nelsson, 'The Collapse of Ronan Point, 1968 – in Pictures', *The Guardian*, 16 May 2018, www.theguardian.com/society/from-the-archive-blog/gallery/2018/may/16/ronan-point-tower-collapse-may-1968.

11. See Christina Horvath, 'Banlieue Narratives: Voicing the French Urban Periphery', *Romance Studies* 26, no. 1–2, 1–4; and Angelique Chrisafis, 'Nothing's Changed': 10 Years After French Riots, Banlieues Remain in Crisis', *The Guardian*, 22 October 2015, www.theguardian.com/world/2015/oct/22/nothings-changed-10-years-after-french-riots-banlieues-remain-in-crisis.

The descriptive vocabulary of modernist architecture reflects its aesthetic severity and association with social depravation and violence. Terms such as 'ugly' and 'violent' are often accompanied by grotesque allegory, such as the notion of modernist blocks as 'concrete monstrosities'.[12] Even brutalism, the genealogy of which comes from the French for raw concrete (*béton brut*), has somewhat become a misnomer, with the terms 'brutal' and 'brutalist' often used pejoratively to critique the movement's harsh aesthetics.[13] Human metaphors describing modernism as 'soulless' and 'bloody-minded' evoke its alienating effects, as well as an image of architects and commissioners as bullish or disturbed.[14] All-encompassing visions and aspirations of efficiency have reinforced this image, criticised as overly functionalist and – in extreme cases – immoral.[15] For, if Mussolini and his government employed modernism's stark form to strengthen the ideological hold of fascism over the Italian people,[16] town planners in Britain utilised its streamlined designs to organise people into ways of living and working that would be productive for society and the economy.[17]

For artists in the exhibition, social and political agendas form the backbone to international histories of architectural modernism. A result of the widespread influence of architects such as Walter Gropius, Le Corbusier and Mies van der Rohe, The International Style – also known as internationalism – adapted modernism's core values of material and functional transparency to local conditions, incorporating elements of vernacular design.[18] In *Horror in the Modernist Block*, prints by Seher Shah (p. 70) and sculptures by Ruth Claxton (p. 38) draw inspiration from the shadows, texture and surface illusions of Le Corbusier's Unité d'Habitation – a prototype for the architect's Capitol Complex in Chandigarh, India – and Louis Kahn's National Assembly in Dhaka, Bangladesh, respectively. The geometrically shaped wall cavities and concrete slats of these buildings protect their interiors from outside heat and humidity. In a visual sense, these features also create the impression of hollowed cages shielding interior caverns which, anatomically, recall the image and function of skeletons (figs. 3, 4). For Shah and artist Shezad Dawood, the shadows cast by internationalism's aesthetics were not only architectural, but political. It was the partitioning of India in 1947, for instance, which led to the establishment of Chandigarh and Le Corbusier's commission; a context which gives the architect's Capitol Complex an air of neo-colonialism.

12. 'The Brutalist Divide: Concrete Monsters or Architectural Icons?', *BBC Arts*, 12 October 2018, www.bbc.co.uk/programmes/articles/1CPtMYghnVMJVv1YphFrWDc/the-brutalist-divide-concrete-monsters-or-architectural-icons; and *Bunkers, Brutalism and Bloodymindedness: Concrete Poetry with Jonathan Meades* (BBC, 2014).

13. Reyner Banham describes how brutalism was originally used as 'a term of Communist abuse … intended to signify the normal vocabulary of Modern Architecture – flat roofs, glass, exposed structure – considered as morally reprehensible deviations from 'The New Humanism''. For Banham, the latter comprised the style of 'picturesque' architecture that involved brickwork, segmental arches, pitched roofs and small windows. 'The New Brutalism', www.architectural-review.com/archive/the-new-brutalism-by-reyner-banham.

14. *Bunkers, Brutalism and Bloodymindedness: Concrete Poetry with Jonathan Meades* (BBC, 2014).

15. Banham highlights how modernist architects' commitment to pure functionalism led to what was widely perceived as an 'abdication of architectural responsibility'. 'The New Brutalism', www.architectural-review.com/archive/the-new-brutalism-by-reyner-banham.

16. Lucy M. Maulsby, 'Material Legacies: Italian Modernism and the Postwar History of Case del Fascio', *Cambridge University Press*, 7 May 2019, www.cambridge.org/core/journals/modern-italy/article/abs/material-legacies-italian-modernism-and-the-postwar-history-of-case-del-fascio/B3A403544469BE225578C7BCF238B2D1.

17. For example, town planner and city engineer Sir Herbert Manzoni played a key role in the modern re-design of Birmingham, including the Inner Ring Road and Central Library. His plans envisaged a 'single-path solution' to the 'complex social, economic and architectural problem' of the city following its bombing after the war. Stephen Bayley, 'It's All Change in the Second City… Again', *The Observer*, 29 June 2008, www.theguardian.com/artanddesign/2008/jun/29/architecture.regeneration.

18. Henry-Russell Hitchcock, *The International Style*, revised ed. (New York: W.W. Norton & Company, 1997).

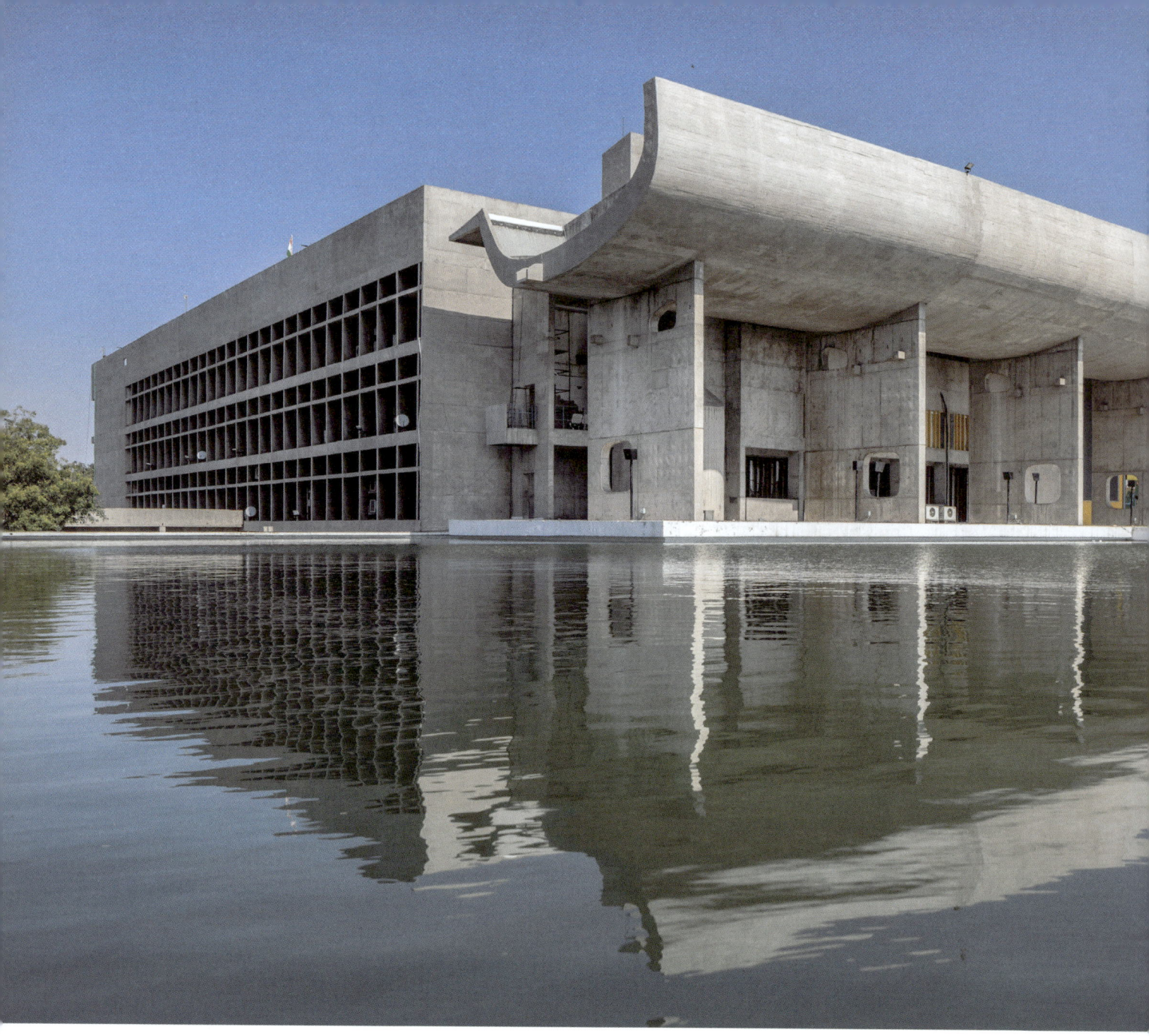

Fig. 3. Le Corbusier, Palace of Assembly, 1951–65, Chandigarh, India. Photo taken in 2019

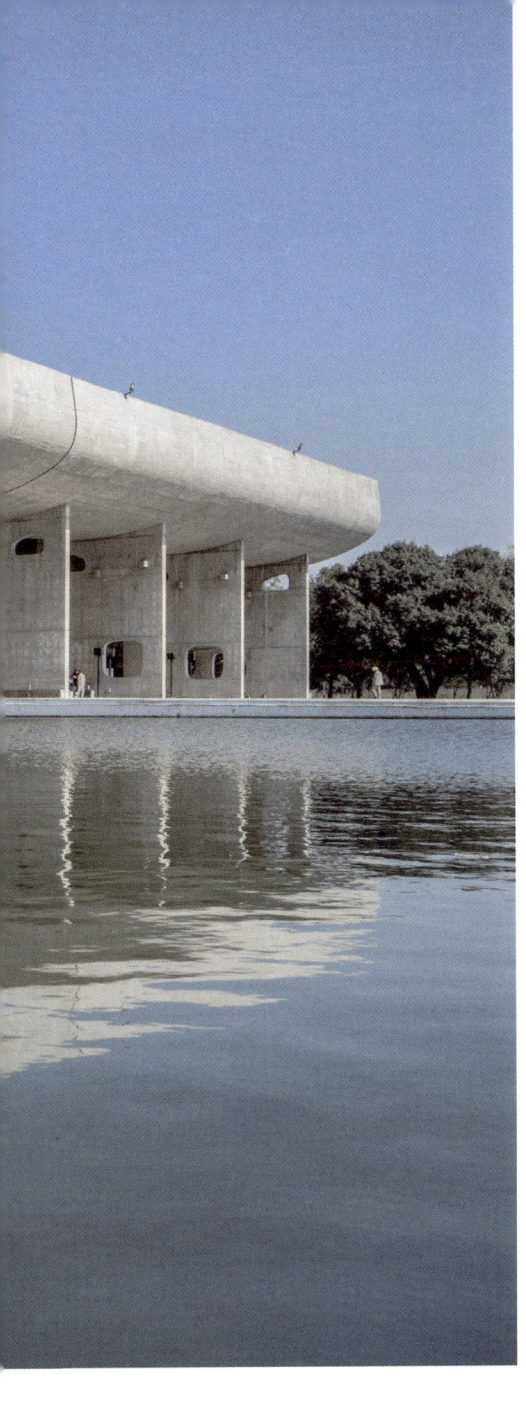

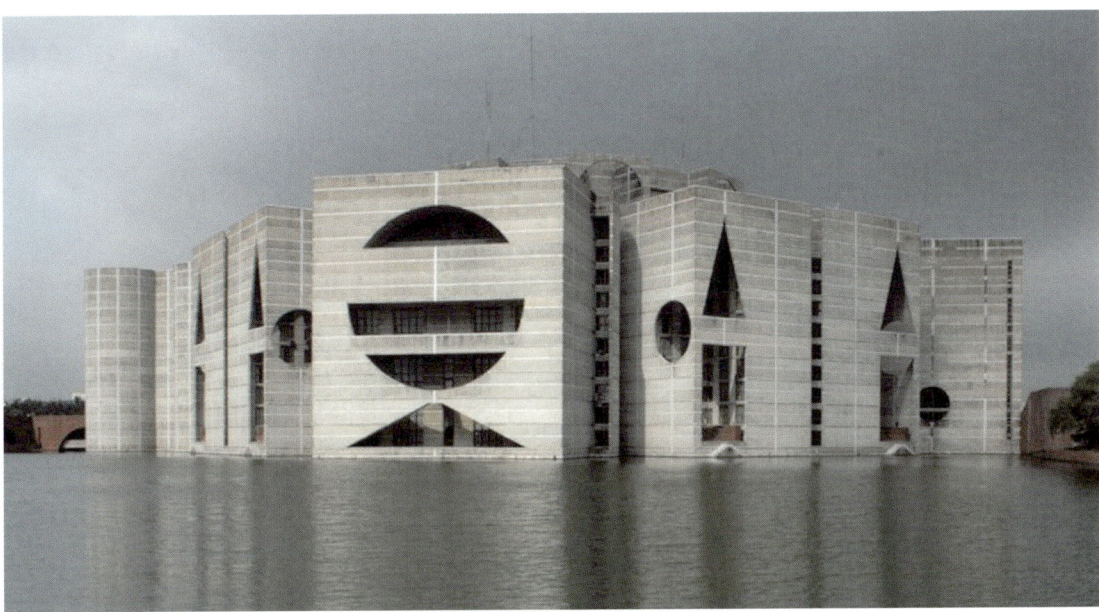

Fig. 4. Louis Kahn, National Assembly, 1982, Dhaka, Bangladesh

In Pakistan, buildings like the former United States consulate, designed by American architects Richard Neutra and Robert Alexander, formed a part of Cold War politics and the US government's ideological war against Soviet communism (fig. 5).[19] In reality, architectural modernism was employed by countries on both sides of the Cold War divide as a means of championing national socialist and western liberal values. In her sculpture *An Early Road Before a Modern One* (2022) and video *The Line That Follows* (2022), Ola Hassanain shows how the 'modernisation' of Sudan's landscape by the British paved the way for the Soviet Union's investment in modernist infrastructure from the late 1950s, precipitating the destruction and displacement of indigenous settlements (p. 42).

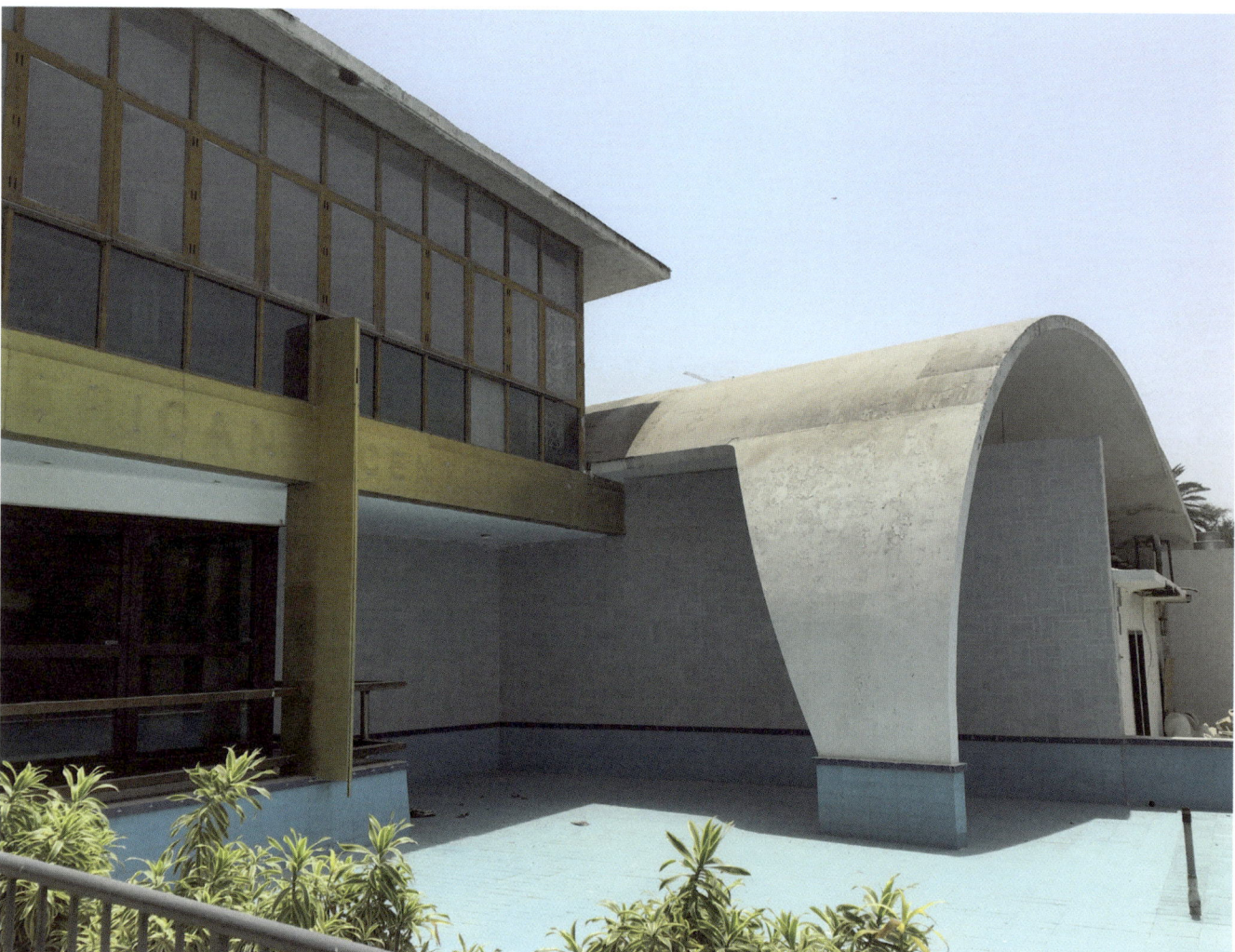

Fig. 5. Richard Neutra and Robert Alexander, former US Consulate, 1961, Karachi, Pakistan. Photo taken in 2018

19. This tendency echoes a similar movement in art, literature, film and music, in which Western modernism was employed as a tool of cultural diplomacy through traveling exhibitions, touring musical shows and publishing. See Greg Barnhisel, *Cold War Modernists: Art, Literature, and American Cultural Diplomacy* (New York City: Columbia University Press, 2015).

Invariably, the most extreme instrumentalisation of architectural modernism occurred under fascist governments. In *Monelle* (2017) by Italian artist and filmmaker Diego Marcon, the Casa del Fascio (1936) in Como – once the local office of the National Fascist Party (PNF) – epitomises the PNF's use of modernist architecture as a form of political theatre (p. 60). Designed by Giuseppe Terragni, the palazzo's cavernous marble hall is impressive and intimidating, its interior and exterior balconies implying the watchful eye of the state (fig. 6).[20] A sense of panopticism – the theory developed by Michel Foucault to describe how prison watchtowers and cells were arranged to 'carry out disciplinary power through knowledge of surveillance'[21] – also emerge in sculptures and drawings by Amba Sayal-Bennett. The forms of her sculptures and drawings recall architectural maquettes and masterplans, while their prototypical scale points to the omnipotence and seemingly infinite reach of architecture constructed by authoritarian regimes (p. 66). Firenze Lai's paintings of figures in abstract landscapes are similarly infused with feelings of oppression and tyranny. Their equivocal compositions bring to mind the kind of dense urbanism that weighs on individual and collective bodies, their figures variously entrapped and corralled by their surroundings (p. 56).

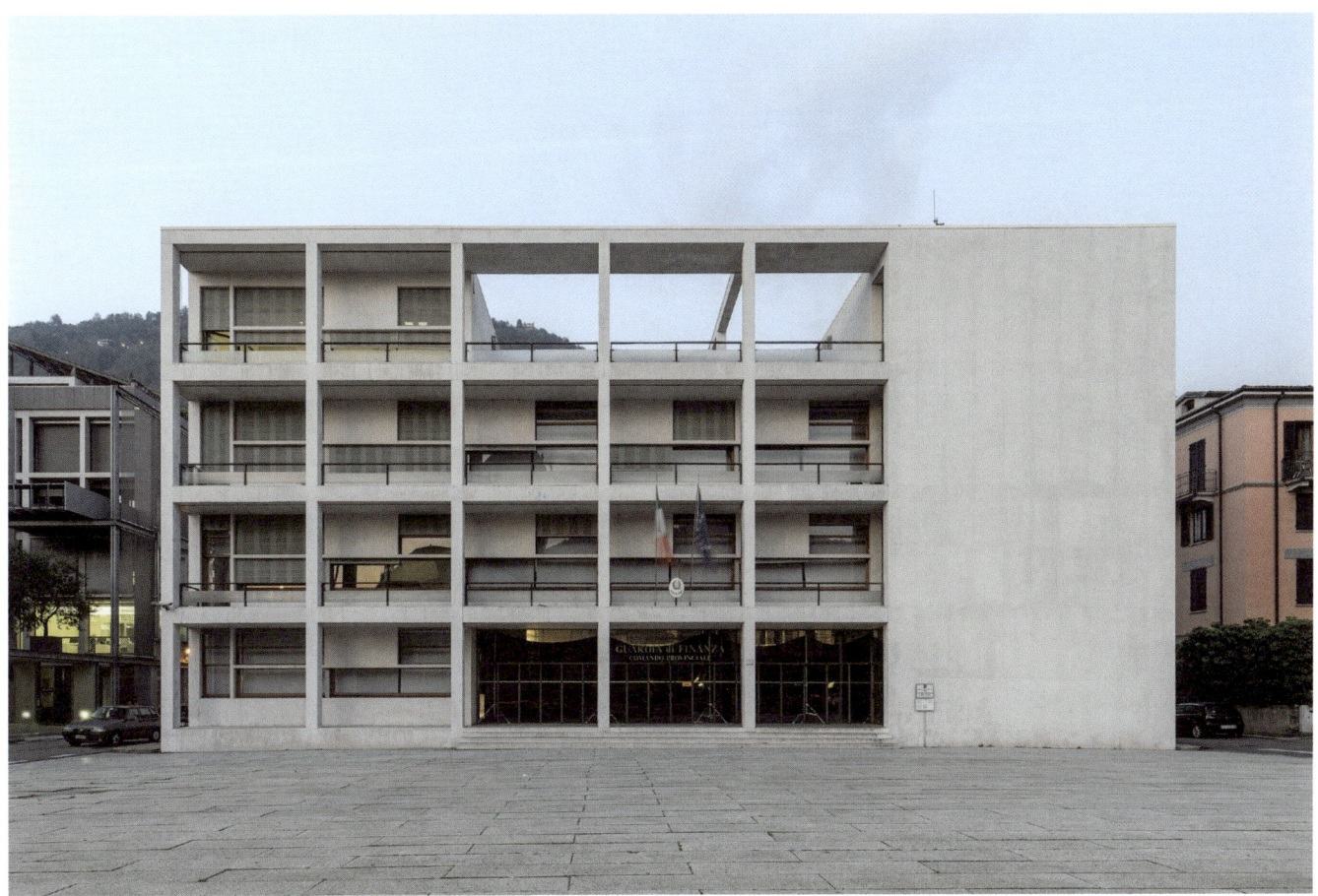

Fig. 6. Diego Marcon, *Monelle*, 2017, 35 mm film, CGI animation, colour, sound, 13:56 minutes, production still

20. Interview with Diego Marcon by Eva Fabbris, 'Lack of Light', *Mousse* 62 (February–March 2018): 182–193.

21. Michel Foucault, *Discipline and Punish: The Birth of the Prison* (New York City: Vintage Books, 1979): 201.

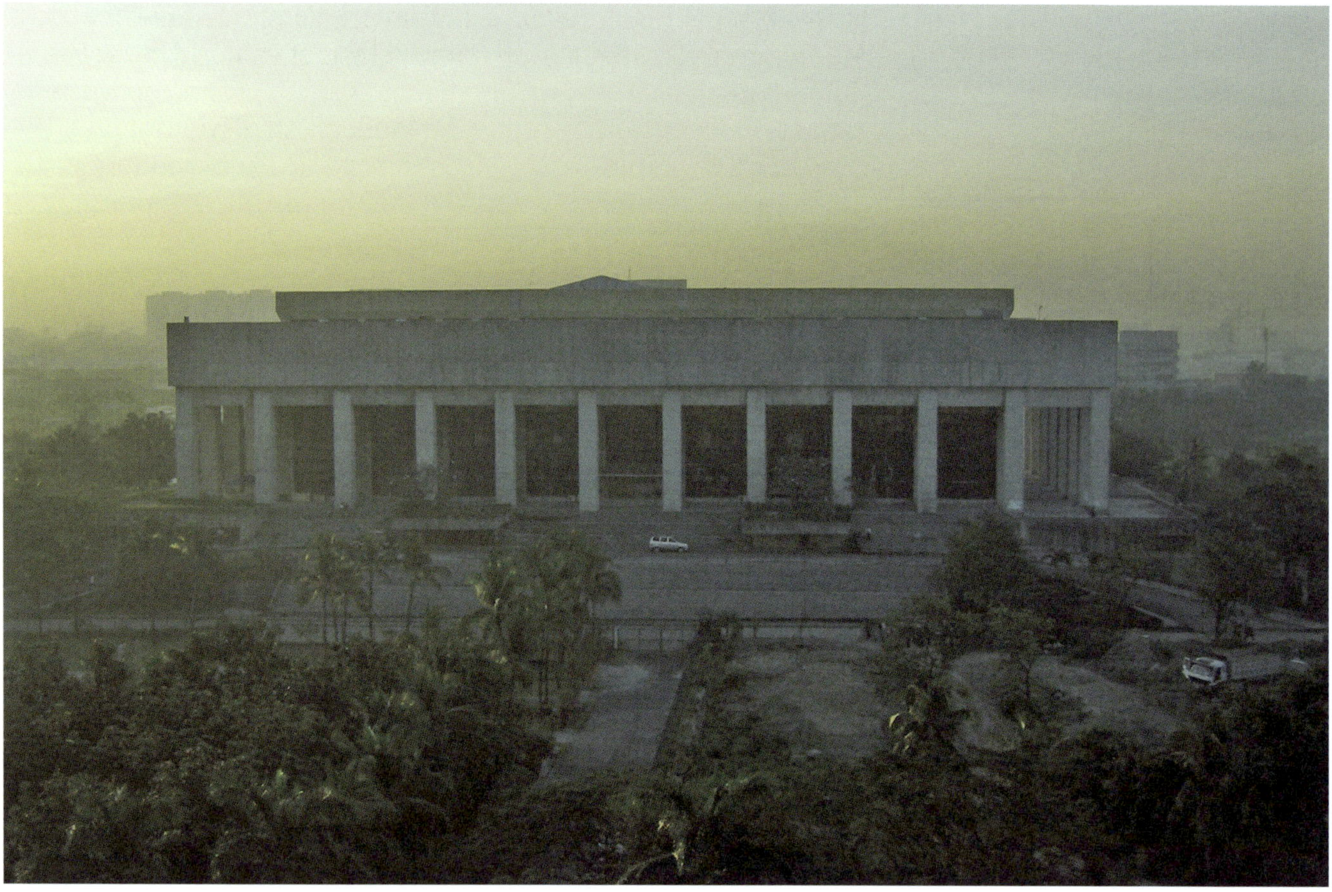

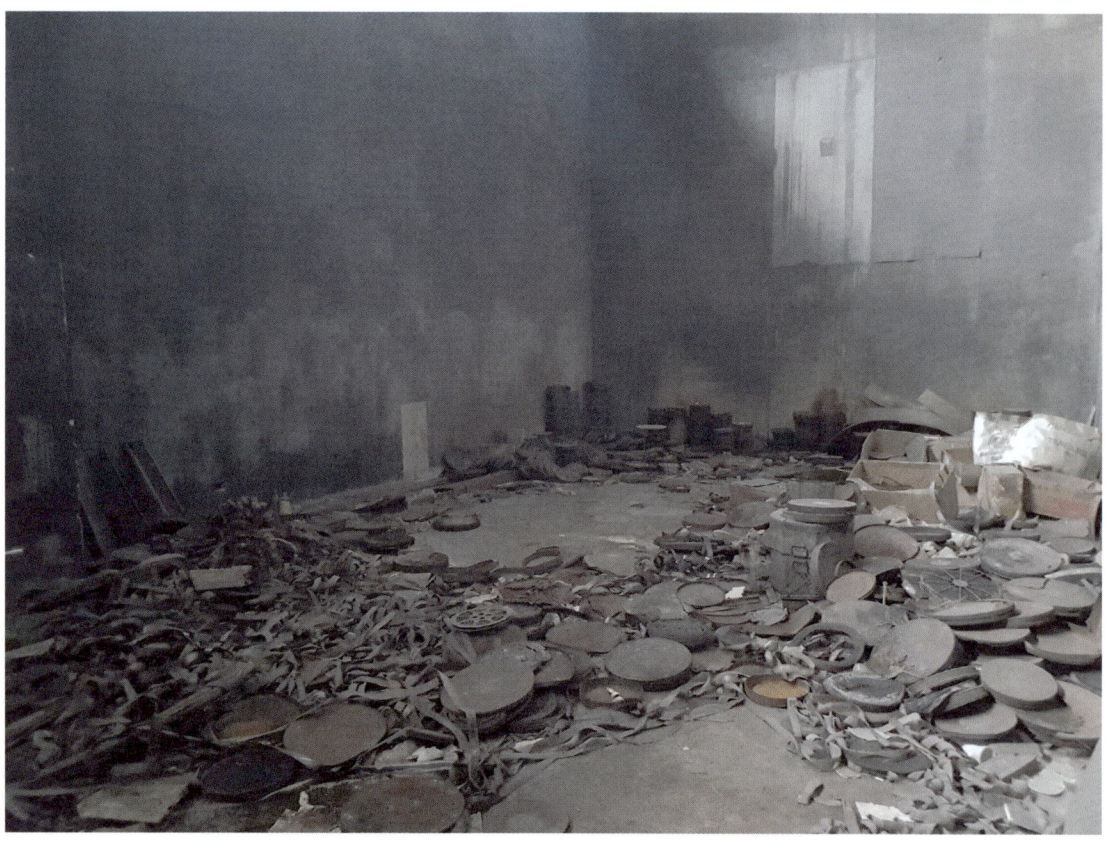

Fig. 7. Froilan Hong, Manila Film Center, 1982. Photo taken 2009

Fig. 8. Inside the now derelict Manila Film Center. Photo taken 2018

In the Philippines, brutalist architecture commissioned by the Marcos regime similarly incarnated fascist values. Under the helm of President Ferdinand Marcos and his wife Imelda, the regime – which lasted from 1965 to 1986 – ordered the construction of more than a dozen large-scale buildings, including the Cultural Center of the Philippines (1966) and Philippine International Convention Center (1974). Combining tenets of classicism, modernism and traditional architecture, these huge concrete buildings not only symbolised the absolute power of the Marcos regime but its illusion of economic prosperity.[22] Spurring the construction of this architecture was what art historian Gerard Lico describes as the Marcoses' 'edifice complex', '... an obsession and compulsion to build edifices as a hallmark of greatness'.[23] This megalomaniac aspiration reached grotesque levels with the Manila Film Center (1982), a brutalist Parthenon that was commissioned by Imelda Marcos as the venue for the Manila International Film Festival (figs. 7, 8). Part way through its construction, a section of scaffolding collapsed, resulting in the deaths of more than 160 workers. Refusing to stop the construction, Imelda Marcos reportedly ordered the workers' bodies to be covered in concrete – entombed in its edifice – so that the centre could be completed on time.[24]

Today, many Filipino people believe the centre is haunted; a mythology which feeds into local artists' associations of modernist architecture in the country with political and physical horror.[25] In Maria Taniguchi's film *Mies 421* (2010), Mies van der Rohe's Barcelona Pavilion (1929) forms the setting for an ambiguous horror narrative. The film's bullet-like metronome soundtrack gives the black-and-white images of the pavilion an unsettling undertone, as if – like the Manila Film Center – cinema and architecture were about to converge to some lethal end (p. 76). Spectres of impending doom or death are also referenced in Polish artist Monika Sosnowska's series of black steel sculptures and wall reliefs. The contorted forms of works such as *Tower* and *Truss* (both 2019) are inspired by the hyperboloid structures of Vladimir Shukhov, an avant-garde designer who was active at the time of Vladimir Lenin's Soviet Russia (p. 74).[26] During the fabrication of one of the architect's commissions for a radio tower, the process of fatiguing metal that was required to twist it failed, resulting in the collapse of the tower and the deaths of several workers.[27] Despite the tragic accident, Shukhov's tower was completed in 1922, and is widely regarded today as an important example of Leninist Soviet architecture. A photograph of the partially collapsed tower from 1921 nonetheless forms a haunting memento of the workers who perished during its construction (fig. 9).

22. Gerard Lico, *Edifice Complex: Power, Myth, and Marcos State Architecture* (Quezon City: Manila University Press, 2003): 51.

23. Ibid.

24. Ibid. 81, 122.

25. See Nicai de Guzman, 'The Mysterious Curse of the Manila Film Center', *Esquire* (Philippines), 7 November 2019, www.esquiremag.ph/long-reads/features/manila-film-center-haunted-a1729-20191107-lfrm2. My conversations with artist Maria Taniguchi about Marcos state architecture and its association with political violence informed the theme of *Horror in the Modernist Block*. Email correspondence with the author, 30 April – 8 September 2020.

26. Adam Heardman, 'Monika Sosnowska (Review)', *Art Monthly* (September 2019): 28.

27. Ibid.

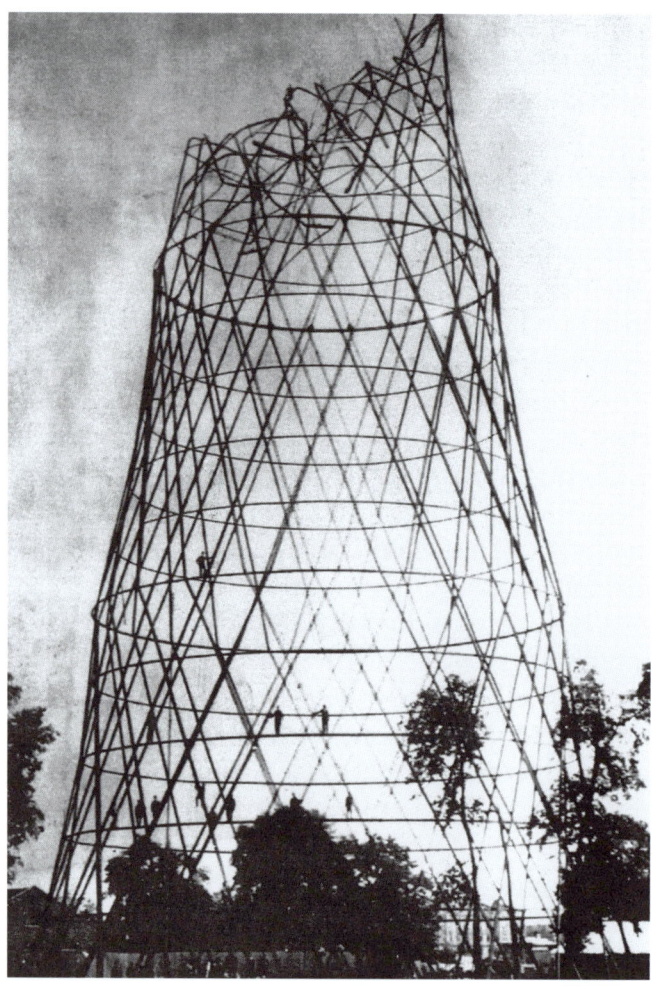

Fig. 9. The Shukhov Radio Tower in Moscow after the collapse that occurred during the construction of the tower on 29 June 1921

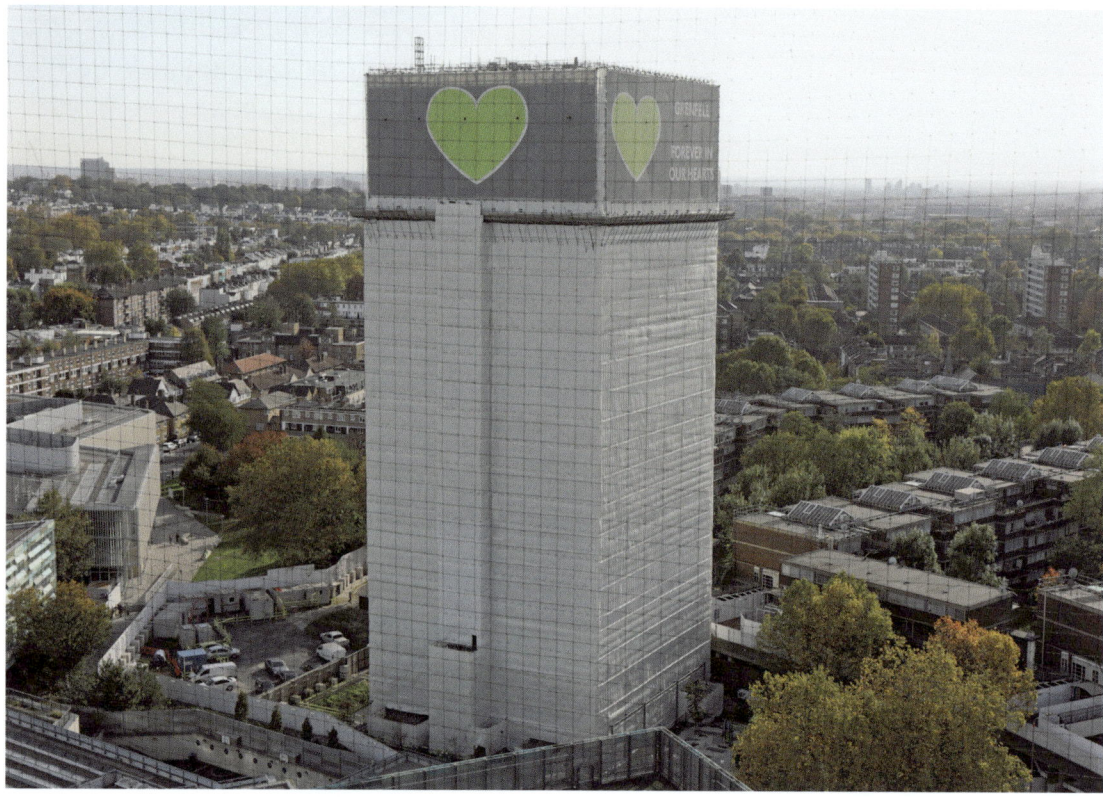

Fig. 10. Grenfell Tower. Photo taken in 2020

Certainly, construction-related deaths are not unique to modernist architecture. Yet they often feel horrific because of the politics and power behind them, in which the lives of working-class or ordinary people seem expendable. There is also a sense of regret – that such tragedies could have been avoided if safe and ethical methods of construction had been implemented. A similar mourning surrounds the deaths of residents of modernist tower blocks caused by architectural faults and incendiary material. In 2017, a fire – provoked by flammable insulation and cladding – claimed the lives of 72 residents of Grenfell Tower in west London. A poignant reminder of the lethal nature of insulation which clads many modernist towers in Britain, Grenfell's fire was also evidence of the kind of horror brought about by political negligence.[28] Through his artistic practice, Abbas Zahedi subtly and explicitly touches on these issues by reworking infrastructural elements within and around the sites where he works. By shifting the vocabulary of the built environment, Zahedi reminds us how we can resist the neglect of these estates by local authorities, and the negative impact this neglect has on the people who live in them. In the case of the fire at Grenfell, it is now recognised that insulation and cladding companies willingly exploited the local authority's failure to vet their products according to accepted safety standards (p. 78).

Currently, the charred remains of Grenfell are wrapped in scaffolding and scrim, printed with text that honours the victims of the fire (fig. 10). In its integral form, the tower no longer exists; a fate which applies to many modernist blocks and estates. Whether due to their faulty design or maligned public image, the absence or demolition of these buildings creates an inverse form of horror – that of erasure. While some might find the continued presence of Grenfell in London's urban landscape unsettling, others would be traumatised by its demolition, because of its status as a memorial to the people who died in the fire. Indeed – if the Manila Film Center reminds people in the Philippines of a regime they would rather forget, its continued existence forms a reminder to younger generations of the perils of authoritarianism.[29]

---

28. In an article published in *The Sunday Times Magazine* on the fifth anniversary of the fire at Grenfell Tower, journalist Martina Lees outlines several failures of the British government to prevent the tragedy. Faults in safety tests allowed cladding products with a highly flammable core to be coated with a thin fireproof surface and still pass. Tests on the foil surface of insulation – instead of the foam insulation itself – also enabled insulation products to achieve a Class 0 fire rating. 'Grenfell: An Investigation', *The Sunday Times Magazine* (12 June 2022): 10–23.

29. It is worth noting that Ferdinand 'Bongbong' Romualdez Marcos Jr. – the son and heir of Ferdinand and Imelda Marcos – became the 17th President of The Philippines in June 2022. Many Filipinos see his election as the product of a misinformation campaign that sought to whitewash the crimes of the first Marcos regime. Michael Beltran, 'Disinformation Reigns in Philippines as Marcos Jr Takes Top Job', 29 June 2022, www.aljazeera.com/news/2022/6/29/disinformation-reigns-in-philippines-as-marcos-jr-takes-top-job.

The question of demolition is not only relevant to modernist architecture marred by tragedy. Many buildings revered by community groups and architects have been torn down because of modernism's negative image in the public and media.[30] Nowadays, architecture of this kind is earning listed or protected status from city councils and heritage bodies like UNESCO, which are keen to safeguard what they increasingly perceive as cultural heritage.[31] In many cases, modernist architecture is simply demolished so that urban developers can profit from the value of the land it occupies.[32] Somewhat ironically, the privatisation of several modernist estates, such as the Barbican in London, has also led to their gentrification, so that they are now seen as desirable residences.[33] In this sense, the 'horror' of modernist architecture can lie in its removal. Undoubtedly, processes of demolition are scary to watch. Despite attempts at cordoning, demolition sites are often highly visible, the detonation of explosives and wrecking balls creating the impression of a war zone (fig. 11).

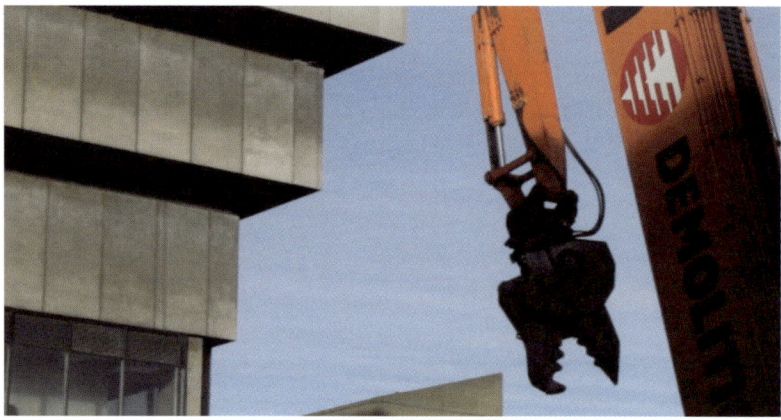

Fig. 11. Diggers moving in to begin demolition of Birmingham Central Library, 2015

Tensions between the redevelopment and razing of modernist buildings surface in Kihlberg & Henry's film *Slow Violence* (2018–22). In the film, the utopic premise of architectural modernism is re-translated for a contemporary era through the language of advertising, digital simulations of 'ideal' homes, and destructive rhetoric (p. 54). In many ways, cycles of destruction and reconstruction are integral to the conceptual and physical foundations of modernist architecture. For writer and journalist Owen Hatherley, the demolition of modernist buildings not only enacts the latter's promise of renewal but provides evidence for the precocious nature of modernism's vision. To quote Hatherley, it was as if modernist architects already had '[its] ruins ... in mind: a death-drive architecture, where ... the corpse has been designed before the living body'.[34]

30. Rowan Moore, 'How Britain is Failing its Modernist Masterpieces', *The Observer*, 29 May 2011, www.theguardian.com/artanddesign/2011/may/29/modernist-architecture-demolished-listed-buildings.

31. Examples include Ove Arup and Partners' brutalist bus station in Preston, which earnt Grade II listed status in 2013 following a public campaign to preserve it, and Le Corbusier's Capitol Complex in Chandigarh, which achieved UNESCO World Heritage Status in 2016.

32. See, for example, the case of Hotel Kyjev in Bratislava, an icon of Slovak modernist architecture, which was demolished to make way for urban development of the area. Charlotte Arden, 'Jewel of Modernist Architecture Slated for Demolition', *The Slovak Spectator*, 18 March 2008, www.spectator.sme.sk/c/20028723/jewel-of-modernist-architecture-slated-for-demolition.html.

33. Colin Wiles, 'A Tale of Two Brutalist Housing Estates: One Thriving, One Facing Demolition', *The Guardian*, 13 January 2016, www.theguardian.com/housing-network/2016/jan/13/brutalist-housing-estates-private-barbican-social-london.

34. Owen Hatherley, *Militant Modernism* (Zero Books, 2009): 49.

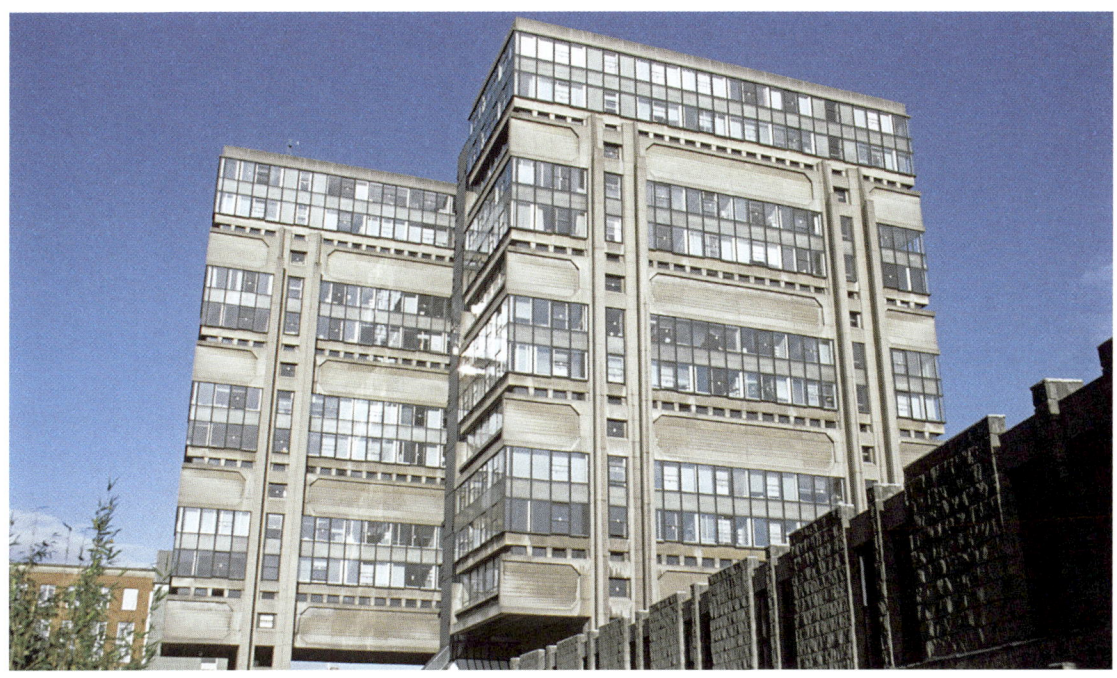

Fig. 12. Philip Dowson of Arup Associates, Muirhead Tower, 1971, University of Birmingham, as originally built

Perhaps no-where is the 'death drive' of modernism more apparent than in Birmingham, where brutalist architecture survives alongside contemporary developments. Home to maverick designs such as the Signal Box (1964) and Muirhead Tower (1971) (fig. 12), the city's landscape is equally marked by the absence of modernist icons, notably the Central Library (1974), designed by local architect John Madin (fig. 13). The Central Library formed part of a complex known as Paradise Circus, which was intended to transform Birmingham's city centre into a pedestrianised zone of accessible, public buildings. Although the Central Library – an inverted ziggurat structure made of concrete – was arguably Madin's greatest achievement, it was also his most vilified.[35] Thus, in 2015, just forty years after opening, the Central Library was deemed 'no longer fit for purpose' and demolished to make way for a contemporary building.[36] Whilst the original library was criticised for its convoluted layout and the safety of its underpasses at night, these same spaces were also highly valued by the city's young, counter-culture generation for the freedom of expression these infrastructures enabled.[37] For Birmingham-born artists Richard Hughes and Simon & Tom Bloor, the concrete fabric of the city has had a lasting impact, its textures and traces of humanity mimicked and cast into their sculptural installations (p. 46 and 36). Indeed, Hughes himself remembers growing up in Birmingham and skateboarding with friends in the concrete 'underbelly' of the Central Library (i.e. the former Paradise Circus). In this way, both modernism and brutalism form an inherent part of the city's cultural identity and mythology.

35. *Paradise Lost, History in the Unmaking*, directed by Andy Howlett (2021).

36. Nick Clark, 'First Look: Birmingham's New £188m Library – a Sparkling Cornerstone of the City's Rebirth', *The Independent*, 29 August 2013, www.independent.co.uk/arts-entertainment/architecture/first-look-birmingham-s-new-ps188m-library-a-sparkling-cornerstone-of-the-city-s-rebirth-8788527.html.

37. *Paradise Lost, History in the Unmaking*, 23:20 to 26:02.

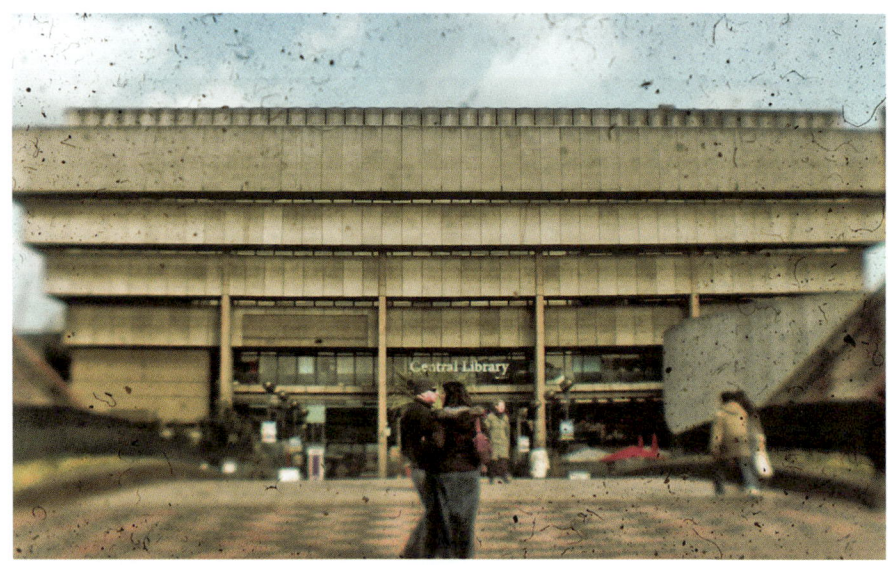

Fig. 13. John Madin, Birmingham Central Library, 1974

In addition to absent and extant modernist architecture, Birmingham has a large number of neo-gothic buildings. A legacy of the city's industrial past, this architecture would, at first, seem to have little to do with its modernist equivalent. Yet, as the descriptive vocabulary of modernism shows, ideas of modernism as 'monstrous' originate in Victorian horror and the 'uncanny' spirits written into its architecture.[38] Several architects and academics also trace the simplified and repetitive forms of modernism to the 19th century factory, and its scale to the exponential development of industrial capitalism.[39] For architect Joshua Comaroff, increases in the speed of production and flourishing consumerism resulted in 'the manic repetition of bits' that characterise early modern skyscrapers, such as the former Pullman Building in Chicago (fig. 14).[40] In the documentary *Bunkers, Brutalism and Bloodymindedness: Concrete Poetry* (2014), British poet Jonathan Meades also draws links between the sublime qualities of Victorian neo-gothic architecture and brutalism, highlighting how buildings in both styles were similarly derided by critics as 'coarse', 'violent' and 'ugly'.[41] For Meades, these visual parallels extend to their parallel affects, with neo-gothic buildings serving as 'the emotional precursors' of brutalism; '... antecedents which provoked the same mood' and that caused inhabitants and onlookers 'to shiver with the same undoubted horror'.[42]

38. In the 19th century, the myth of the haunted house was popularised in works such as Edgar Allan Poe's short story *The Fall of the House of Usher* (1839). The sense of a strange 'atmosphere' – that all is not as it seems – is evidence of what Anthony Vidler describes as 'the architectural uncanny.' This 'uncanny power' is all 'the more disquieting for the absolute normality of the setting, its veritable absence of overt terror.' Anthony Vidler, *The Architectural Uncanny* (Cambridge: MIT Press, 1992): 18.

39. Owen Hatherley emphasises the genealogy of modernist architecture in 'the factories and mills of the 19th century.' He cites Nikolaus Pevsner's study *Pioneers of Modern Design* (1936), which features a photograph 'that proves that Mies van der Rohe's glass grids, that dominate our skylines still, existed in embryo in 1850s Britain in the form of Sheerness Boatstore.' Hatherley, *Militant Modernism*, 19. Le Corbusier also published Illustrations of 19th-century American grain elevators and factories in his book *Towards a New Architecture* (1923). According to academic Maroš Krivý, the attraction of factory design for Le Corbusier and Walter Gropius (who visited the US in 1935 and 1928 respectively) was its 'embodiment of social progress [...] rooted in and driven by the rationality of science, technology and engineering.' Maroš Krivý, 'Industrial Architecture and Negativity: the Aesthetics of Architecture in the Works of Gordon Matta-Clark, Robert Smithson and Bernd and Hilla Becher', *The Journal of Architecture* 15, no. 6 (2010): 829.

40. Joshua Comaroff and Ong Ker-Shing, *Horror in Architecture* (Novato, CA: ORO Editions, 2013), 39.

41. *Bunkers, Brutalism and Bloodymindedness*: *Concrete Poetry*.

42. Ibid (Part 1), 6:15–7:07.

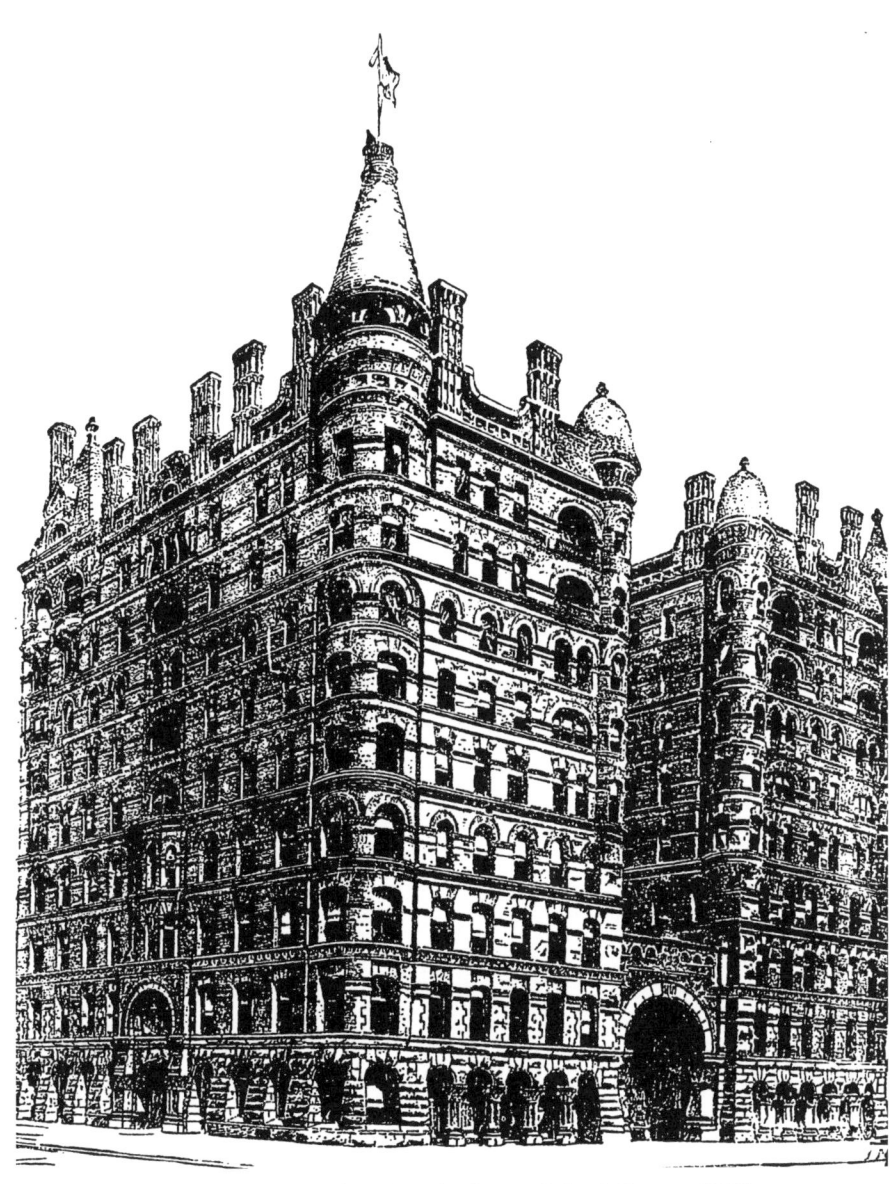

Fig. 14. Illustration of the Pullman Building, (architect: Solon S. Beman, 1884) Chicago, United States

At Ikon, such links between Victorian architecture and modernism are pertinent because of its neo-gothic building (fig. 15). While the gallery's contemporary interior has a certain neutrality, features from the original building such as steel beams and arched ceilings remain. Painted white, they have the absent/present quality of a ghost; remnants from the past which haunt the present. In *Horror in the Modernist Block*, the building inevitably becomes a subject, and our movement within it heightened. As a result, many artists in the exhibition have created or configured work that dialogues with its architecture. Ismael Monticelli's paintings referencing the erasure of vernacular culture in Brazil by modernism, for instance, are arranged in the form of a pyramid which extends to the full height of the gallery (p. 62). Laëtitia Badaut Haussmann's installation interacts with an existing niche, creating a 'para-architecture' that mimics tropes of high modernism (p. 34). Works such as these recall the affects of modernist architecture – how its design and materials make us think and feel – and the ways in which these might trigger a sense of foreboding or marginalisation.

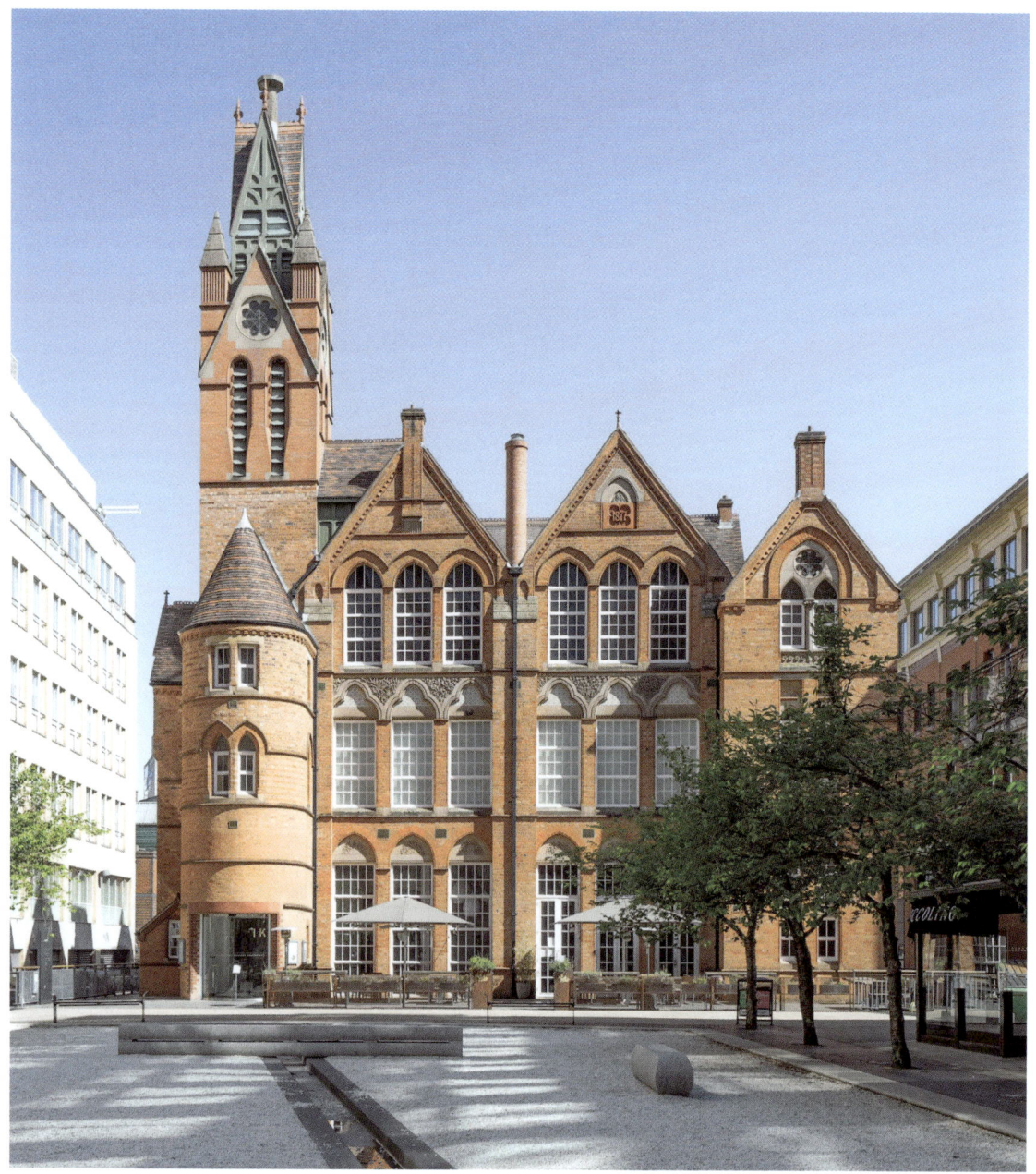

Fig. 15. Ikon Gallery, 2022

For Comaroff, this affective dimension of modernist architecture is integral, but one that is rarely addressed in architectural research.⁴³ Through the sensory realm of aesthetics, artists in the exhibition explore this emotive quality of modernism. The first section of the exhibition iterates this emphasis on affect, inviting viewers to enter a darkened space where they encounter a sequence of moving image and film installations. Projected in a timed sequence in different areas of the space, the audience experiences one work at a time (fig. 16). Playing with tropes of horror such as suspense and darkness, the unobvious order of the sequence reminds us of the role of human projection and imagination in filling gaps in knowledge and space. While the unknown sequence might provoke concern in some viewers, others will undoubtedly take pleasure in its element of surprise. There is also a magical quality to the sequence, the illuminated projections operating like ghosts that mysteriously manifest when the audience is present.

43. *Horror in Architecture*, 7–44.

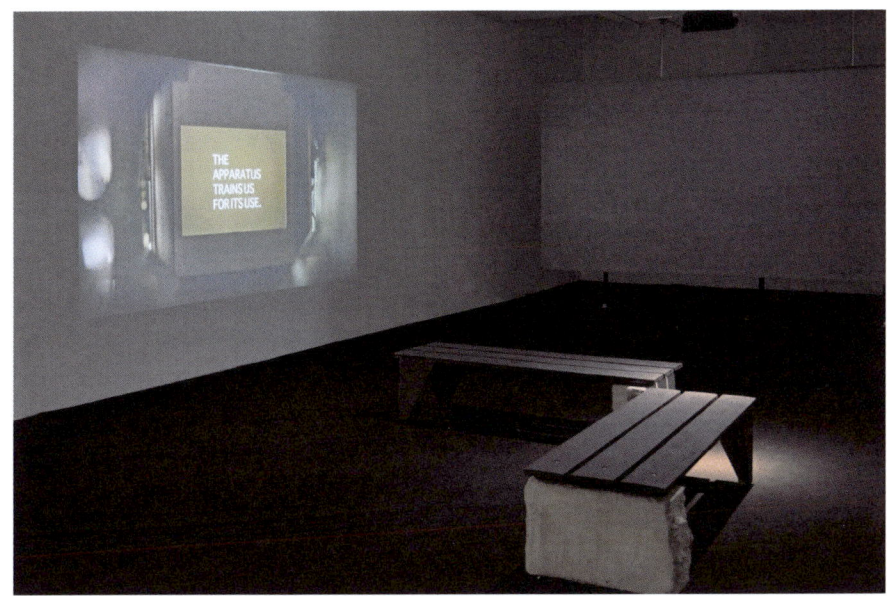

Fig. 16. *Horror in the Modernist Block*, installation view, 2022

In NT's new film *BRUTAL* (2022), tower blocks in the modernist estates of Druids Heath and Aston New Town in Birmingham appear as if they are emerging from the dark, surreptitiously captured by the artist's camera (p. 64). Filmed entirely at night, the film's soundtrack transforms the dormant estates into agents of the imagination. Ho Tzu Nyen's video installation *The Cloud of Unknowing* (2011) similarly takes viewers on a magical realist journey through various floors of a residential block in Singapore. Towards the end of the work, the walls and ceilings of flats entrap residents, a monsoon downpour penetrates the interior, and a cloud engulfs the building (p. 44). The meaning of the cloud is uncertain; an ambiguity which is implied in the work's title. As real as it appears, the cloud is also a fiction; a conclusion reinforced by the characters' seeming obliviousness to its presence.

Horror, as the exhibition shows, is not one, but many things. In works of horror, tragedy, trauma, seduction and the sublime often converge, the incongruity of these emotions increasing their terror. Politicians and governments have often exploited such incongruities, the power of many liberal, fascist and postcolonial states reinforced by the impervious nature of modernism's geometry and material. Throughout history, we see how horror is literally *in* modernist architecture – its faulty structures and concrete blocks. It is a horror that is shaped by place and culture, as well as shared internationally through the global propagation of the modernist idiom. In Birmingham, horror and modernism have a particular resonance, borne from the city's past as a crucible of industrialisation and gothic culture. Yet the contemporary fate of the modernist block – one that is not mired in local politics and capitalist agendas – is possible to reimagine. With the help of the artists in *Horror in the Modernist Block*, audiences can feel and observe multiple horrors of modernism, as well as its fictions. In this way, the exhibition forms both an invitation and provocation; a statement of fact as much as doubt. It is a building in progress; a narrative to be retold.

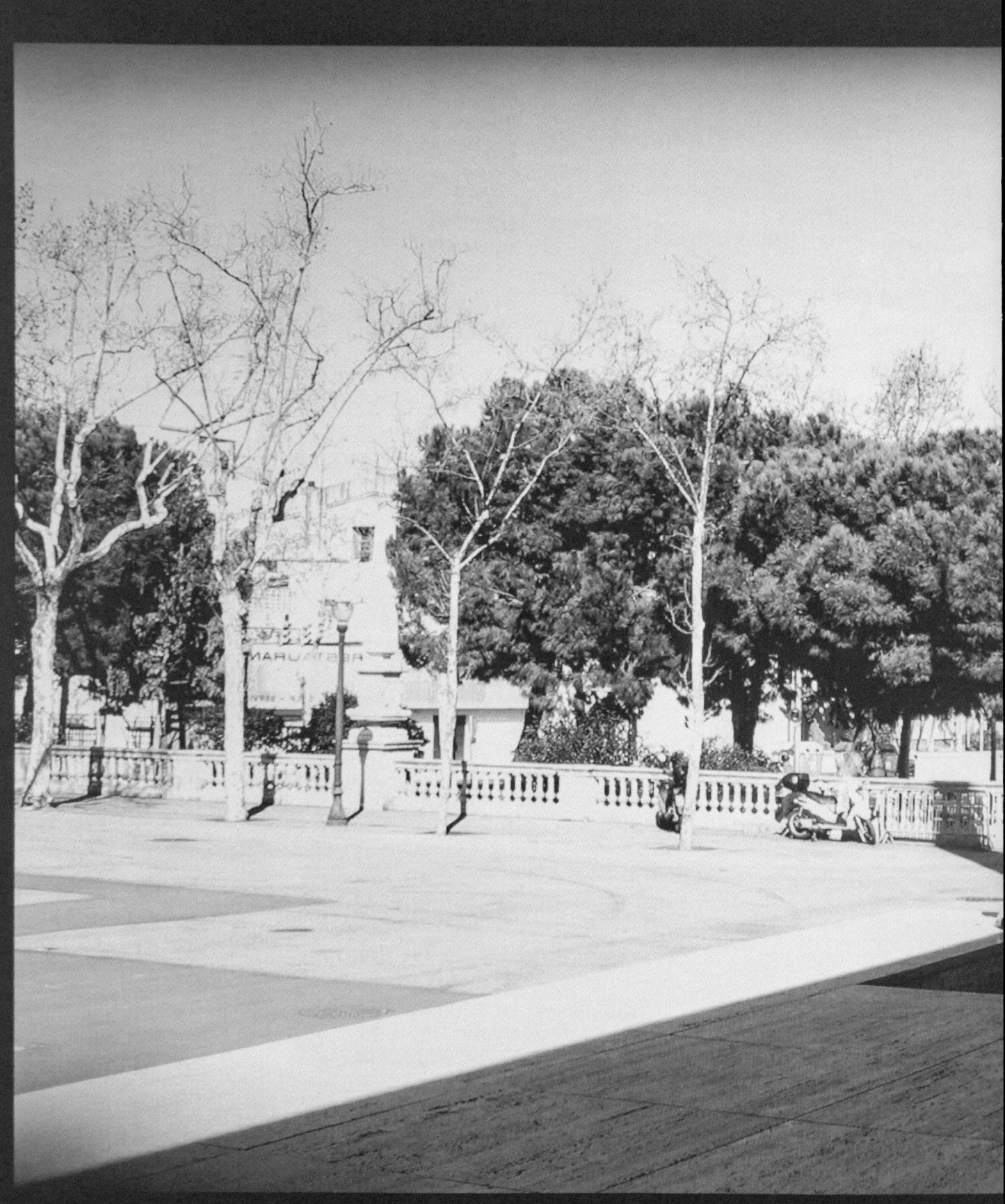

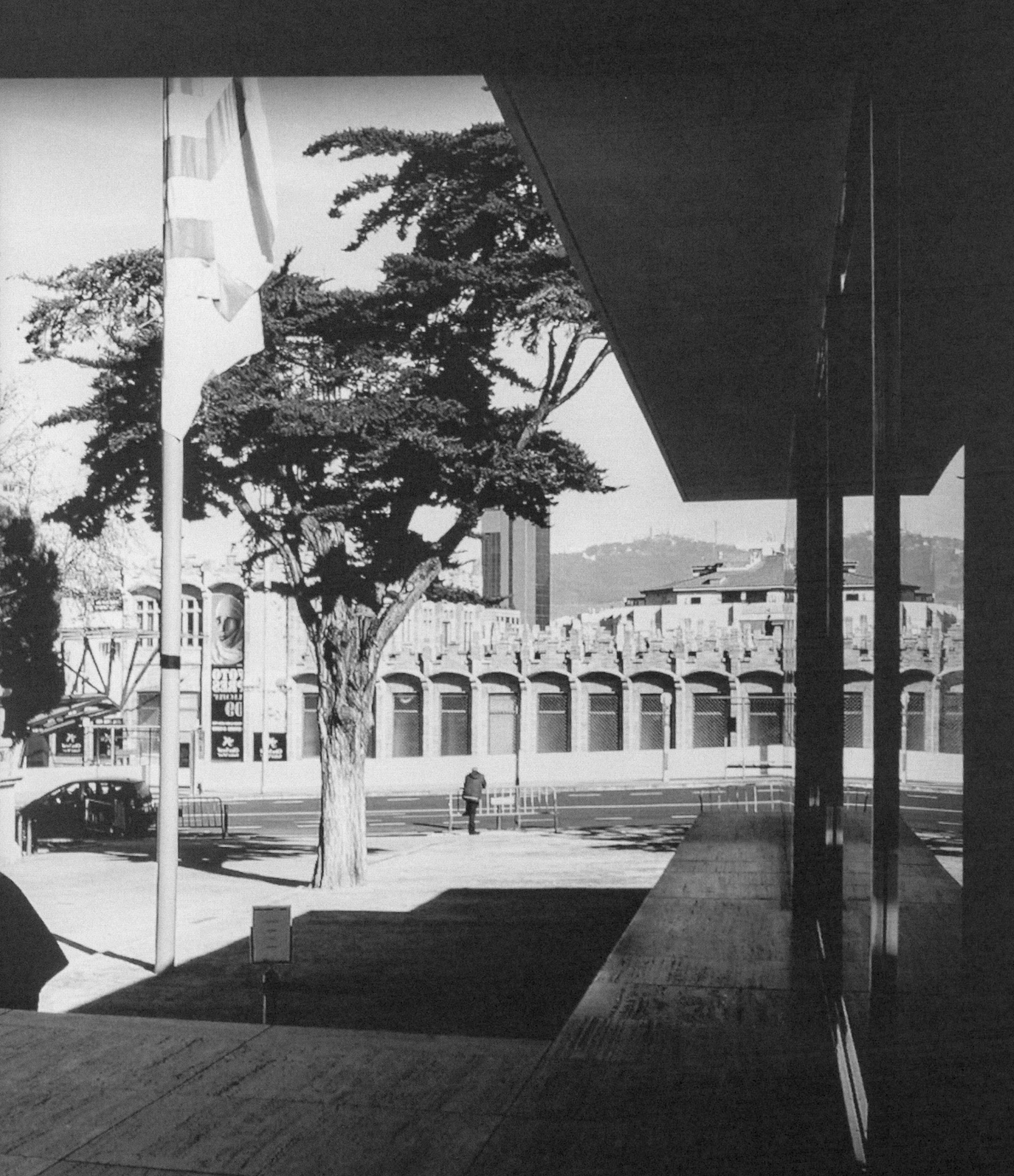

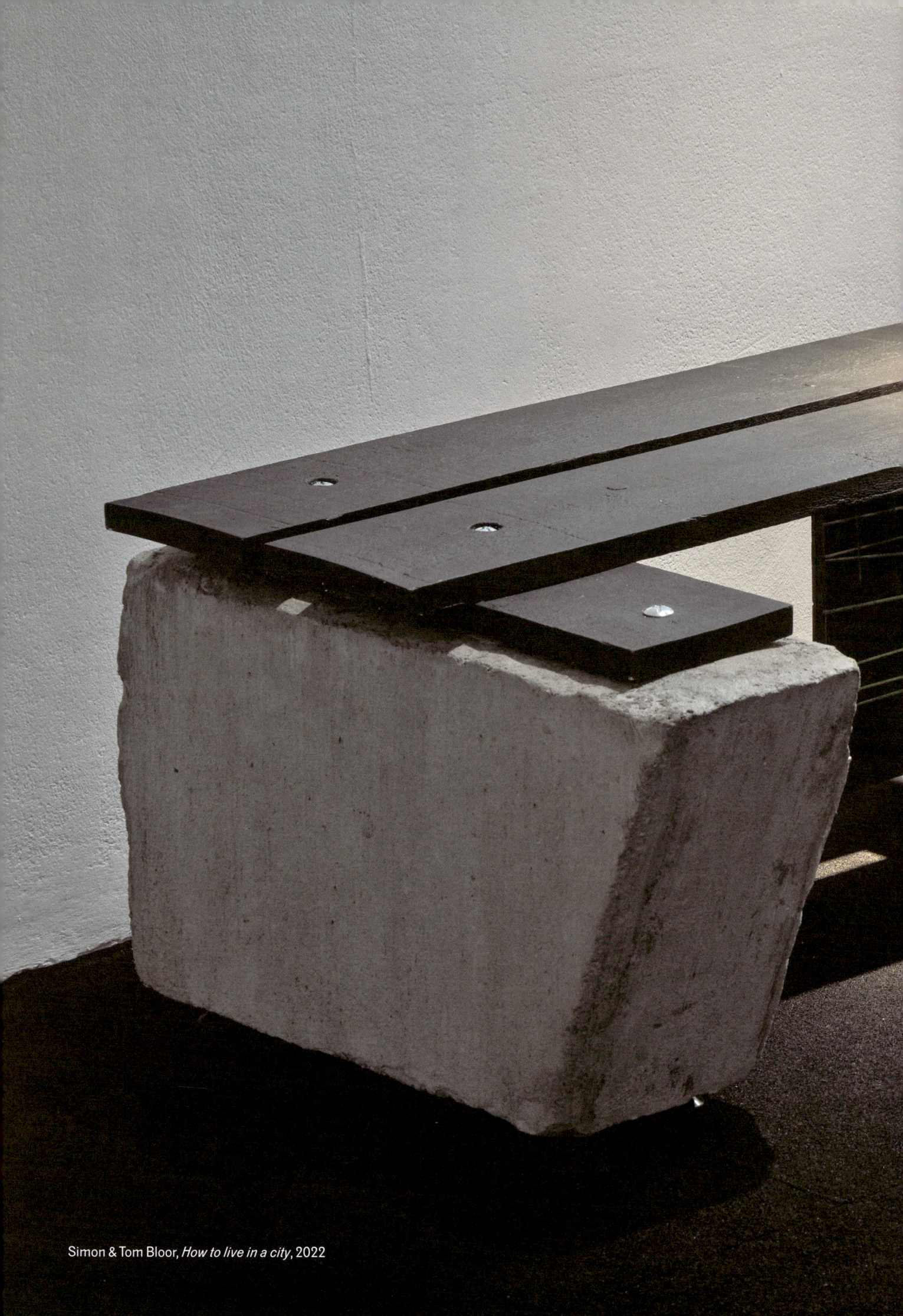

Simon & Tom Bloor, *How to live in a city*, 2022

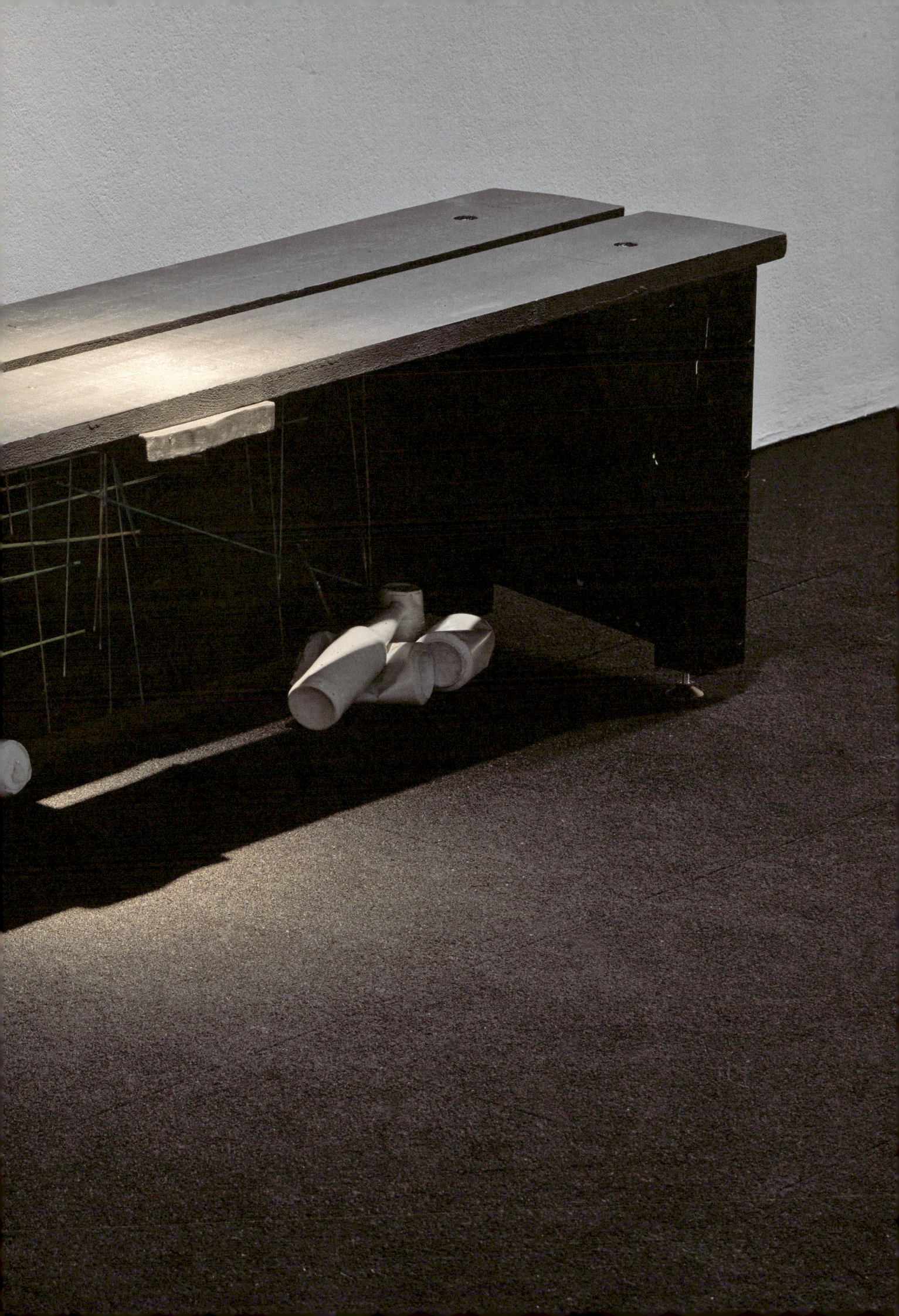

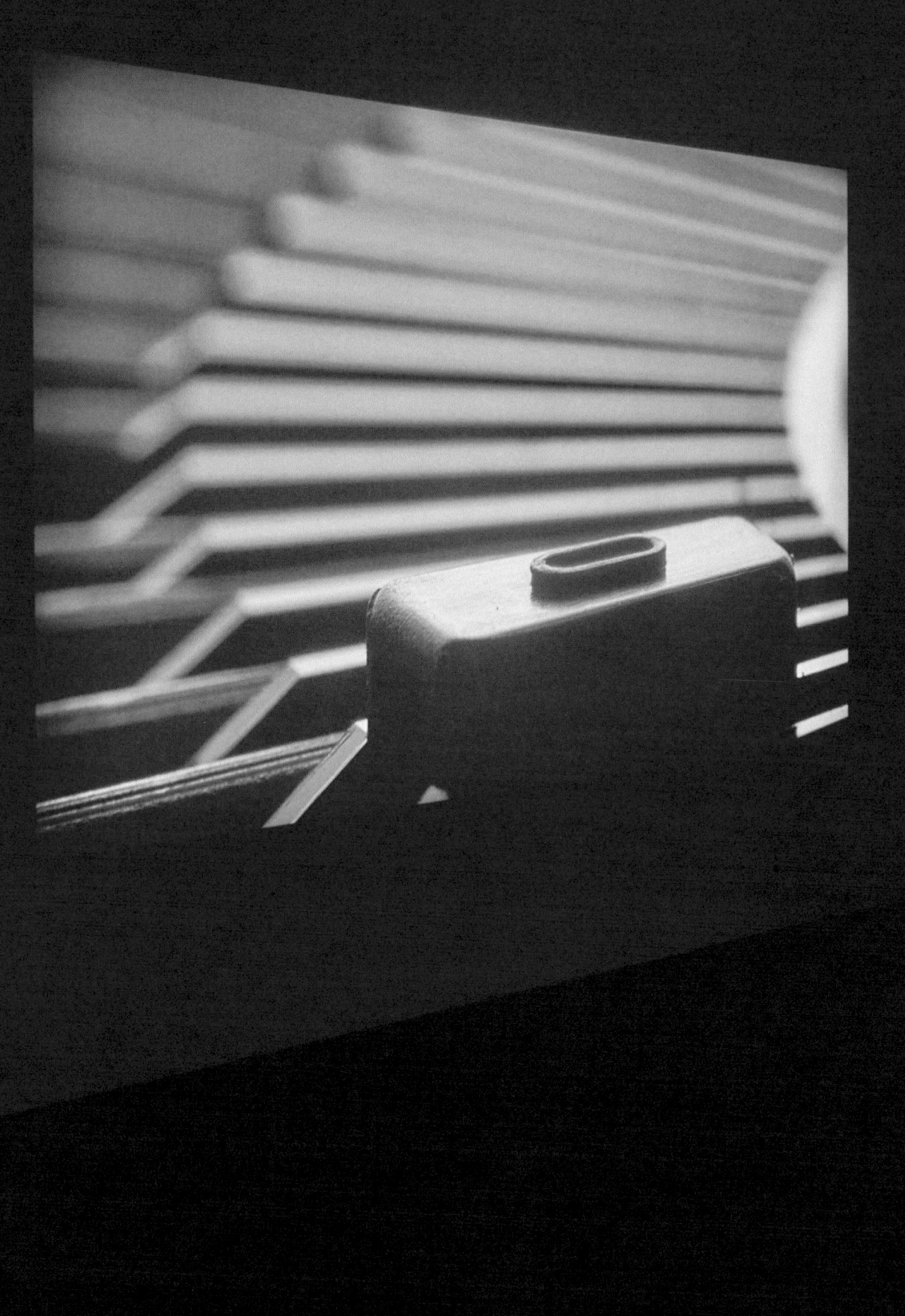

Kihlberg & Henry, *Slow Violence*, 2018–2022

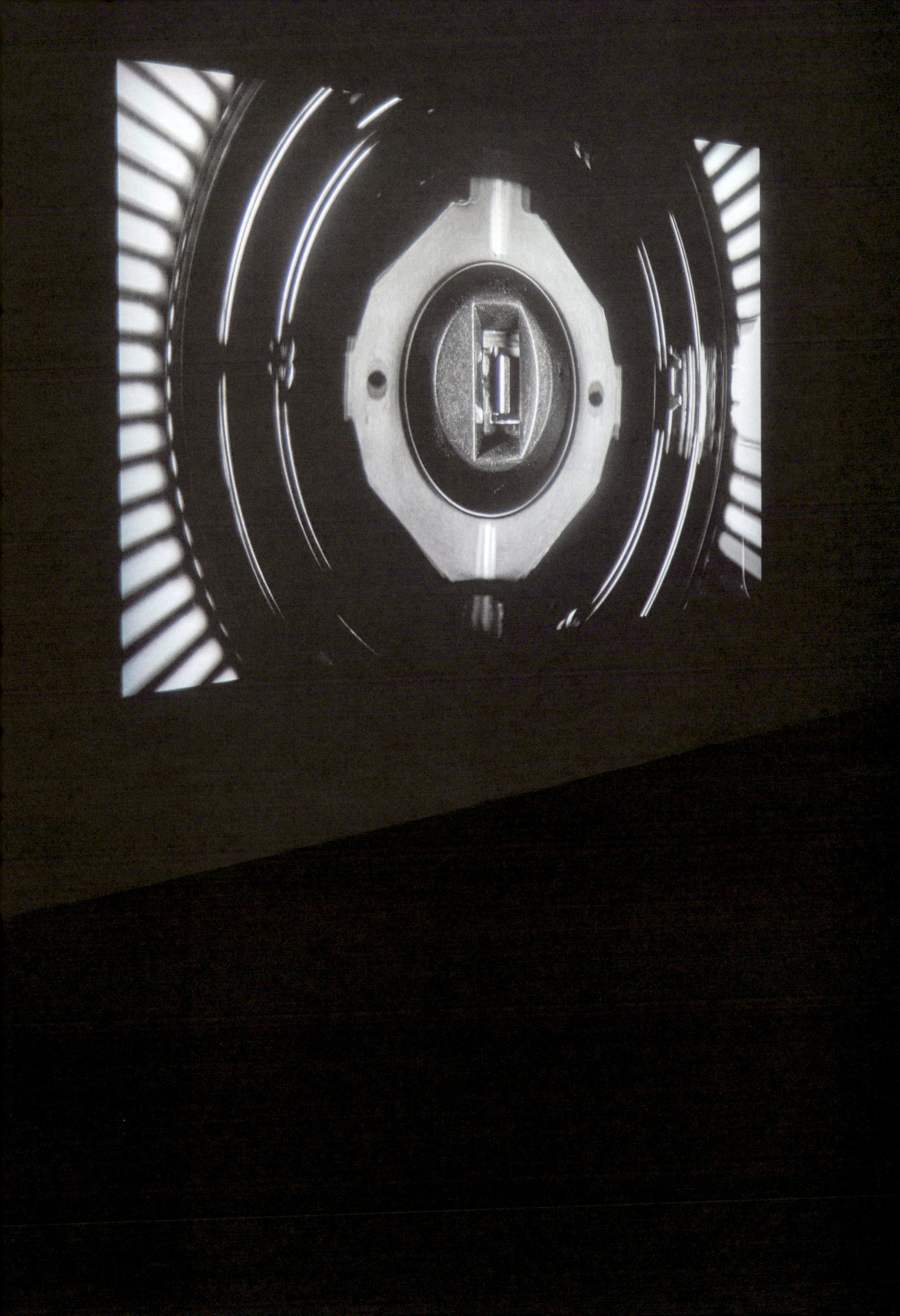

Left to right: Kihlberg & Henry, *Slow Violence*, 2018–2022;
Simon & Tom Bloor, *How to live in a city*, 2022

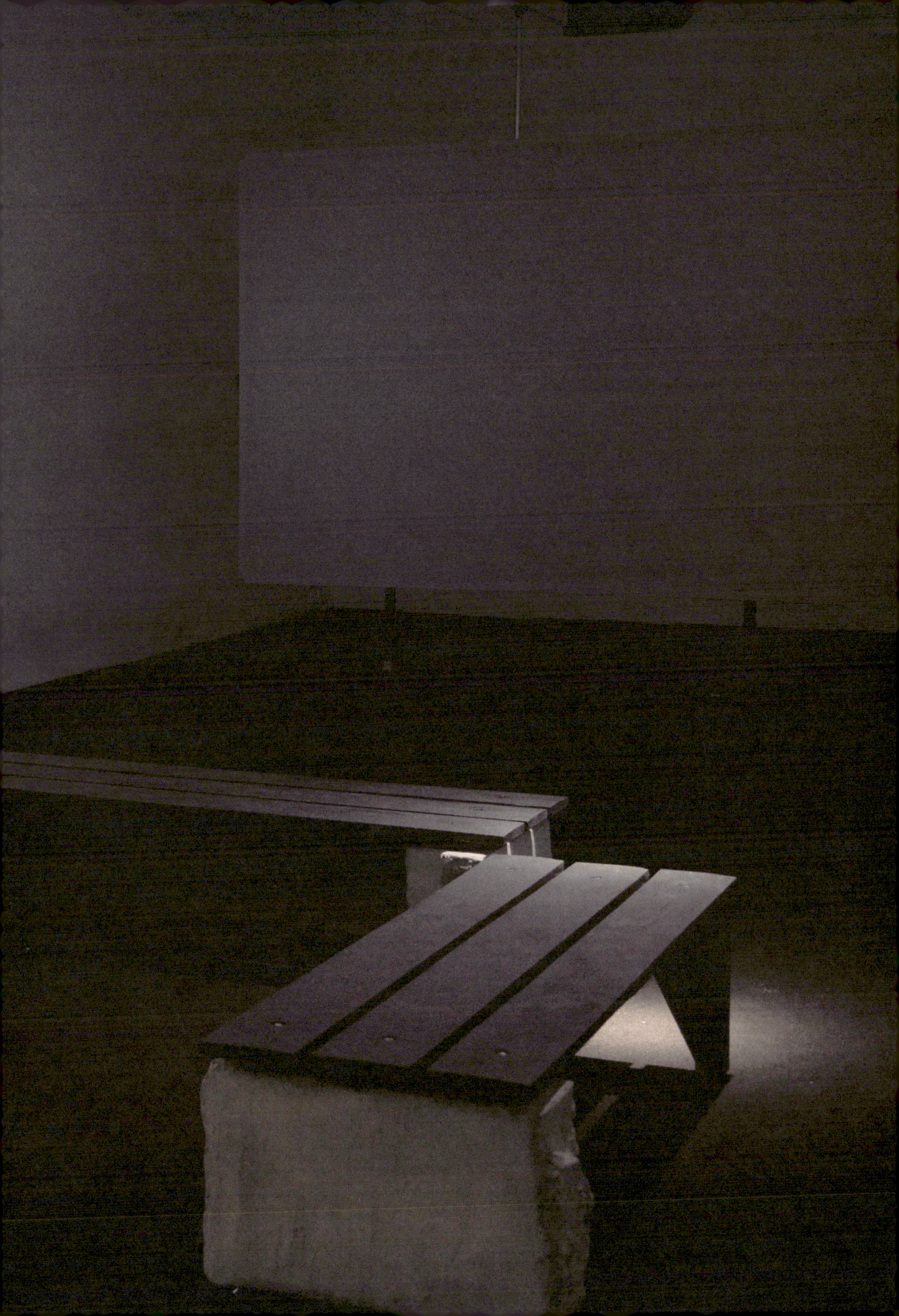

Horrid Objectivity

Joshua Comaroff

Why does horror stalk the modern block?

'Horror', here, might mean several things. In common parlance, it refers to a spectrum of negative affect, carefully parsed by Gothic author Ann Radcliffe: aversion and revulsion, the creep of the unheimlich,[1] dreadful anticipation in the form of 'terror', or the paralytic shock of encountering an object of fear ('horror' in its precise sense).[2] Increasingly, this term signifies frightful or traumatic event, as well as a range of media intended to deliver thrills associated with violence and anxiety. In architecture, horror is often communicated through distorted and monstrous forms, configurations that compromise human control and comfort, and social histories of crime and abuse.[3]

Houses, as principal spaces – and imaginaries – of intimacy, easily lend themselves to uncanny projections. All that invades, all that is alien, appears to contradict most horribly that world expected to be safe and 'kind' (in the older sense, of kindred). The home, old or new, might simply be understood as a spatial figuration of the category of 'inside', or 'us', as the familiar that is at risk of incursion by outsiders or outré behaviours. This was the seminal insight of Mary Douglas' *Purity and Danger* (1966): that social scandal and disgust does not arise from the *content* of things or actions, but rather from their *location*. 'Dirt', she famously wrote, 'is matter out of place'.[4] In this model, the architecture of intimacy simply stands for intimacy itself, as that which may be violated.

Given this, one might argue that there is nothing particularly special about the glass tower or the brutalist stack. Rather, these are simply iterations of the home-as-self, or home-as-society – and are thus no different from the haunted Victorians or suburban 'ranch' dwellings of supernatural horror films such as *Amityville Horror* (1979), *Poltergeist* (1982), or more lately *Stranger Things* (2016–present). Isn't a house just a house? Considered in this way, the exhibition *Horror in the Modernist Block* might struggle to justify the sexiness of its premise.

---

1. The uncanny (a translation of the German *unheimlich*) refers to a sensation of creeping unease upon the realization that the intimate is also deeply alien. This concept was developed in Sigmund Freud's *The Uncanny* (London: Penguin, 2002).

2. See Anne Radcliffe, 'On the Supernatural in Poetry', *New Monthly Magazine* 16, no.1 (1826): 147.

3. For an extensive discussion of this subject, see Joshua Comaroff and Ong Ker-Shing, *Horror in Architecture* (Novato, CA: ORO Editions, 2013; forthcoming edition, University of Minnesota Press, 2023), and Anthony Vidler's *The Architectural Uncanny: Essays in the Architectural Unhomely* (Cambridge, MA: MIT Press, 1994).

4. In *Purity and Danger: An Analysis of Concepts of Pollution and Taboo* (London: Routledge, 1984), 36.

The *modern* block, however, has other associations. It is not merely architecture writ large, or contemporary. Quite the contrary. It carries a great weight of ideological and historical baggage – much of which has to do, ostensibly, with the eviction of traditional terrors and violences. This produces an interesting tension; the *frisson* of this show's title arises, in part, because we see horror, and the modern block, as somehow in contradiction. The progressivist and utopian strains of ideology in architectural modernism promised a world without ancient fears, and without the social abuse and degradation associated with 19th century industrialism. This was to be a realm of social justice, just as it would be the domain of scientific, enlightened modes of thought.

This went beyond buildings. A canonical assumption of modern social theory was the progressive retreat of supernaturalism from the world. Max Weber theorised this process as 'rationalisation' and 'disenchantment'. The instrumental logic of capitalism had ostensibly come to dominate as a habit of thought – and with it, the human mind dismissed magical explanations for the doings of the world.[5] What had once been a mental orientation to reduce the agonies of Calvinist cosmology became (after the exit of the Holy Spirit during the Enlightenment period) an 'iron cage' of productivism and accumulation. Frankfurt School critic Theodor Adorno, who read the rise of productive rationality in yet more negative terms, saw any lingering belief in ghosts as the worst kind of irrational atavism, an infantile refusal to see one-dimensional society for what it was.[6] The increasingly common spectacle of the modern block represented nothing if not bureaucratisation, extended into the sphere of domestic life: the 'iron cage' in its most literal guise.

However we might feel about this condition, it appeared to leave little room for ghosts or irrational terrors. The ongoing haunting of the era was depicted in more straightforward and psychoanalytic guises: symbolic projections for stress and anxiety, or the collective shock of war and industry among the 'discontents' of contemporary civilisation.[7] In Henrik Ibsen's *Ghosts* (1881), the titular beings were a metaphor for sexual violence and venereal disease – an emergent symbolic system for speaking about the shadow of trauma in the industrial age.[8] The theories of split and shaken subjects, as in Georg Simmel's *The Metropolis and Mental Life* (1903) or Emile Durkheim's *The Division of Labor in Society* (1893), find their culprit in over-stimulation, depersonalisation, and anomie.

5. 'Science as Vocation', in *From Max Weber: Essays in Sociology* (Abingdon, UK: Routledge, 2009), 129.

6. Theodor W. Adorno, 'Theses Against Occultism', In *The Stars Down to Earth*. (London: Routledge, 1994), 174.

7. Of course, there has long been a counter-discourse among academics and artists – not least, those of the Spectral Studies school – to counter Weber's assumptions about disenchanted conditions. These point out, to the contrary, that modernity is an inherently spectral condition, and that this is clear when we consider such phenomena as the cyclical return of spiritualism. The point I am making, here, is not that terror and haunting went away – but rather, that they were *thought* to have gone away in the vanguard theories of the time.

8. Henrik Ibsen, *Ghosts and Other Plays* (London: Penguin, 1964).

There is truth to this. As Michel Foucault argued in his *History of Sexuality* (1976), the era of humanism produced more mass death than those past times associated in the cultural imagination with the arbitrary violence of kings and mobs.[9] And as modern buildings replaced antique ones, these became the new sites of age-old abuses: murders, domestic and sexual violence, and inhumane treatment. However, we might still ask: why is the modern block, in particular, so open to claims of horrible event and association? Is it simply the neutral backdrop (or symbolic materialisation) of generalised or individualised trauma? What is it about contemporary architecture that seems to offer itself as a site of terrors and apprehensions?

In *Time, Labor, and Social Domination* (1993), the late and brilliant social theorist Moishe Postone offers a more penetrating clue.[10] Postone unfolds a substantive reinterpretation of Karl Marx's critical theory, in part, around the objective character of work and the commodity. In an historically unprecedented way, Postone argues, labour and its products have become the medium by which all people are related. To survive, and to relate to humanity via a hegemonic marketplace, we must make and consume. Hence, our productive behaviour is twofold: it has a precise, or 'concrete' component, in the realisation of useful things; and it has an 'abstract' aspect, in generating value.[11] Our activity is dialectical in a manner that reflects the commodity itself, which likewise embodies both utilitarian properties and a quantum of pure fungibility. Both production and product represent discrete and physical instances, while being objective and universal.

Importantly, for Postone, it is this that determines the appearance of capitalism (and, we might add, its architectures) as inevitable, external and natural. Throughout history, transactions have had a personal basis; they were a mode of interaction among people. By contrast, modern fetishism lends objects an *objective* character. A horrid new animism arises; these appear not merely to possess value, and to exchange with one another in the marketplace, but to exist as forces and facts despite their clear artificiality as social products. The thing-for-sale has a substantial 'magic' with which we, as participants in a system that requires certain behaviours and modes of thought for survival, are persuaded to believe in.

As the inhabited commodity, architecture gains an impression of objectivity to an unusual degree; its rules, expectations and aesthetic standards do not appear arbitrary but as the basic and realistic constraints within which life, and the creative process, occur. The perception of these as existing *beyond* the realm of human determination is embodied in objects that appear to have their own independent agency and legitimacy. The necessary arrangements, the *habitus* of the home or the office, stands apart from and beyond ourselves.

9. Michel Foucault, *History of Sexuality, Volume 1: An Introduction* (New York: Patheon Books, 1976), 137.

10. Moishe Postone, *Time, Labor, and Social Domination* (Oxford, UK: Oxford University Press, 1993).

11. Ibid., 123.

A leitmotif (and prerequisite) of the uncanniness of the modern block is found here. In their objective and self-determining aspect, buildings *possess themselves* and 'act' free from our intentions. Spectral understandings, and a deep sense of human victimisation, seem practically inevitable in this context. The house that inhabits itself – its parts moving by independently, possessed of their own will and sinister intelligence – is merely an over-determined imaginary of the commodity-building as both magical repository and autonomous fact. The dwelling that can be neither properly owned nor domesticated, in a profound sense, is at the core of horror, and links many of its varied manifestations. This objectivity, a force apart from and beyond the reach of subjective agency, makes the block an alien and potentially harmful thing, with its own strategies of desire and violent intent. These are not 'social', in imagination or in practice, and exist without any recourse to intervention or negotiation on our part.

Objectivity cements ancient terrors and new abnormalities. Postone's account stands as a fully theorised analogue of Mark Fisher's 'capitalist realism' – in which the anthropogenic environment increasingly embodies the action of a perverse system, and colludes in the impression that this system is the only 'real'.[12] The horrid is not merely a cultural imaginary; instead, it permeates the very substance of the material world and tolerates no alternative. This self-same objectivity likewise lies at the heart of modern architecture's project of benevolent social engineering; here, too, it frightens. As in J.G. Ballard's *High Rise* (1975) (fig.1), it is precisely the function of the building, as an autonomous medium of benign order, that causes everything to go so dreadfully wrong.[13] In this respect, the discipline's utopianism, and its role as a site of commodity-production, are separable.

We build our life worlds inside this spectral objectivity; our spaces of domestic care and retreat are also the product of alien regimes, political orders and financial dispensations. Their social violence resonates in our rooms and corridors, which represent such foreign logic as something organic, and necessary. It falls to art, then, to make this not merely apparent – but, once again, horrifying.

12. Mark Fisher, *Capitalist Realism: Is There No Alternative?* (London: Repeater Books, 2009).

13. J.G. Ballard, *High Rise*, (New York: Harper Perennial, 2006) was also the subject of a 2016 cinematic adaptation directed by Ben Wheatley.

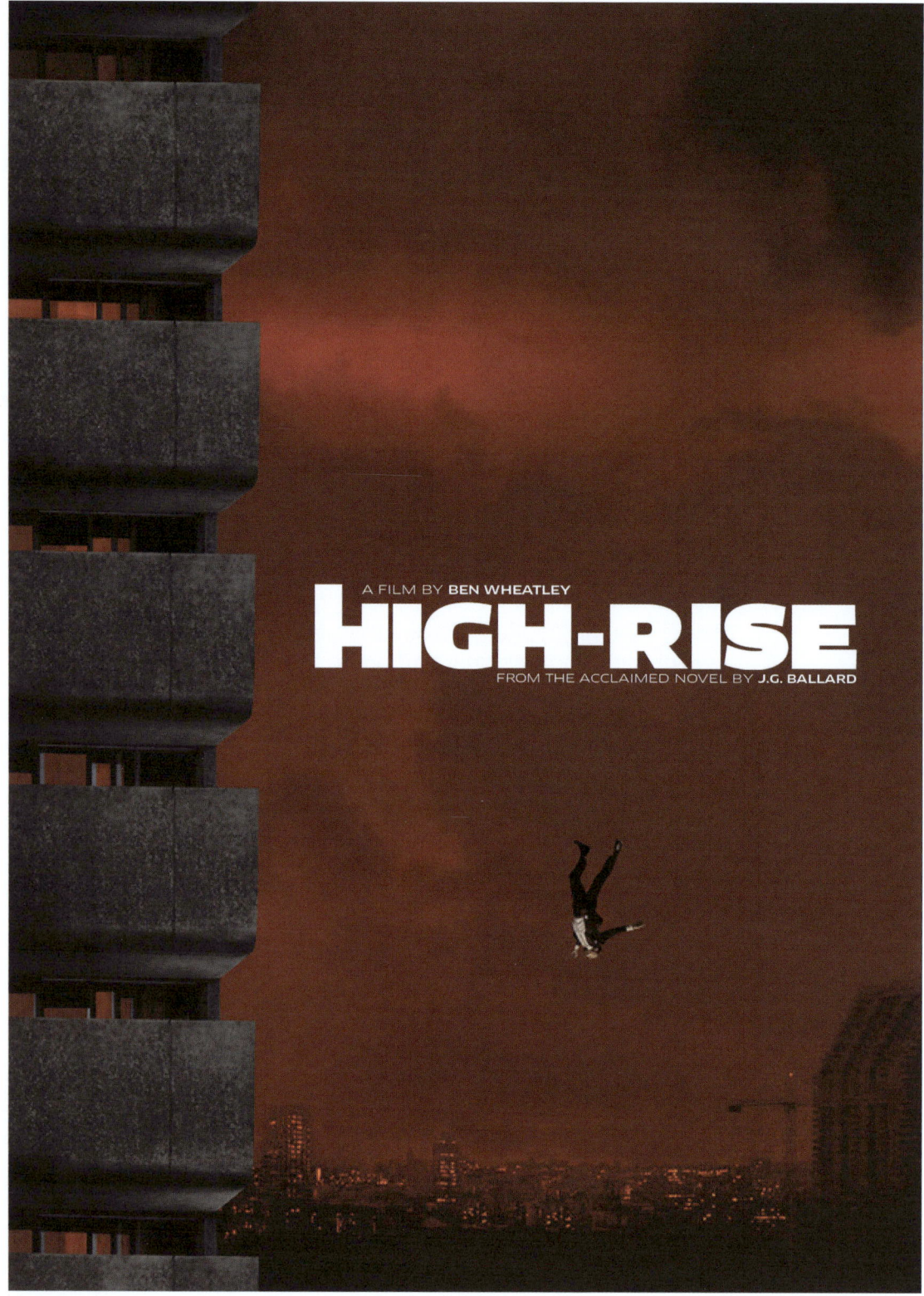

Fig. 1. *High Rise*, 2015, film poster, directed by Ben Wheatley

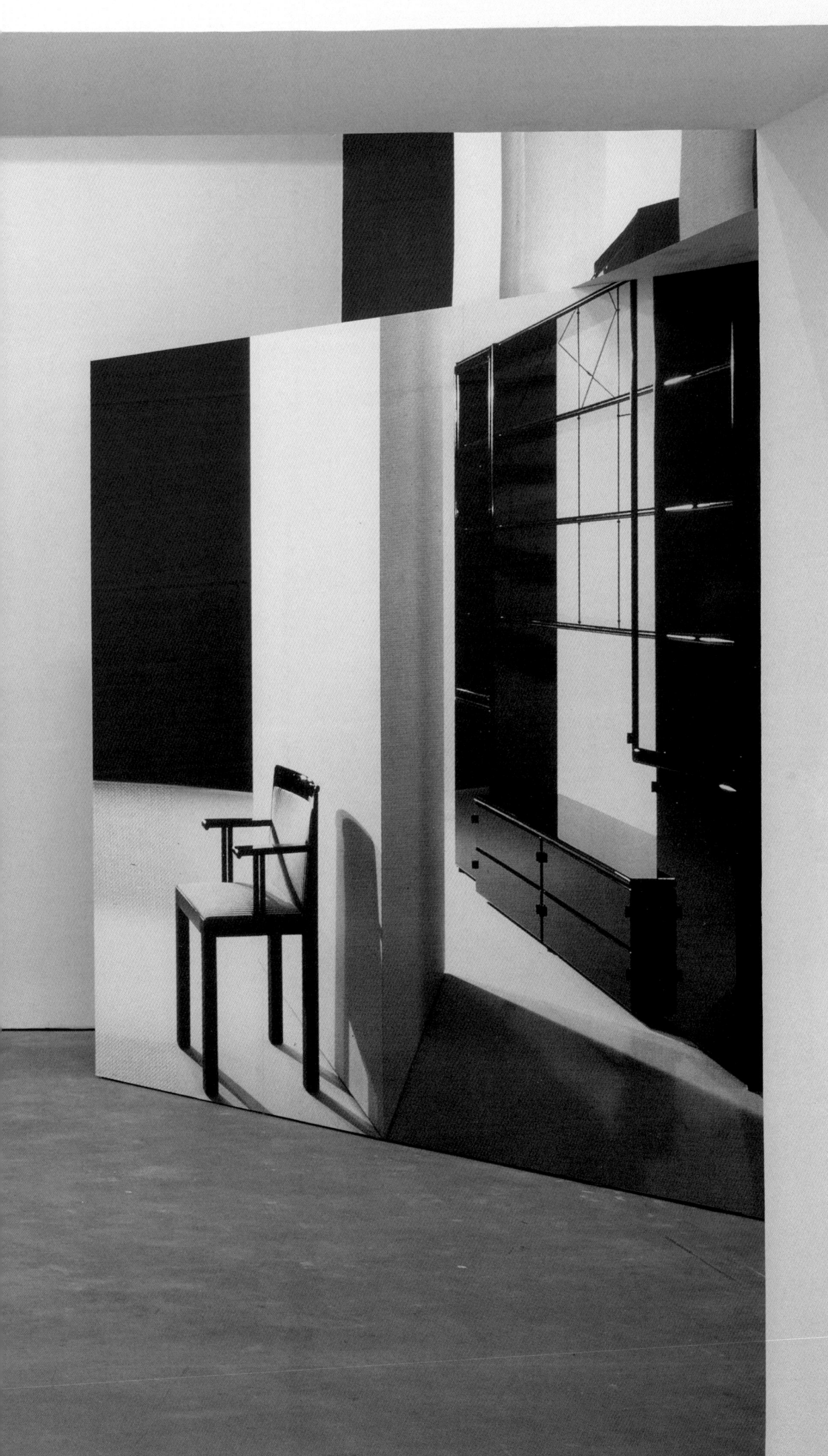

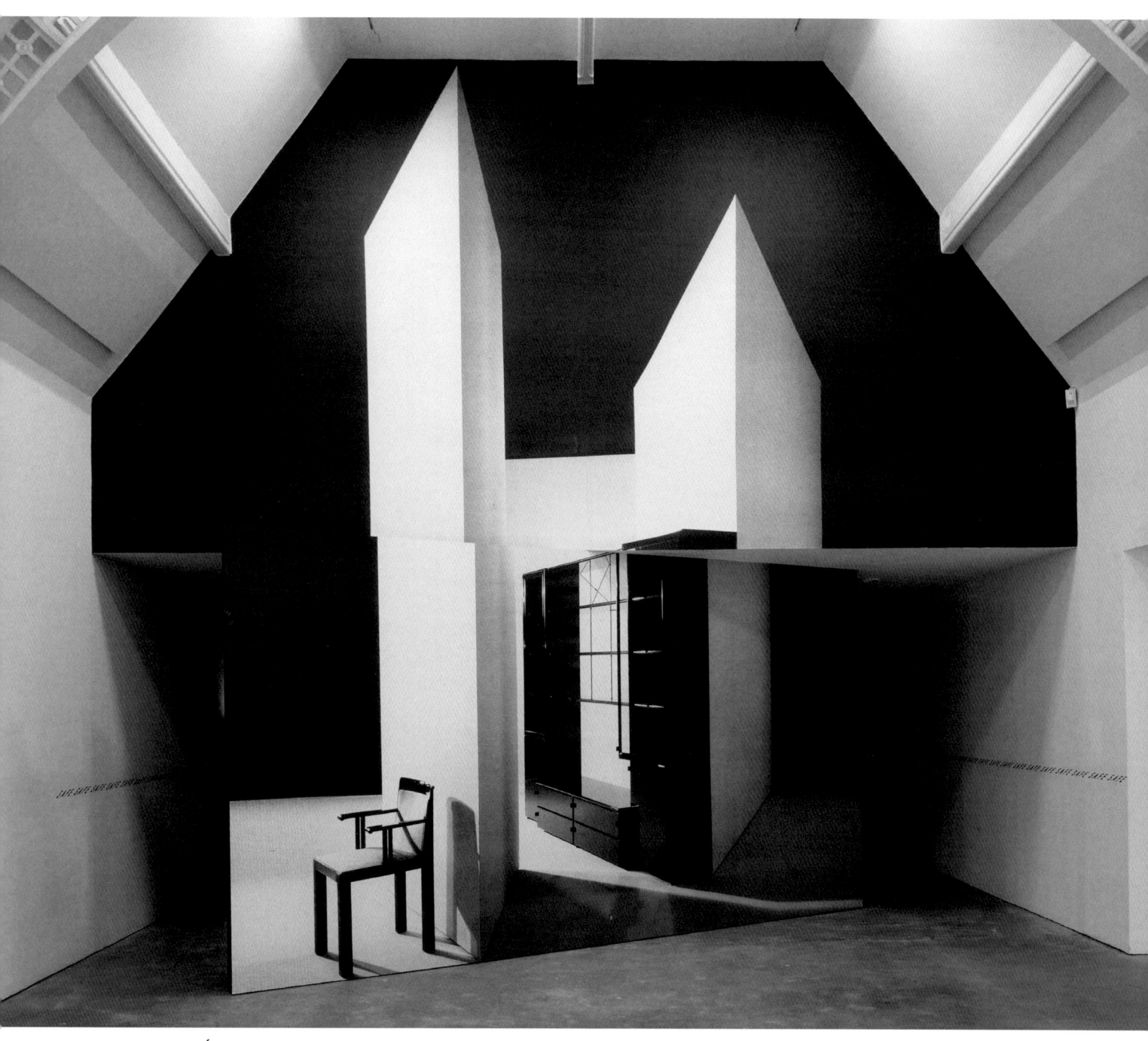

Espace vaincu, Énergie contrôlée (Vanquished space, Controlled energy), 2022, vinyl, paint, screen-print, lacquered and painted wood, carpet, glasses, water, gin, metal, mirror, light, photography, sound, 35 minutes (looped), 6071 × 474 × 268 cm, installation view from *Horror in the Modernist Block* at Ikon Gallery

Laëtitia Badaut Haussmann

Laëtitia Badaut Haussmann's practice is multi-disciplinary in scope, often incorporating sculpture, installation, image, text, video and sound. She is interested in 'para-architecture', a notion which refers to temporary structures that resemble architecture, but which for Badaut Haussmann is also an abstract generalisation of architectural concepts such as space and infrastructure. The artist's previous installation *La Politesse De Wassermann* (2017) used the setting of the Maison Louis Carré – designed by the Finnish architects Alvar and Elissa Aalto – to highlight the often-overlooked role of women in the field of architectural design.

Badaut Haussmann's site-specific installation *Espace vaincu, Énergie contrôlée* (Vanquished space, Controlled energy) (2022) playfully examines materials and tropes of high modernism to challenge representations of women within modernist architecture in film. The installation transforms a 6-metre-wide (usually hidden) niche within Ikon's Second Floor Galleries into a domestic interior. An angled wall extends into the main exhibition space, disrupting the gallery's neo-gothic features. Covering this structure and the upper wall of the exhibition space is a black-and-white image of a mid-20th century modernist interior from Badaut Haussmann's series *Maisons Françaises, une collection* (2013–ongoing).

Inside are existing works by Badaut Haussmann that create a 'feminist space' and alternative to the modernist homes of women in horror films. *Safe Maîtresse* (2020), a black-and-white screen-print lining the interior walls, appropriates the titles of two films – Barbet Schroeder's *Maîtresse* (1976) and Todd Haynes' *Safe* (1995). *Stage Circle Marble* (2020), a sculptural representation of the BDSM dungeon in *Maîtresse*, doubles as a coffee table. A new sculpture, *Falling Stairs* (2022), interacts with an existing trap door, with two stainless steel poles that connect the carpeted floor to an infinity mirror. A sound piece, *Fading Away* (2021), comprises excerpts from different interviews with Marguerite Duras, Marianne Faithfull and Todd Haynes. The freestanding sculpture *Scenius II (Rouge Noir)* (2018) provides the only source of light, enhancing the installation's ominous atmosphere and ambiguous sense of scale.

Espace vaincu, Énergie contrôlée reflects on the possibility of a feminist architecture. Can a dungeon in *Maîtresse* and a New Age clinic in *Safe* be considered feminist? These questions are further explored through still images taken from Italian director Dario Argento's film *Tenebrae* (1982), which show lesbian journalist Tilde in the home she shares with her lover moments before she is killed. Dispersed throughout the installation, these images show a woman who – until her cinematic death – inhabited the 'modernist dream'.

LM

Born 1980, Paris
Lives and works in Paris and London

Laëtitia Badaut Haussmann's work revolves around the notion of para-architecture. Her research is situated at the intersection of several fields including domesticity, psychology and feminism. Her practice centres on the concept of design and its history as forms of social and political expression. She works with sculpture, installation, image, text, video and sound; the exhibition being her main medium.

A graduate of the École Nationale Supérieure d'Arts, Paris-Cergy (2006), Haussmann was awarded the 2017 AWARE Prize (Archives of Women Artists, Research and Exhibitions). Her work has been the subject of numerous solo and group exhibitions at Campoli Presti (2022); Musée d'Art Moderne de Paris (2022); Fondation d'entreprise Pernod Ricard (2021); The Community, Paris (2021); A Tale of A Tub, Rotterdam (2021); Centre Pompidou (2020); Beeler Gallery, Columbus, Ohio, USA (2020); Museum of Contemporary Art of Rome (2020); MRAC – Musée Régional d'Art Contemporain Occitanie (2019); Musée d'art contemporain de la Haute-Vienne – Château de Rochechouart (2018); Kettle's Yard (2018), MUSEION | Museo d'arte contemporanea di Bolzano (2017); Mudam Luxembourg – Musée d'Art Moderne Grand-Duc Jean (2017), and Centre Pompidou-Metz (2017), among others. She has undertaken residencies at the Secession, Vienna (2022); Villa Kujoyama, Kyoto, Japan (2016), and Palais de Tokyo Pavillon Neuflize OBC (2011–12). Haussmann is represented by Galerie Allen, Paris, and collaborates with Ellen de Bruijne, Amsterdam.

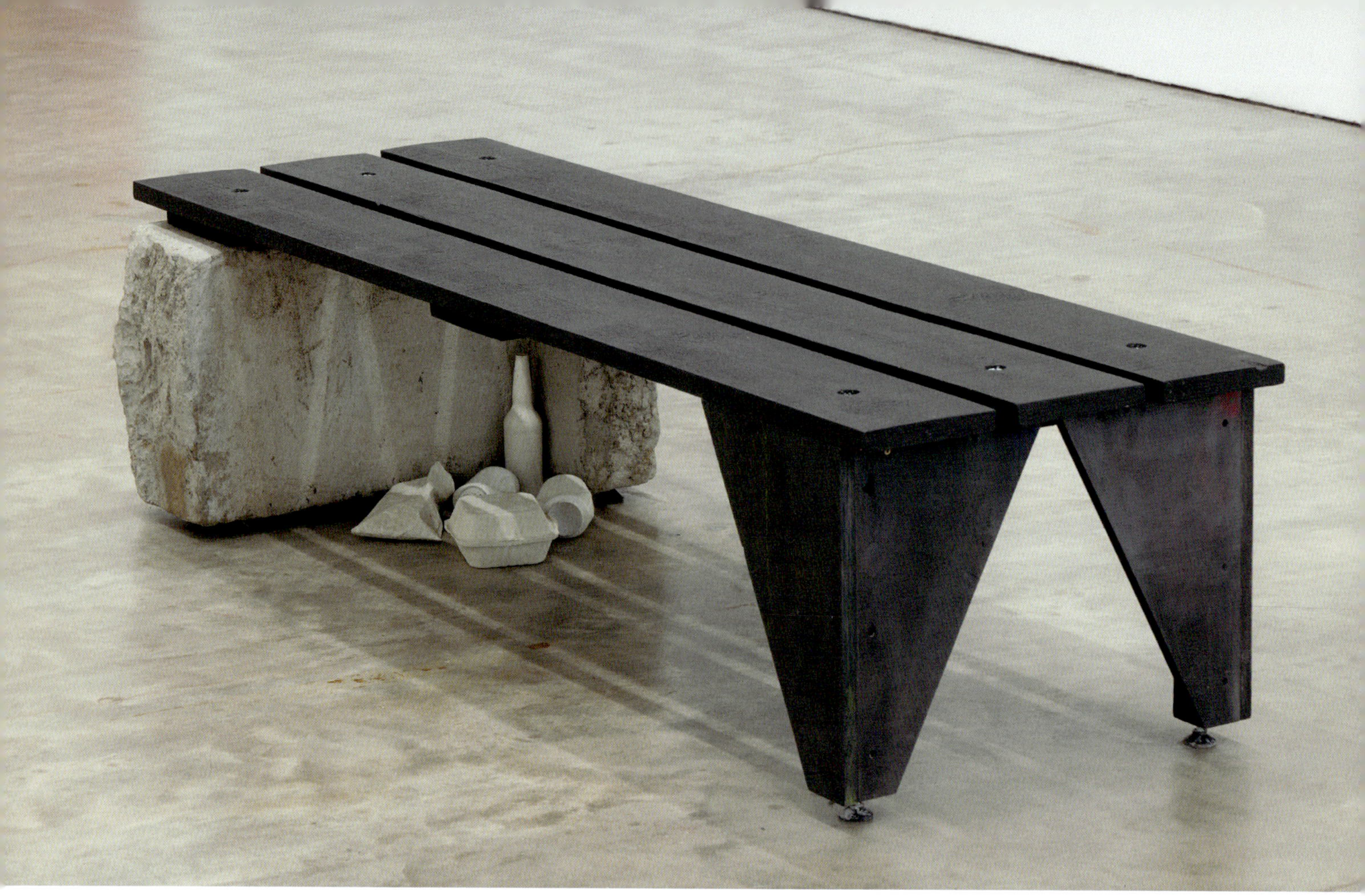

How to live in a city, 2022, concrete, polystyrene, wood, paint, fixings, 46 × 180 × 66 cm, installation view from *Horror in the Modernist Block* at Ikon Gallery

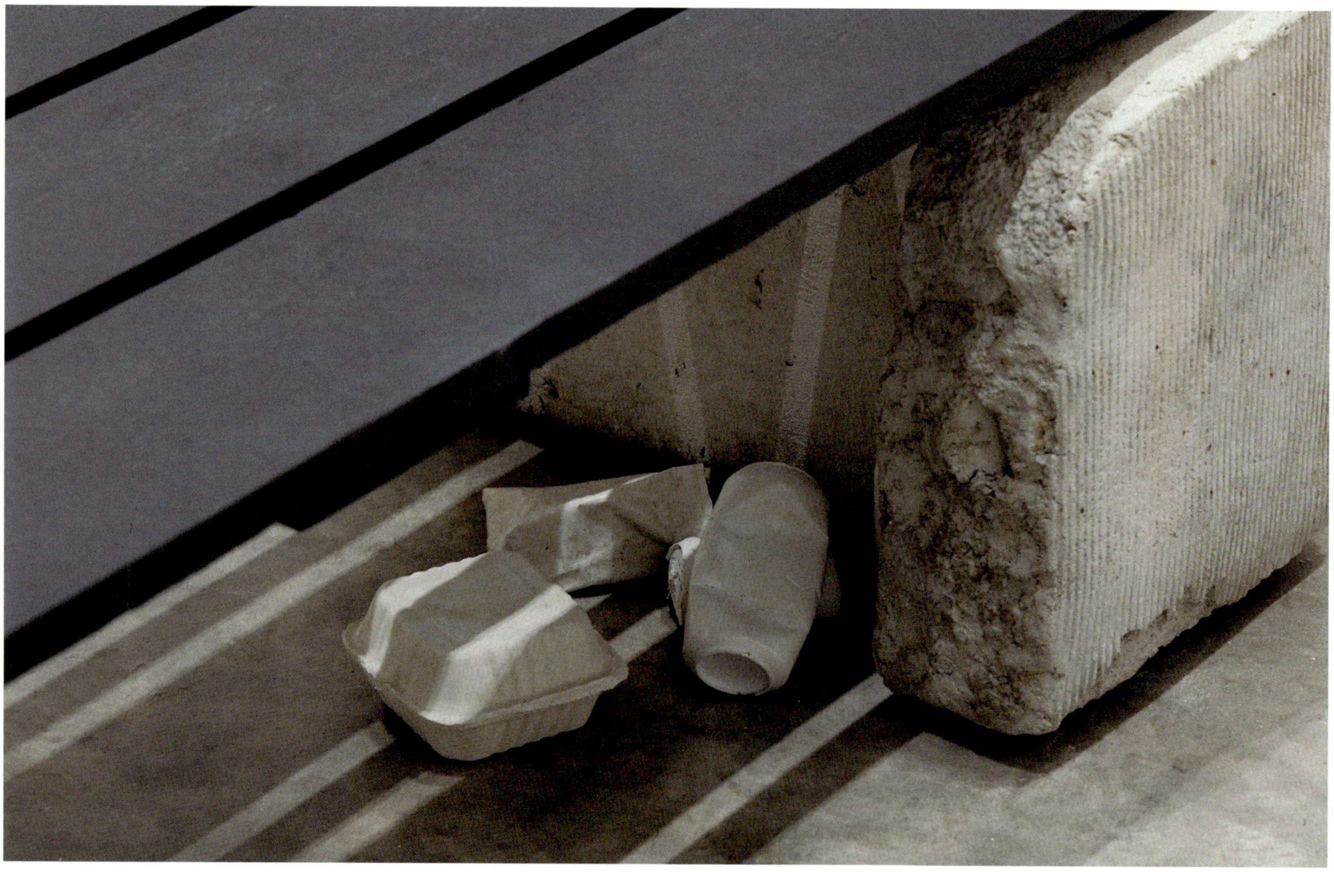

Simon & Tom Bloor

Simon & Tom Bloor's practice explores post-war urban landscapes and inner-city regeneration schemes, with particular emphasis on civic monuments and modernist sculptures. They use a range of media to connect with the utopian potential of the recent past, with works focussing on public spaces such as housing developments.

How to live in a city (2022) is a series of four sculptures that double as seating. Resembling street furniture in design, their use of recycled materials associated with the aesthetics of architectural modernism suggest that they have been put together from the ruins of a disaster – as if a post-apocalyptic society were attempting to reproduce a post-war municipal environment. The angular legs of the benches reference Czech designer and architect Vlatislav Hofman's (1884–1964) cubist *Chair* (also known as *The Hofman Chair*) that was part of a commission by sculptor Josef Mařatka. In referencing the aesthetic language of Hofman through recycled materials, the Bloors recall the high modernist aspirations of post-war town planners. Cost-cutting and reduced budgets meant that many of these developments were not fully realised, or – in the case of John Madin's Central Library for Birmingham – modified and not subsequently maintained.

Underneath two benches are concrete sculptures cast from beer bottles, cans and takeaway food boxes resembling the detritus often found underneath public seating. Facing Karim Kal's *Entourage 1, Lyon / Guillotière* (2017), the bench in Ikon's Second Floor Galleries is evocative of public furniture whose function has been made redundant due to the demolition of nearby residential housing. Remaining in their original orientation towards public parks and residential spaces, such benches are humorous signifiers of changes in contemporary town planning. *How to live in a city* highlights the role of public benches as important spaces for social gathering and sites of transgression.

LM

Born 1973, Birmingham
Live and work in Birmingham

Simon & Tom Bloor are artists who make works and projects for and about public space, developed from their experience of growing up in a post-industrial city and its legacy of regeneration. Addressing the histories and fabric of the built environment, they view the urban landscape half through rose tinted spectacles and half a cynical gaze. Running throughout their practice is a playful optimism about the design of the built environment and the people who use it.

Past exhibitions, commissions and public artworks include Pallet Stack, Warwick Arts Centre, Coventry (2022); Bluecoat Platform, Bluecoat, Liverpool (2021); *The Aerodrome*, Ikon Gallery (2019); THE CITY IS WHERE WE'RE GOING NEXT, Baltic, Gateshead, (2019); Structure for the City Observatory, Collective Gallery, Edinburgh (2016); Festival of Love, Southbank Centre, London (2015), and *Loose Parts*, Whitechapel Gallery, London (2013).

Ruth Claxton

Ruth Claxton's studio practice explores the mediation of space through reflective material, sculpture and architectural intervention. Her work often addresses the cultures of art institutions which shape how art is viewed in these spaces.

Here I am, waiting (2014–22) is an installation of sculptural forms made from cast plaster and aluminium foil. In the installation, some forms are fixed slightly out from the wall, as if floating. Others are placed on support structures of rebar; a form of reinforced steel used to improve the tensile strength of concrete. Each sculpture is coated with the light reflective paint typically used on high-vis workwear and road signs. The brightness and form of the sculptures vary according to light levels and the movement of viewers. These variations make the sculptures seem 'alive' – as if they were subjects instead of inanimate objects.

In one sculptural arrangement, sheets punctuated by holes reveal stacked forms behind: a layering reminiscent of Louis Kahn's National Assembly Building (1982) in Dhaka, Bangladesh. Other forms contain multiple indentations, evidencing the trace of the artist's hand. The mixture of fabricated materials and handcrafted gestures evokes the complex combination of artistry and manufacturing within architectural modernism, such as designer William Mitchell's concrete murals (1968) at Hockley flyover in Birmingham.

The title of the work references a line of *Everybody Here Wants You* (1998), a song by Jeff Buckley in which he sings: 'I'll be waiting right here just to show you.' The song conveys its subject's affection for and estrangement from their popular lover. This simultaneous sense of intimacy and distance is reflected in the work's dual materiality. Upon approach and without light, the sculptures lose their reflective quality and become opaque, eluding vision. Yet their visibility (from a distance) also depends on the presence and engagement of viewers to activate them.

For this installation, Claxton invites audiences to view the works using the torch on their phone or to take a picture with flash. In the resulting images, the sculptures appear like digital ghosts, manifesting as if by magic from the black abyss.   MP

Born 1971, Ipswich, UK
Lives and works in Birmingham

Ruth Claxton's practice takes a variety of forms. She makes artworks for exhibitions and public spaces, resources (Birmingham Art Map), infrastructure for artists (STEAMhouse, The Syllabus), and multiverses such as Eastside Projects, which she co-founded in 2008.

Spanning sculpture, drawing and installation, her studio practice reflects on space, the architecture of the gallery, and how art is viewed, often using reflective surfaces to create multiple perspectives within a single work. Claxton trained at Nottingham Trent University and the Royal College of Art (MA Sculpture). Solo exhibitions and public artworks include *once solid now dissolved*, Quench, Margate (2022); *In Intimacy, New Solitudes*, New Art Gallery Walsall (2016); *Specular, Spectacular*, Pippy Holdsworth, London (2013); *Synthetic Worlds (Two Women)*, Grundy Art Gallery, Blackpool (2013); *House of Beasts*, Meadow Arts (2011–12); *Synthetic Worlds*, SITE, Santa Fe, New Mexico, USA (2011); *Land's End*, Ikon Gallery; Oriel Davies Gallery, Newtown, Wales; Spike Island, Bristol, and Grundy Art Gallery, Blackpool (2008–09), among others.

Here I am, waiting, 2014–22, plaster, foil, rebar, retroflective pigment, installation view from *Horror in the Modernist Block* at Ikon Gallery

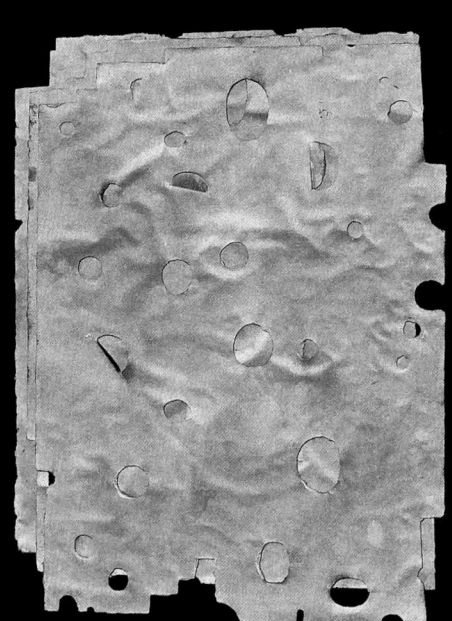

Shezad Dawood

Shezad Dawood's richly layered artworks imagine alternative pasts and futures, drawing on history, philosophy, ecology and architecture. Much of his work centres on the geopolitics and legacy of modernism in India, Pakistan and Bangladesh following Partition in 1947. His project *Encroachments* (2020) explores the 'illegal' structures established on and around private and state properties in Pakistan; a form of 'shadow' architecture that counters the linearity of state- and capitalist-driven architecture.

The Directorate (2019) is a tapestry which depicts a view of the vacant pool adjoining the former US Consulate in Karachi, Pakistan, designed by Richard Neutra and Robert Alexander. Neutra and Alexander's modernist design was originally intended to serve as the site of the US Embassy but was downgraded to a consulate after the country's capital was moved to Islamabad in 1967. In Dawood's tapestry, the empty pool serves as a reminder of this fate, and how such architecture was used during the Cold War to project an image of the United States as dynamic and modern. A veil of red and yellow particles recalling specks of blood partially obscures the view. Their arrangement mirrors the coloured patterns of the black terrazzo flooring of the consulate, which is represented in the fabric wallpaper behind Dawood's tapestry. Enhancing the eerie atmosphere of the image is a line of iridescent green, which slices through the picture plane.

Dawood's research on the history of the consulate has uncovered several interesting facts and stories. It is believed to have housed a CIA supercomputer; a fact ostensibly proven by gouges in the terrazzo flooring that were left after its removal. It was also allegedly built around the burial plot of a Sufi saint, a shrine to whom exists as a makeshift wooden construction just outside the consulate's perimeter.

MP

Born 1974, London
Lives and works in London

Shezad Dawood is a multidisciplinary artist who interweaves stories, realities and symbolism to create richly layered artworks, spanning painting, textiles, sculpture, film and digital media. Fascinated by ecologies and architecture, his work takes a philosophical approach, asking questions and exploring alternative futures through what Dawood describes as 'world-building' and 'imagineering'. His practice is animated by research, working with multiple audiences and communities to delve into narrative, history and embodiment.

Selected exhibitions and commissions include: St. Pancras International (2022); DesertX AlUla, KSA (2022); Toronto Biennial of Art (2022); Sea Art Festival, Busan (2021); Paradise Row, London (2021); Folkestone Triennial (2021); Guggenheim, New York (2021); Southbank Centre, London (2020–21); Kai Art Center, Tallinn (2020); New Art Exchange, Nottingham (2020); WIELS, Brussels (2020); Manifesta 13 (2020); Lahore Biennial (2020); Dhaka Art Summit (2020); Sharjah Biennial 14, UAE (2019) – Jury Prize for *Encroachments*; The Bluecoat Liverpool (2019); MOCA Toronto (2019); Kunstverein, Munich (2019); Gwangju Biennale (2018); Rubin Museum of Art, New York (2018); Fondazione Querini Stampalia, Venice (2017); The Museum of Modern Art, New York (2015); Modern Art Oxford (2012); Tate Triennial: *Altermodern* (2009), and the 53rd Venice Biennale (2009).

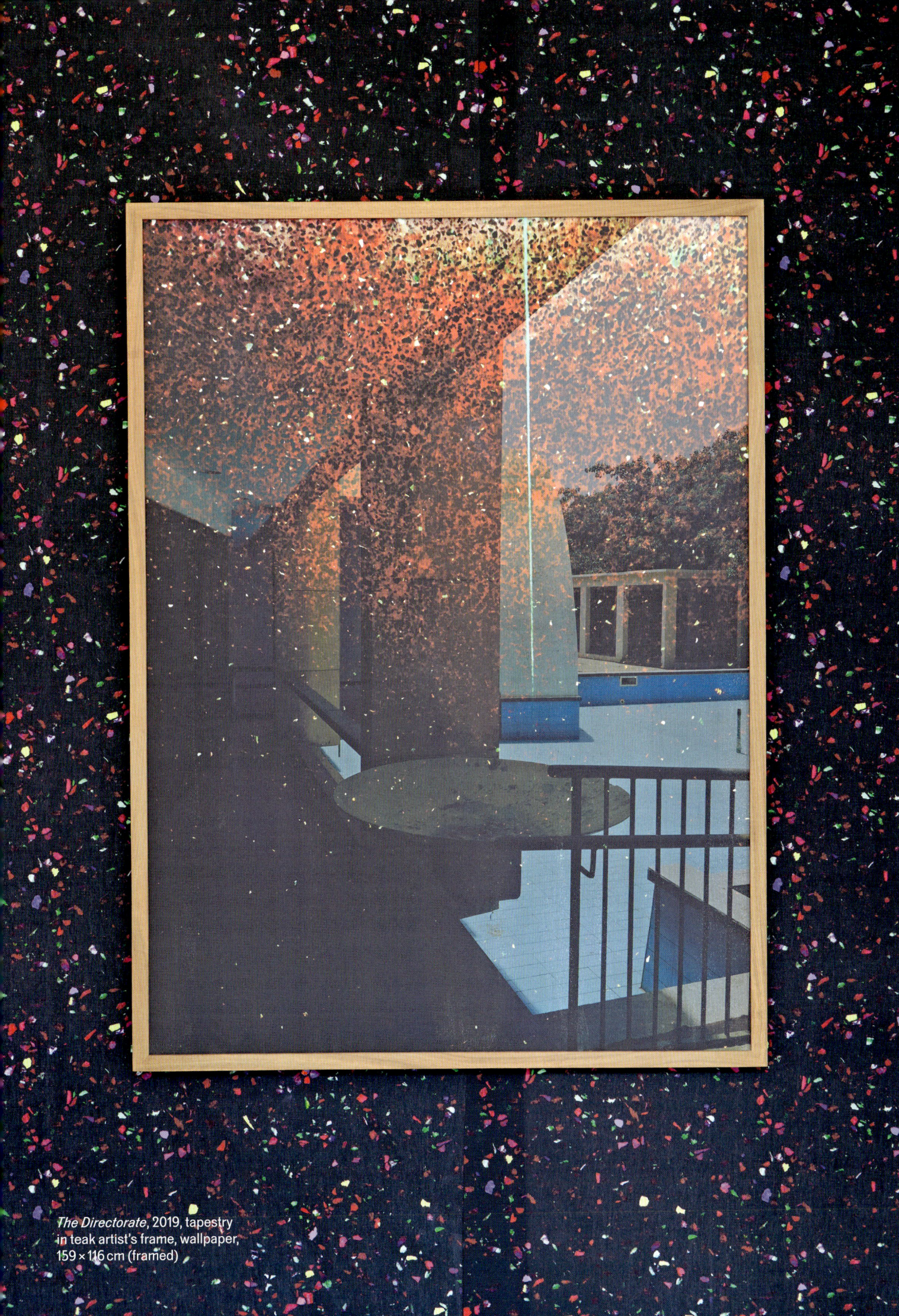

The Directorate, 2019, tapestry in teak artist's frame, wallpaper, 159 × 116 cm (framed)

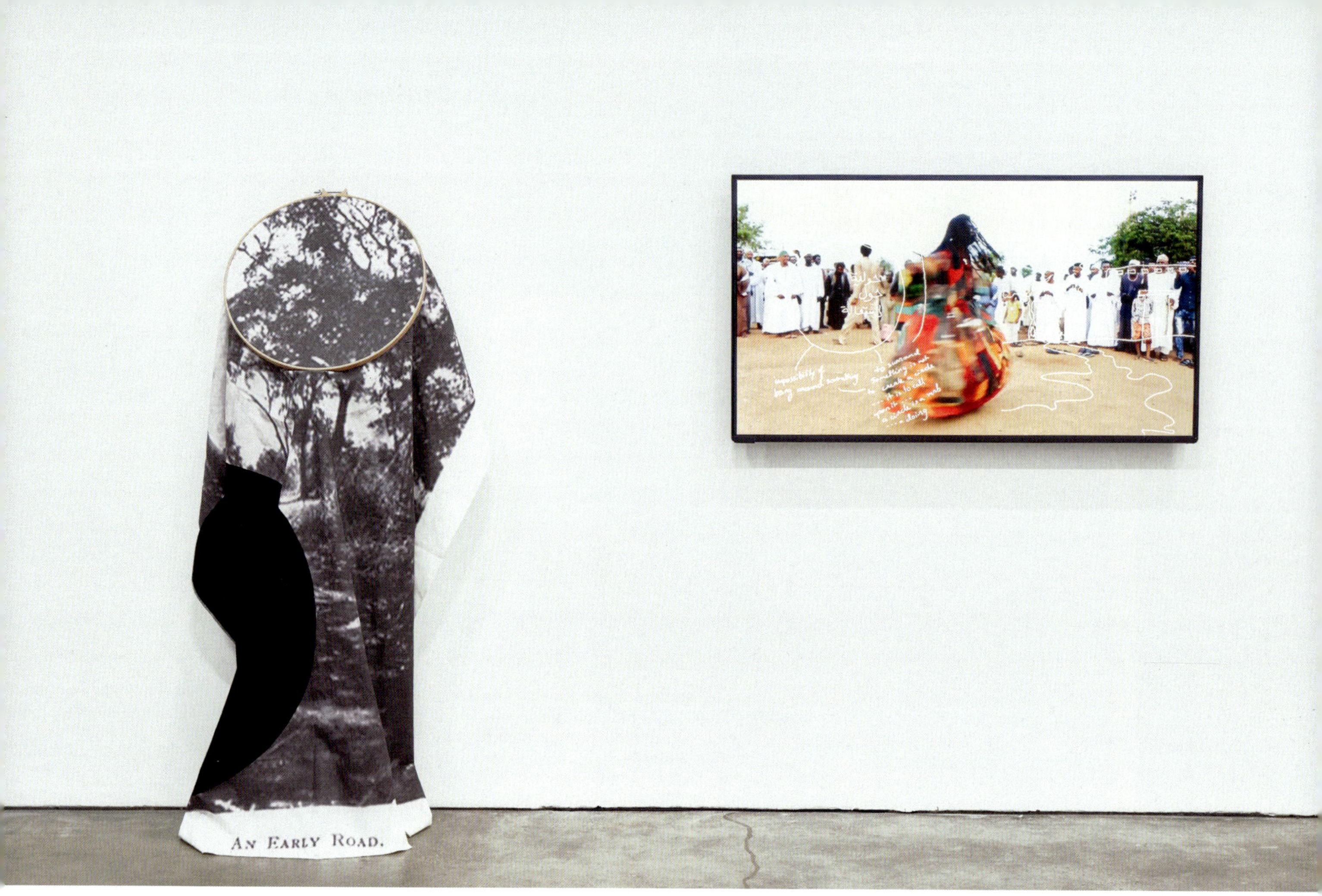

Above: *An Early Road Before a Modern One*, 2022, beech wood embroidery hoop with black-and-white print on fabric, 150 × 200 cm, installation view from *Horror in the Modernist Block* at Ikon Gallery

Above and below: *The Line That Follows*, 2022, 4K video with archival footage montage, 11:52 minutes, installation view from *Horror in the Modernist Block* at Ikon Gallery

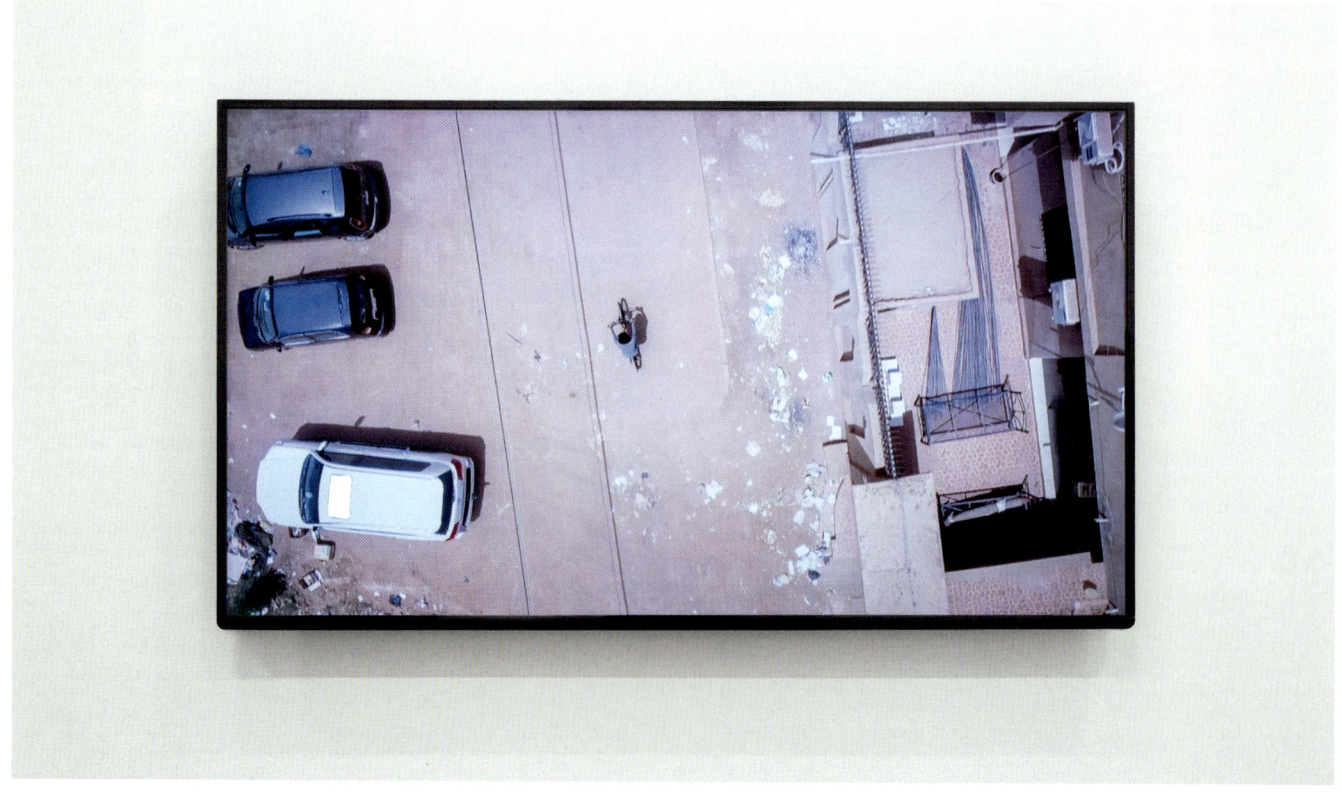

Ola Hassanain

Ola Hassanain's artistic practice responds to the politics of space, specifically in relation to Khartoum, the capital of Sudan. Her research and works identify the ways in which state violence is encoded in architecture, and how the built environment regulates the lives of the people who use it. Having trained as an architect, Hassanain is developing a practice that centres on what she describes as 'spatial literacy'. She is interested in 'informal' architectures shaped by individual, collective and social needs.

The Line that Follows (2022) is a short film overlaid with sound and a digital script that flows freely between text, abstract shapes, schemas, and maps representing spaces in Khartoum. At the beginning of the film, a man slowly cycles through quiet, tree-lined streets with gated buildings, accompanied by the sound of an unseen crowd. Interspersed are sequences of whirling Sufi dancers, the overlaid script plotting the circular movements of the dance and surrounding crowd.

An Early Road Before A Modern One (2022) is a sculpture that traces the history of Sudan's subjugation under British colonial rule and its impact on the landscape. The embroidery hoop creates an enclosure of space and references the circular Sufi dance for which the material is used. Printed on the fabric is an image showing a trodden passageway through vegetation; a reproduction of a black-and-white photograph that Hassanain found during a research visit to The National Records Office of Sudan. The photograph is part of an archive documenting Anglo-Egyptian rule from 1899 to 1955, when Sudan was first 'modernised' by the British. During this time and the latter part of the 20th century, when the Soviet Union exerted economic and political influence in the country, many Indigenous settlements were cleared to make way for modernist constructions. LM

Born 1985, Khartoum
Lives and works in Amsterdam and Khartoum

Ola Hassanain is an artist with degrees in architecture, cultural identity and globalisation. A Rijksakademie resident (2021–22), she is Head Tutor of the Blacker Blackness MA Course at the Sandburg Institute and Lecturer at HKU University of the Arts, Utrecht, where she received her MA in Fine Art (with distinction) in 2016.

Hassanain's work focuses on developing spatial literacy through the idea of 'space as discourse', an expanded notion of space that encompasses a scavenging mode of analysis and the re-presentation of space. Her artistic research responds to the politics of space – how architecture positions 'building' as an ecological 'emptying' of territories and an infrastructure for continuous cycles of 'catastrophe', such as forced migration. Her practice is also informed by the cultural, political and societal position of women in Khartoum, including her own experiences and her family's diaspora. Her project Back and Forth (2016–ongoing) deals with the link between women, public space and policies in Khartoum. Her work has been presented at Casco Art Institute (2021–22), Sharjah Architecture Triennial (2019–20) and Chicago Architecture Biennial (2019–20), among others. From 2017–18, she was a fellow at BAK basis actuele voor Kunst, Utrecht.

Ho Tzu Nyen

Ho Tzu Nyen's immersive works often take the form of multimedia installations. Non-linear narratives draw inspiration from art history, philosophy and mythology, combining pictorial strategies of painting with technologies of live theatre. Many of Ho's works explore the complex history of Southeast Asia, re-imagining the region's folklore, colonial past and historical figures.

The Cloud of Unknowing (2011) was created by Ho for the Singapore Pavilion at the 54th Venice Biennale. Titled after an anonymous 14th-century mystical treatise intended for contemplative prayer, the video work explores the meaning and representation of clouds in art. From the luminous clouds of works by Antonio da Correggio (1489–1534) to the mists that envelope Chinese landscape paintings, clouds have often been used to evoke ascension, metamorphosis and the divine. Yet, as Ho reflects: 'when we look up at clouds in the sky, we are always reminded of the downward pull of gravity and the weight of our flesh'. Ho thus sets *The Cloud of Unknowing* in a dilapidated public housing block in Singapore that was earmarked for demolition at the time of filming. In the artist's words, the block 'would soon follow the way of all flesh', its materials returned to ground zero.

Located in Taman Jurong in western Singapore, the housing block in *The Cloud of Unknowing* was one of many residential projects set up by the Housing Development Board to combat the country's housing crisis in the 1960s. In the work, each apartment is occupied by a character imagined by the artist, based on the block's former residents. Their actions seem plagued by daily struggles and unspoken fear, alluding to the threatening messages from creditors that Ho found on walls and doors of apartments in the block. As a mysterious cloud engulfs the characters, the soundtrack escalates, ending in a dramatic climax akin to an audio-visual apocalypse. In the calm that follows the storm, another cloud – released by a smoke machine – creates both a sense of transcendence and grounding, merging the imaginary realm of the work with the real world of the exhibition space.

MP

Born 1976, Singapore
Lives and works in Singapore

Ho Tzu Nyen works primarily in film, video and performance. His films and multimedia works investigate the construction of history and the plurality of identity. Drawing on historical events, documentary footage, art history, music videos and literary sources, his complex works explore the many possible relationships between still images, moving images, sound and text. Ho often collaborates with theatre professionals to create multisensory and often highly theatrical works, emphasising the ambiguity and doubt which permeate individual and collective myths.

Solo and group exhibitions include *Scheherazade, at Night*, Palais de Tokyo, Paris, France (2022); *The 49th Hexagram*, Hammer Museum, Los Angeles, USA (2021); *Night March of Hundred Monsters*, Toyota Municipal Museum of Art, Toyota City, Japan (2021); *Voice of Void*, Yamaguchi Center for Art and Media [YCAM], Kyoto, Japan (2021); *2 or 3 Tigers*, Haus der Kulturen der Welt, Berlin, Germany (2017); *The Cloud of Unknowing*, Guggenheim Museum, Bilbao, Spain (2015), and *The Cloud of Unknowing*, Mori Art Museum, Tokyo, Japan (2012). His work was also presented at the Singapore Pavilion at the 54th Venice Biennale in 2011. Together with Taiwanese artist Hsu Chia-wei, he co-curated *The Strangers from Beyond the Mountain and the Sea*, the 7th Asian Art Biennale, at the National Taiwan Museum of Fine Arts in 2019. Ho has a BA in Creative Arts from Victorian College of the Arts, University of Melbourne (2001), and an MA in Southeast Asian Studies from the National University of Singapore (2007). He is represented by Kiang Malingue, Hong Kong.

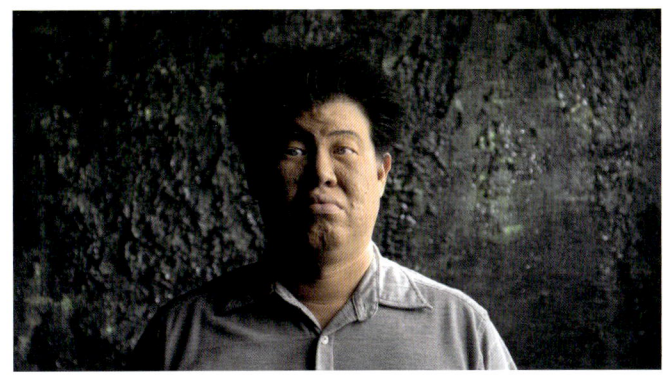
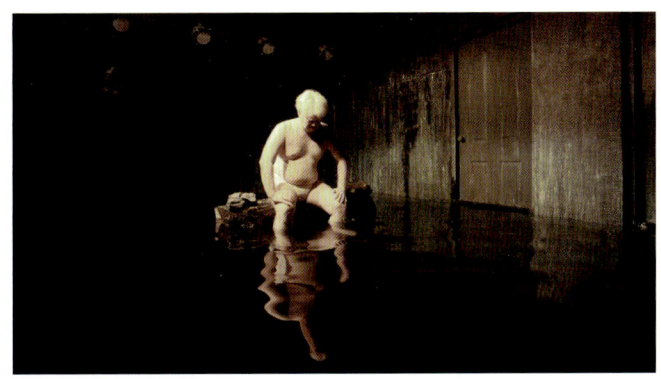
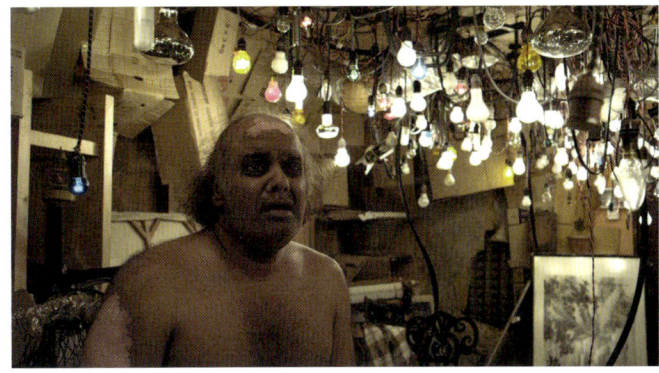
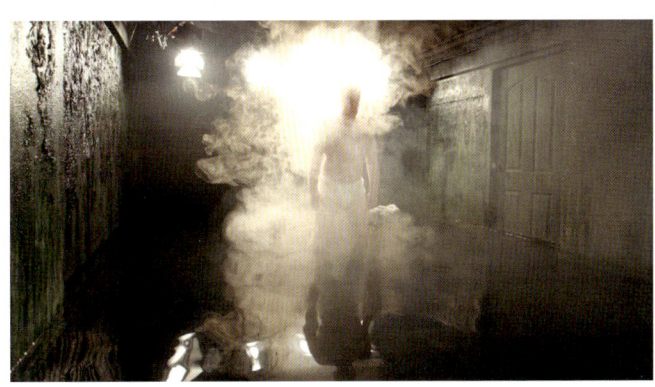
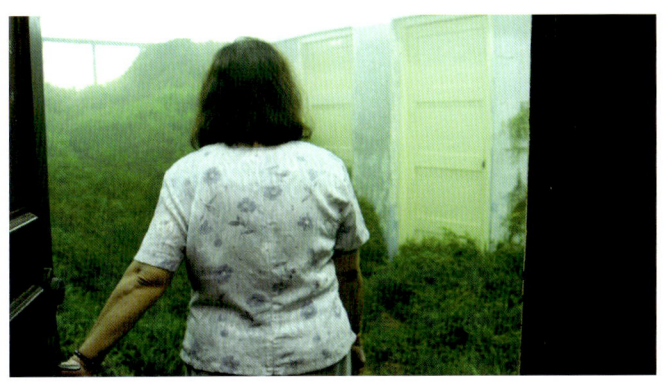
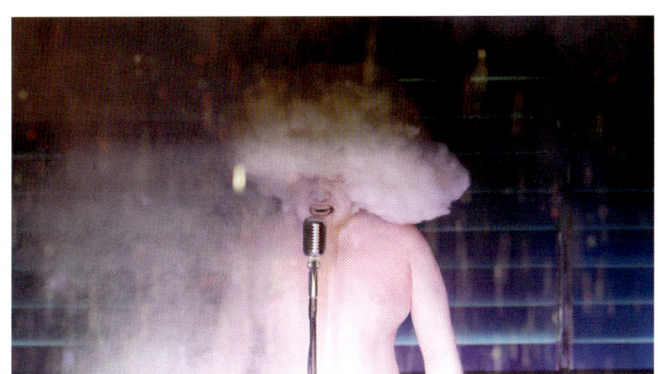
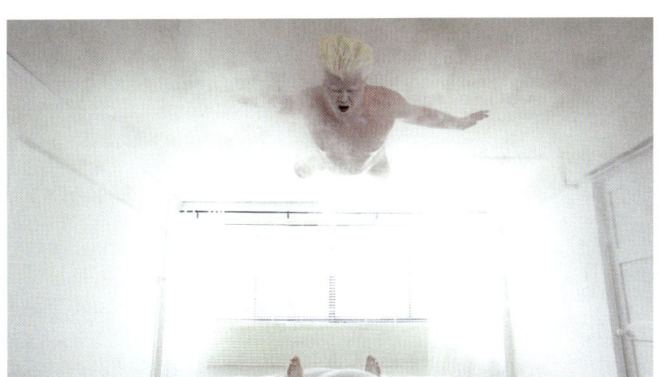
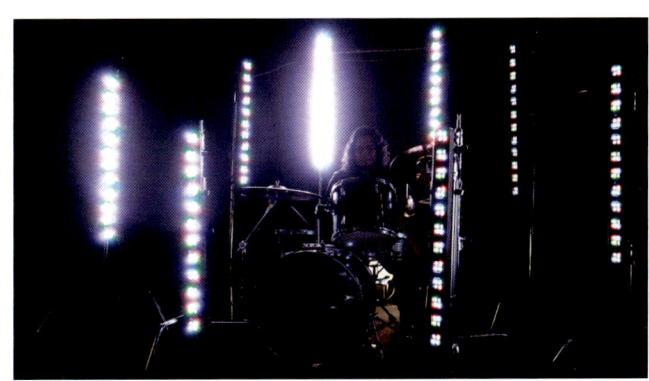
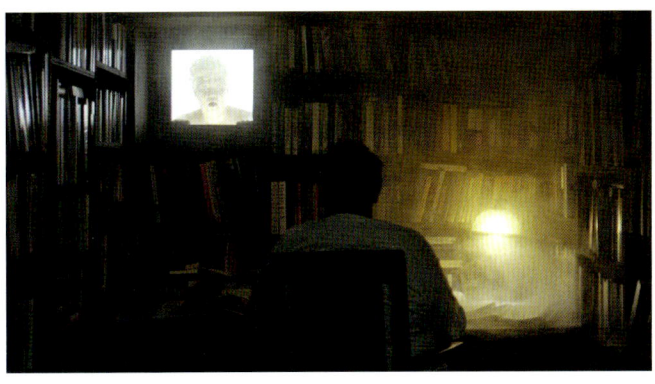
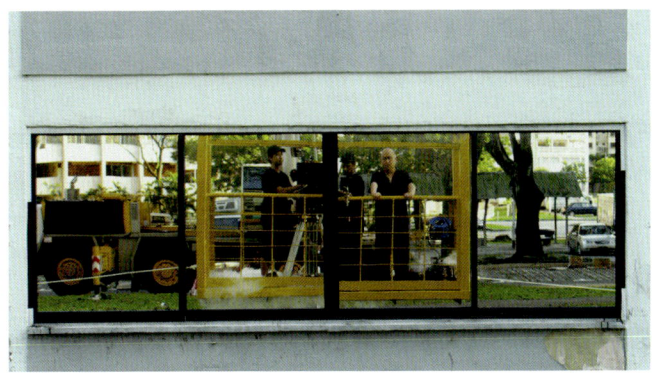

The Cloud of Unknowing, 2011, HD video, colour, 5.1 sound, synchronised smoke machine, 28:28 minutes, film stills

Richard Hughes

Richard Hughes' sculptural installations recall dilapidated urban environments. Painstakingly crafted, they raise questions about the cultural value of decaying infrastructure and its neglect by society, developers and authorities. The realistic quality of his works evokes conflicted memories of post-war estates, from nostalgia and progress to violence and depravation.

At first glance, *If Socks Aren't Pulled Up Heads Will Roll* (2009) looks like a sculpture that has been made from found items. What appears to be the remnants of a football have been skewered to the top of a rusty Victorian lamppost. Broken stiches in the ball create holes resembling the empty eye sockets of a skull. Orange lining pokes out of one gap to create a 'tongue', giving the ghostly object a human character. However, despite its realism, the sculpture is in fact a ruse, its structure entirely made of forms of resin that have been cast, textured and painted to mimic the objects represented. The humour of the sculpture is enhanced by its reference to an emblem of death (the skull), which could be read as a pun on its 'life-like' illusion.

Lithobolia Happy Meal (2022) is a new mobile installation made by Hughes for *Horror in the Modernist Block*. Its title partly references the artist's memories of skateboarding and eating McDonald's chicken nuggets in the underground square and thoroughfares of Birmingham's former brutalist Central Library. The title also refers to a 17th-century tale about a 'Lithobolia' – or 'stone throwing devil' – by Richard Chamberlayne. The folk narrative is considered an early example of supernatural horror and inspiration for modern poltergeist stories. The frontispiece of the tale describes the 'actions of infernal Spirits or (Devils Incarnate) Witches or both ... in throwing about (by an Invisible hand) Stones, Bricks, and Brick-Bats of all sizes, with several other things, as Hammers, Mauls, Iron-Crows, Spits, and other Utensils'.

In Hughes' mobile, the items thrown by the Lithobolia take the form of several large blocks resembling concrete fragments. A semi-deflated space hopper is both a toy from a McDonalds Happy Meal and a wrecking ball. Interconnected steel rods and trampoline parts hold the elements in a delicate equilibrium. Suspended from the gallery's ceiling, the movement of air and fragile balance of the work cause subtle shifts, evoking the 'invisible hand' of Chamberlayne's tale. As with *If Socks Aren't Pulled Up Heads Will Roll*, the sculptural elements of *Lithobolia Happy Meal* are cast from resin and painted to simulate the kind of detritus often found in derelict concrete estates. MP

Born 1974, Birmingham
Lives and works in Ledbury, UK

Richard Hughes produces sculptural work and installations that reference urban infrastructure and the dilapidated estates of inner cities and suburbs. His intricate sculptures simulate found objects that, outside of their site-specific context, would be viewed as detritus. Challenging judgments of value, his installations offer a social and spatial contextualisation of the rapid urbanisation of post-war Britain, and question collective nostalgia for the past.

Hughes received his BA from Staffordshire University in 1995 and an MFA from Goldsmiths College, London in 2003. Solo exhibitions include *Field Trip*, The Modern Institute, Glasgow (2014); Anton Kern Gallery, New York (2013); *Where it All Happened Once*, Tramway, Glasgow (2012); *Endless Bummer*, Gladstone Gallery, Brussels (2011), and Tate Britain (2006). Group exhibitions include *Colours that no-one knows the name of*, Recent Activity, Birmingham (2018); *The Laughable Enigma of the Everyday*, Arquipélago – Centro De Artes Contemporâneas, Portugal (2017), and *The Noing Uv It*, Bergen Kunsthall, Bergen (2015). Hughes is represented by the Modern Institute, Glasgow, and Anton Kern Gallery, New York.

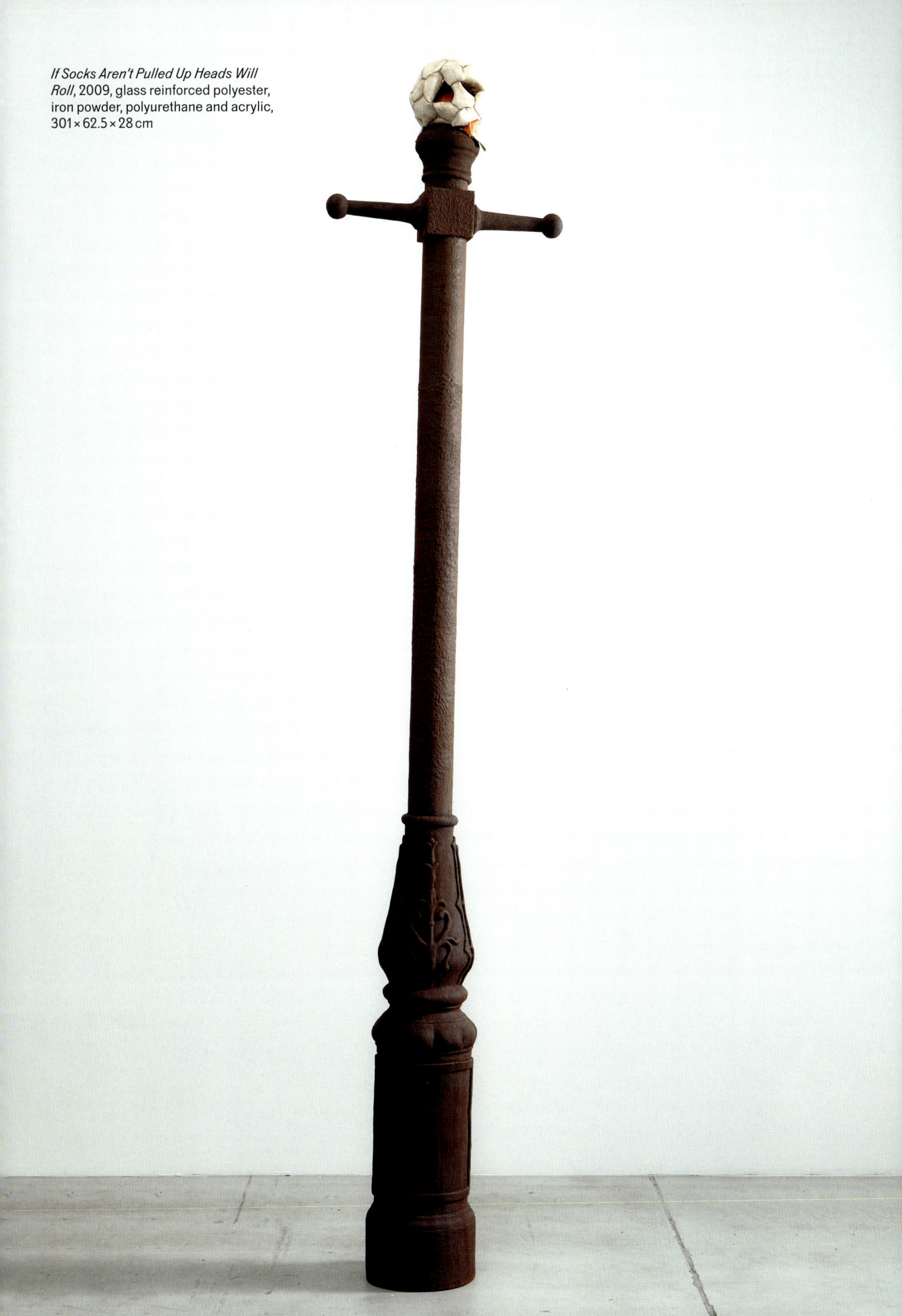

If Socks Aren't Pulled Up Heads Will Roll, 2009, glass reinforced polyester, iron powder, polyurethane and acrylic, 301 × 62.5 × 28 cm

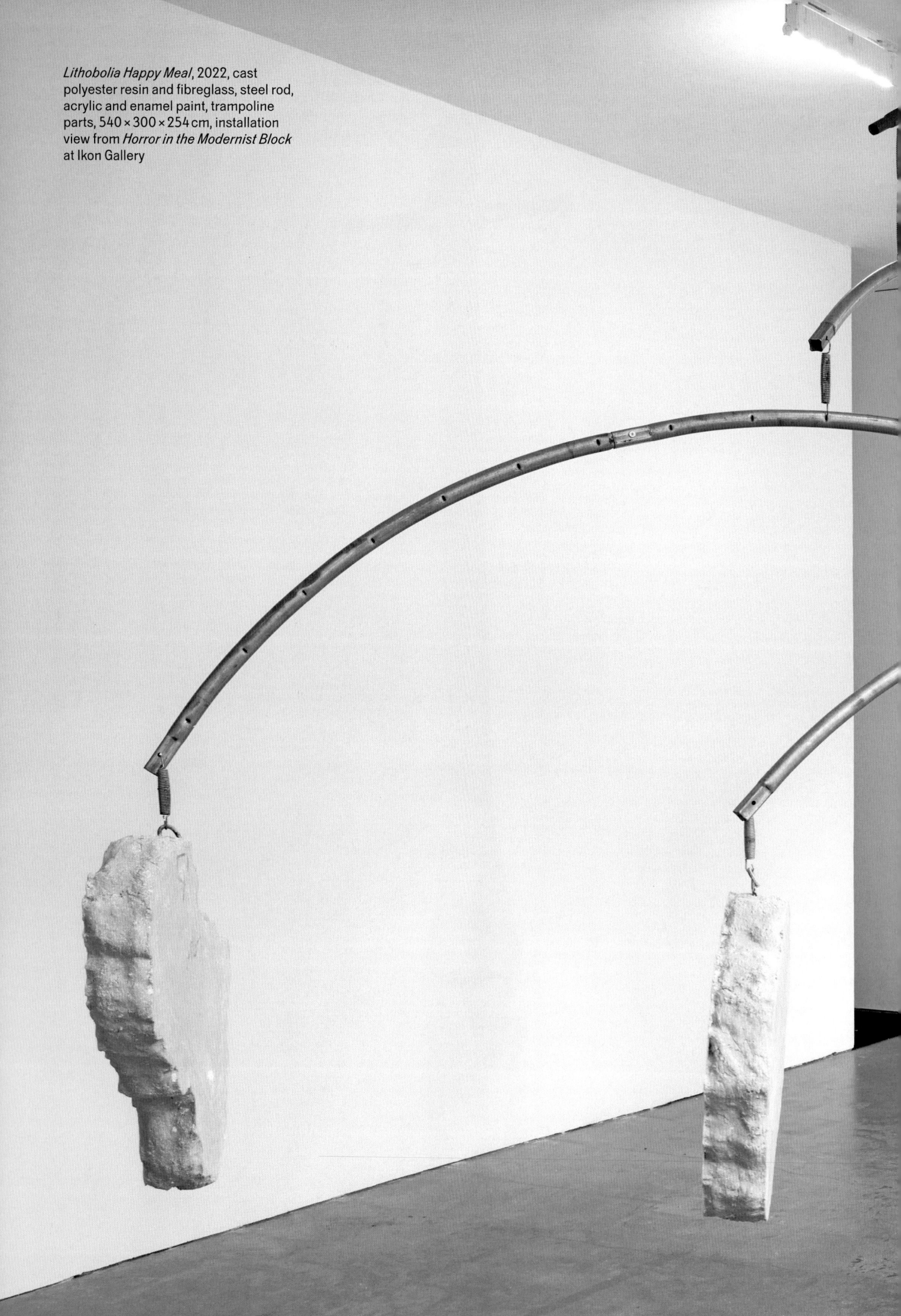

Lithobolia Happy Meal, 2022, cast polyester resin and fibreglass, steel rod, acrylic and enamel paint, trampoline parts, 540 × 300 × 254 cm, installation view from *Horror in the Modernist Block* at Ikon Gallery

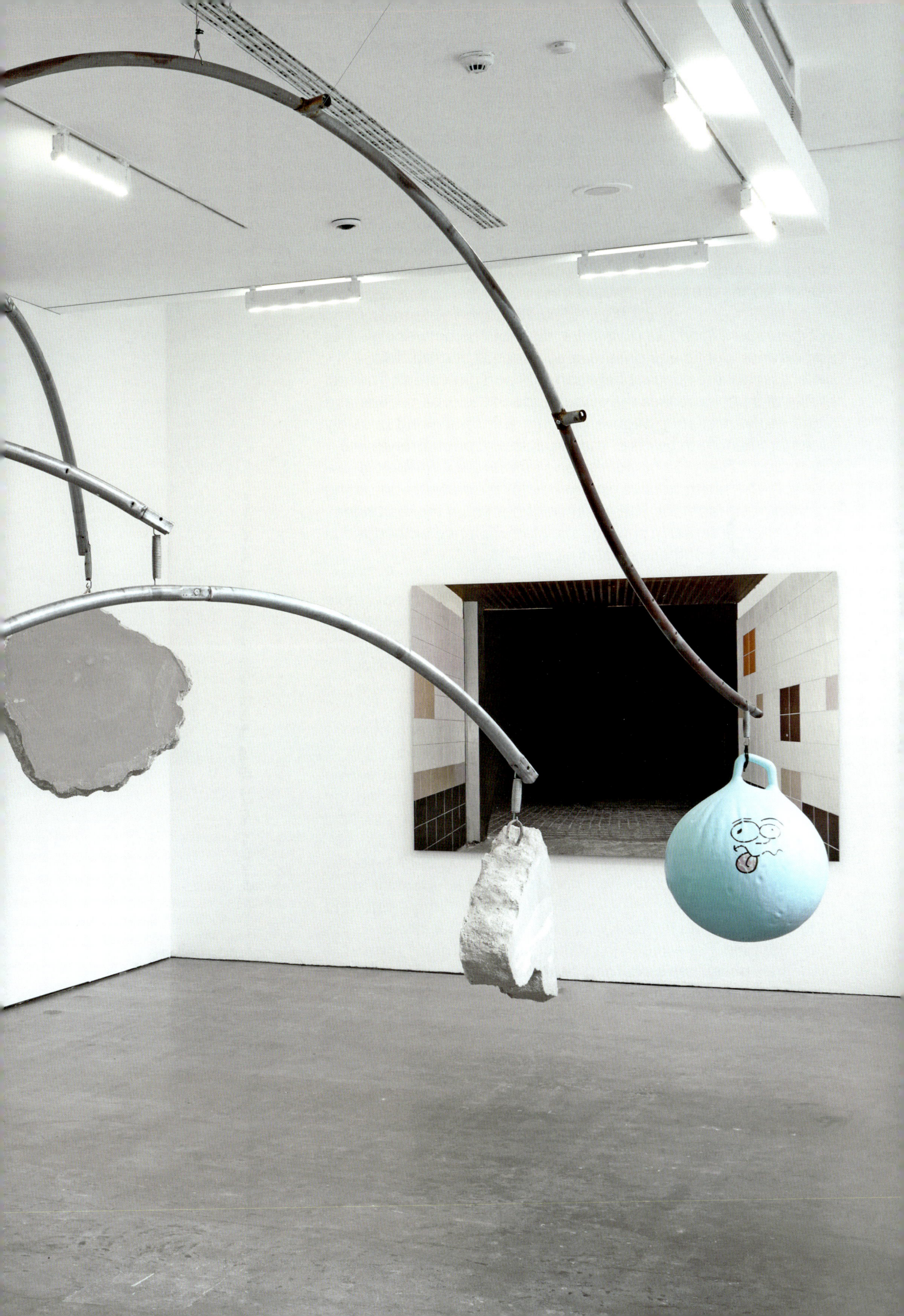

Karim Kal

Karim Kal's *Entourage* (2017) series, photographed in housing estates in Lyon, France, highlights the often marginalised and neglected underpasses, shelters and alleyways which have come to represent urban neglect. Taken at night, the images evoke the tension between the conception and perception of these spaces. The artist's use of flash pushes the resulting images towards abstraction, while imparting the sense that hidden worlds are being revealed.

In *Entourage 1, Lyon / La Guillotière*, distinctions between interior and exterior, public and private space appear blurred. Two bollards mark the contrast between light and dark areas. The half profile of a bin increases the disquietude of the urban scene and signifies the presence of governmental authorities and possibly commercial private owners. The large size of photographs like *Entourage 1, Lyon / La Guillotière* and *Entourage 7, Rillieux-la-pape* creates an immersive experience for the viewer, reinforcing a sense of entrapment. The absence of people in these images reflects Kal's interest in showing the state violence embedded in the architecture of these estates.

The passageway in *Entourage 1, Lyon / La Guillotière* is navigable only by foot or moped, the bollards discouraging the access of large vehicles. Like many modern estates, these passageways were designed as pedestrianised zones to streamline on-foot and motorised traffic. The primacy of motorways in post-war urban planning, coupled with the labyrinthine nature of pedestrianised passageways, led to the creation of informal shortcuts by residents. Both these shortcuts and formal passageways quickly became places of fear and neglect – even if their sheltered and secluded nature made them sites of refuge for homeless people.

Sol 2, Noisy-le-sec (2021) is one of several photographs taken by Kal in the Parisian suburb. The image contains a furtive air of mystery; the composition is mostly black, the dimly lit ground fades vertically into the dark surroundings and the sky is imperceptible. Revealed in the darkness is an organic form – plane tree pollen, which carpets the ground. The surprising substance produces an image that is abstract, but which also indicates tensions between organic and concrete environments.

LM

Born 1977, Switzerland
Lives and works in Lyon

Karim Kal's photographic practice reveals the social, cultural and political dimensions of urbanism through the lens of migration. His work draws attention not only to the physicality of architecture, but the power dynamics of, and local residents' struggles for representation. Taking influence from the philosophical ideas of Foucault, Kal observes discrimination within the city, and as part of his inquiries, seeks to capture moments of transgression.

Exhibitions include *À Corps Défendant*, La Galerie Centre d'art Contemporain de Noisy-Le-Sec, Paris (2021); *Dernières Acquisitions*, Musée d'art Moderne et Contemporain, Saint-Priest-en-Jarez, France (2020) and *Images Résistantes*, Fondation Bullukian, Lyon (2015), among others.

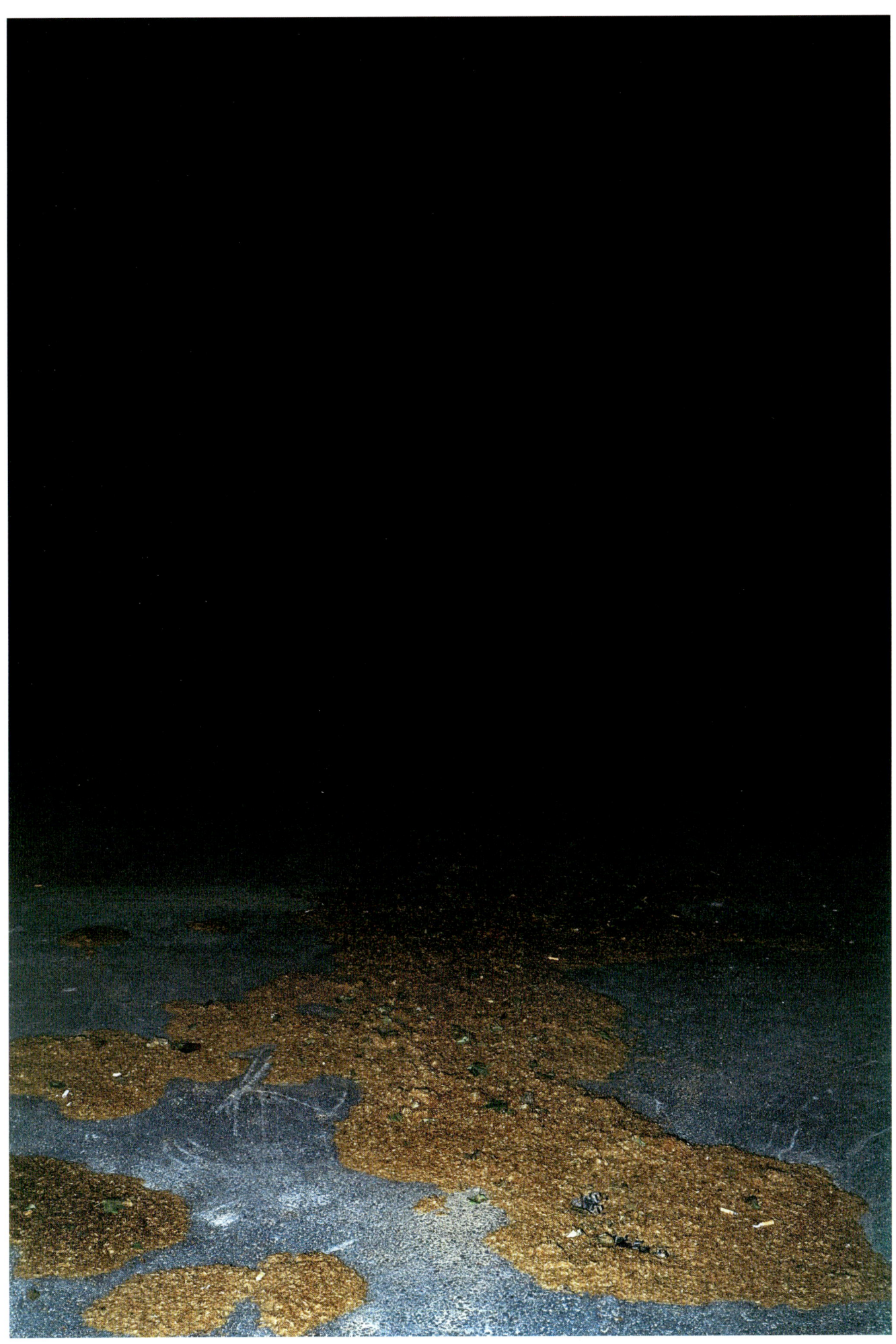

Sol 2, Noisy-le-sec, 2021, inkjet print on baryta paper,
laminated on dibond, 120 × 80 cm

Entourage 1, Lyon / La Guillotière, 2017, inkjet print on baryta paper, laminated on dibond, 150 × 225 cm

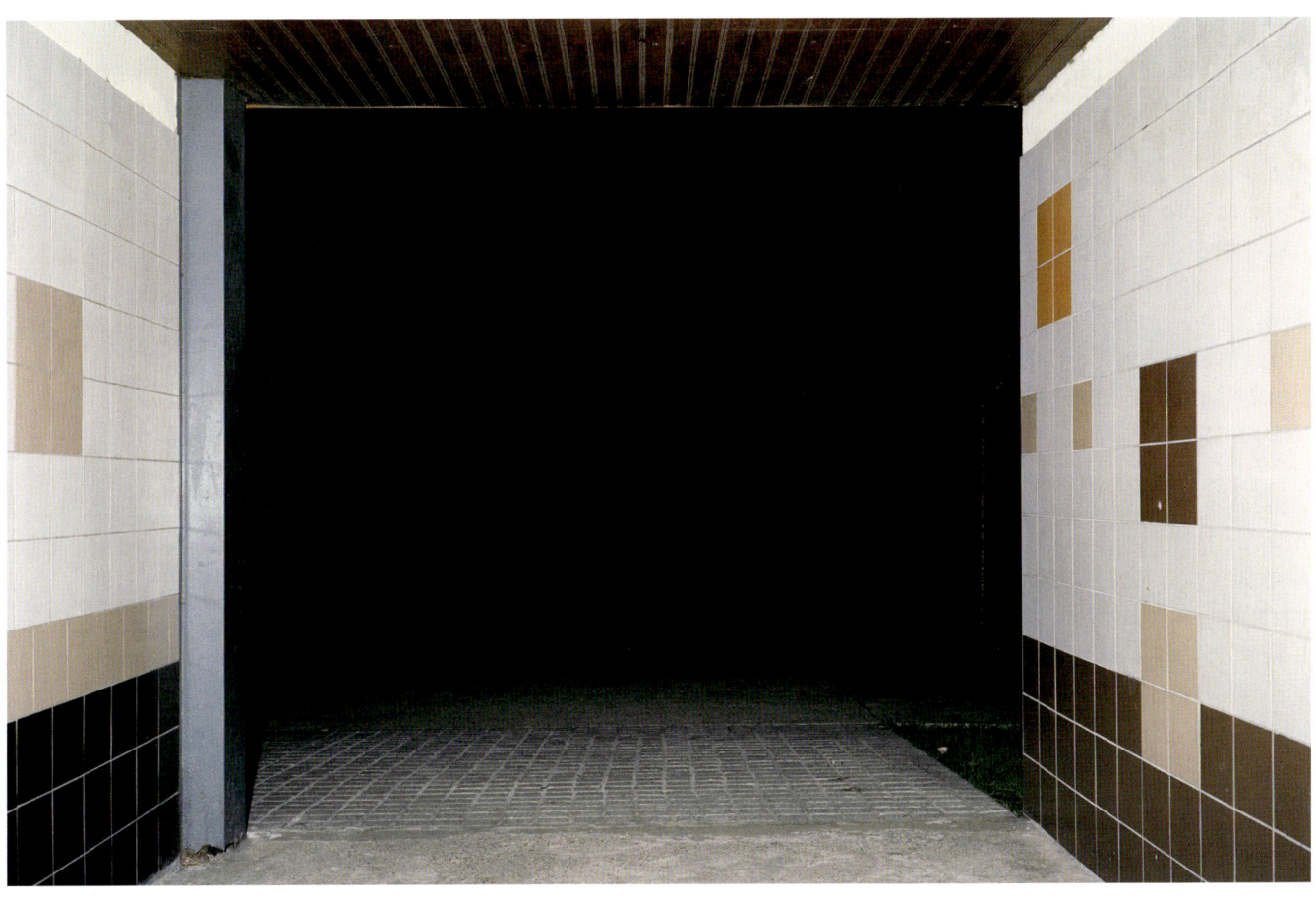

Entourage 7, Rillieux-la-pape, 2017, inkjet print on baryta paper, laminated on dibond, 150 × 225 cm

Kihlberg & Henry

The work of Kihlberg & Henry is strongly influenced by cinema and architecture. The artists' films often make use of performativity, a concept in which language has the capacity to effect change in the real world through inscription or pronouncement.

Between 1999 and 2008, Kihlberg & Henry lived in Birmingham, where they set up the international residency programme Springhill Institute (2003–08) in the apartment of a modernist housing estate. Local and international legacies of modern architecture surface in works such as *Inbindable Volume* (2010), a multi-channel video set in Birmingham's former brutalist Central Library, and *A Mountain Close Up is Only Rock* (2016), a film that traces the digital footprint of architect Jørn Utzon.

Slow Violence was originally commissioned by the Whitstable Biennale in 2018. For *Horror in the Modernist Block*, the artists have created a 16-minute version of the film. A flat in central London forms the backdrop for a script primarily performed by three characters: Research, Polemicist and Chaise Longue. The characters' conversation – which doubles as a manifesto – describes the phenomenon of 'slow violence': a process of large-scale and largely unnoticed manmade environmental change.

Utopian images of urban developments, footage of active construction sites, and instructive texts intercut the fast-paced narrative, creating an atmosphere of constant tension. The film's manifesto iterates how images of architecture – propagated in advertising and popular culture – seduce and oppress as much as its design. The characters' dual attitudes towards high-rise developments reflect this phenomenon, oscillating between desire and feelings of entrapment. A final climatic sequence centres on a slide projector. Appearing to take on a life of its own, the animated projector jolts the characters into an awareness that they do not live in a city, but in a machine – 'a machine which trains them for its use'.

MP

Born 1978, Gallinge, Sweden, and 1979, Burton-Upon-Trent, UK
Live and work in London

Kihlberg & Henry are Karin Kihlberg and Reuben Henry, a collaborative duo based in London. Their work presents architecture as a biological event, an over-spilling of the human mind into exterior space. They studied Fine Art at Birmingham City University (1999–2002) and ran the international residency programme Springhill Institute from 2003–08. From 2008–10 they were research fellows at the Jan van Eyck Academy, The Netherlands, after which Kihlberg gained an MA in Contemporary Art Theory at Goldsmiths, University of London. Both gained a Masters in Cultural Production from the Linköping University in Sweden through their activities with Vision Forum, which culminated in their work with The Disembodied Voice research group. Their video works are distributed by Film Form (Stockholm).

Kihlberg & Henry have presented solo exhibitions and projects at the Whitstable Biennale; Institute of Contemporary Arts, London; Grundy Art Gallery, Blackpool; Plymouth Arts Centre; Res, London; Artsway, Hampshire, UK; Aspex Gallery, Portsmouth; Gallery Box, Gothenburg; and Danielle Arnaud, London. They have participated in group shows and projects at Camden Arts Centre; Eastside Projects; Fundació Miró, Mallorca; Tate Modern and the Hayward Gallery. They won the Great North Run Moving Image Commission in 2012 and were artists in residence at Wysing Arts Centre, Cambridge, 2011; Futura, Prague, 2007, and Red Gate Gallery, Beijing, 2006.

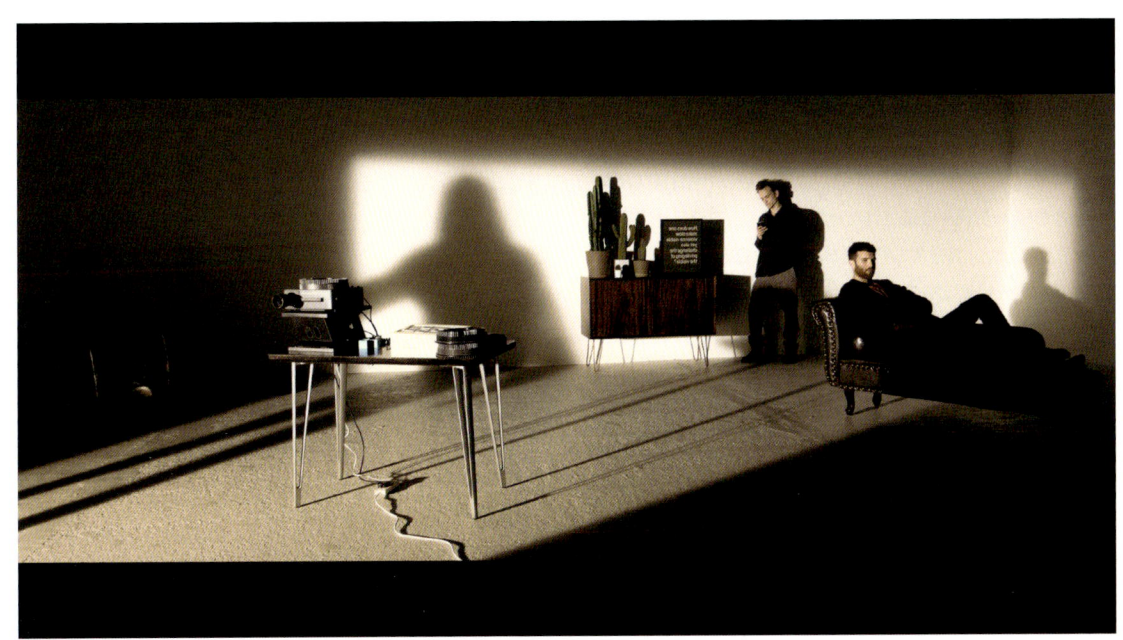

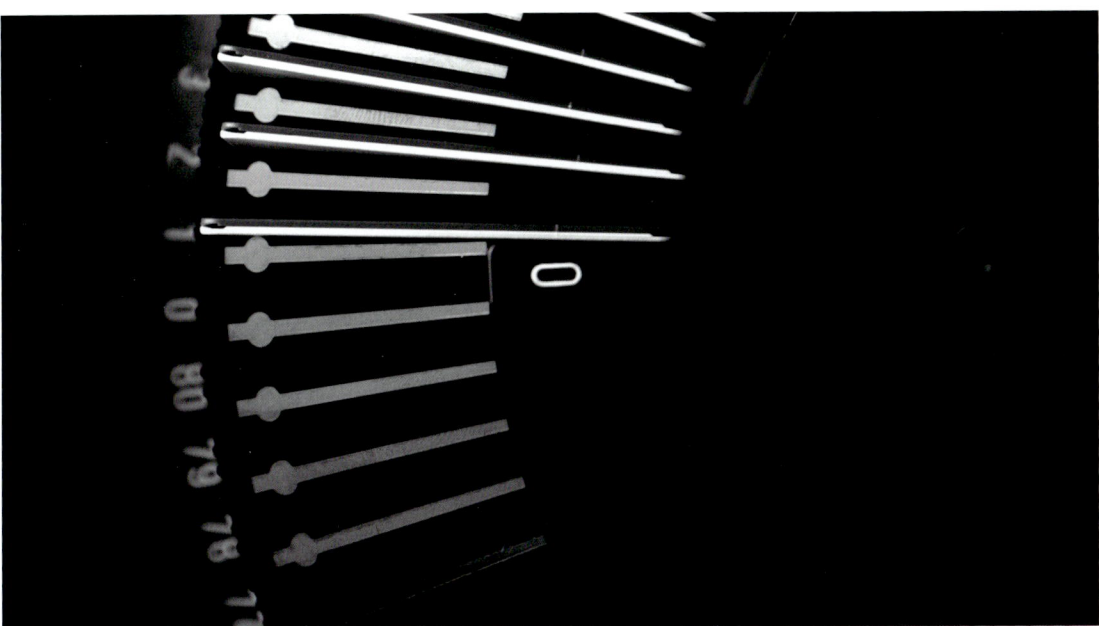

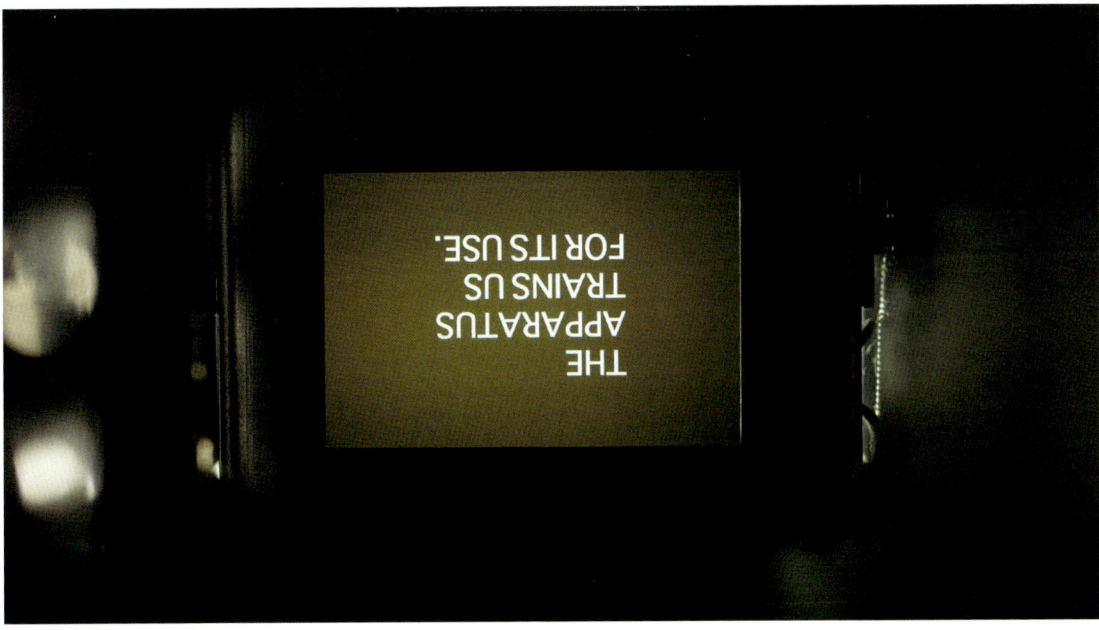

Slow Violence, 2018–22, HD video, colour,
5.1 sound, 16:10 minutes, film stills

Firenze Lai

Born 1984, Hong Kong
Lives and works in London

Firenze Lai's atmospheric paintings show humans in dialogue with their surroundings. Urban interiors, outdoor spaces and figures emerge through painted shapes demarcated by strong contours. The scenes they depict often evoke the densely populated concrete infrastructure of Hong Kong, where Lai lived for many years. Lai's paintings are psychological portraits; expressions of how the human mind and body navigate overcrowded cities and an uncertain modern world.

System #1 (2019) shows a seated figure engulfed by an encroaching mass. The figure appears immobile and drained of life, attempting yet unable to resist the overwhelming force. The grey tones of the figure's body, clothing and chair enhance this feeling, with red outlines suggestive of blood or bodily violence. *Information Center* (2018) depicts a scenario in which a vulnerable individual seeks information from two officials sitting on the other side of a highway. Like high-rise towers, the officials loom over the urban environment. In *Alignment (Pattern)* (2017), criss-crossing lines of charcoal mark the bent body of a crouched figure. The title of the drawing recalls the formal and social streamlining implicit in modernist architecture. *Living and Living Room* (2020) features a human character whose body is unable to fit comfortably within the surrounding apparatus. Swamped in black, the image conveys the dual feelings of comfort and containment common in small apartments in Hong Kong. In *Union* (2022), the thick walls and ceiling of an underpass or tunnel press in threateningly on a group of statuesque figures. Huddled in a corner, their white complexion has a ghostly pallour – as if they were spectres.   MP

Firenze Lai is a painter known for her atmospheric portraits that explore how the human mind and body adapts and reacts to different situations and architecture. Her figurative works often express the interpersonal connections and internal psychological states of people negotiating overcrowded cities and the uncertainty of the modern world.

Recent solo exhibitions include *White Balance*, MAMC+, Saint-Étienne (2019) and *Turbulence*, Mirrored Gardens, Guangzhou (2015). She has participated in international exhibitions and biennials, including *Contagious City: Far Away, Too Close*, Tai Kwun Contemporary, Hong Kong (2019); *A World in a Grain of Sand*, Fosun Foundation, Shanghai (2018); *Viva Arte Viva*, the 57th Venice Biennale (2017); *The World Precedes the Eye*, Institute of Contemporary Arts Singapore (2016); *Surround Audience*, New Museum Triennial (2015); *Social Factory*, 10th Shanghai Biennale, Shanghai (2014), and *A Journal of the Plague Year. Fear, ghosts, rebels, SARS, Leslie and the Hong Kong Story*, Para Site, Hong Kong (2013).

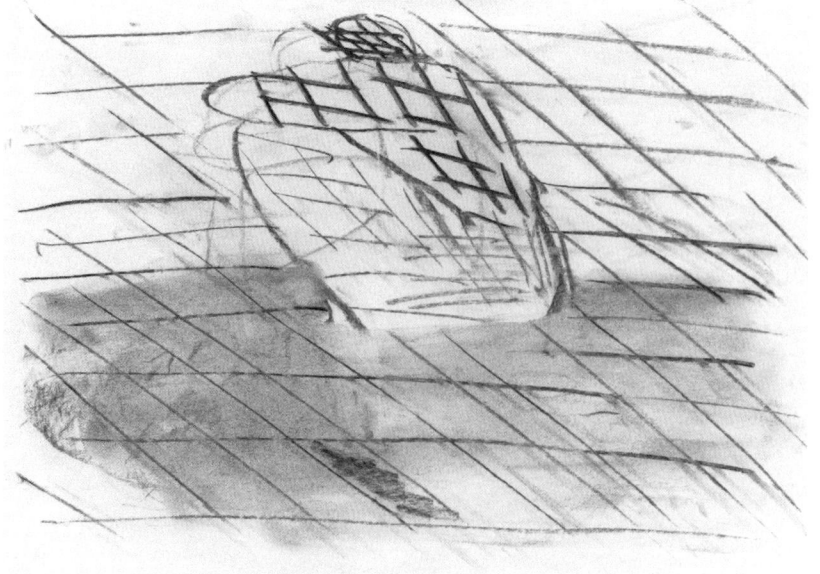

Alignment (Pattern), 2017, charcoal on paper, 23.8 × 31.7 cm

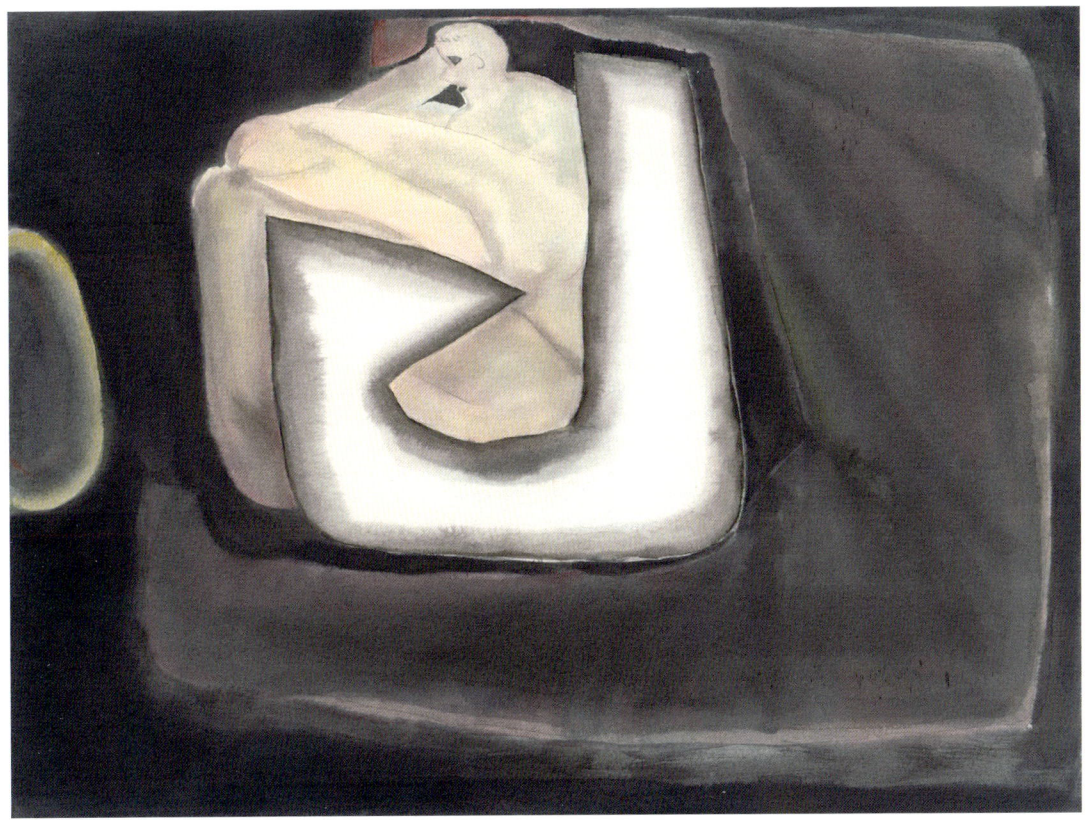

Living and Living Room, 2020, watercolour and ink on paper, 31 × 41 cm

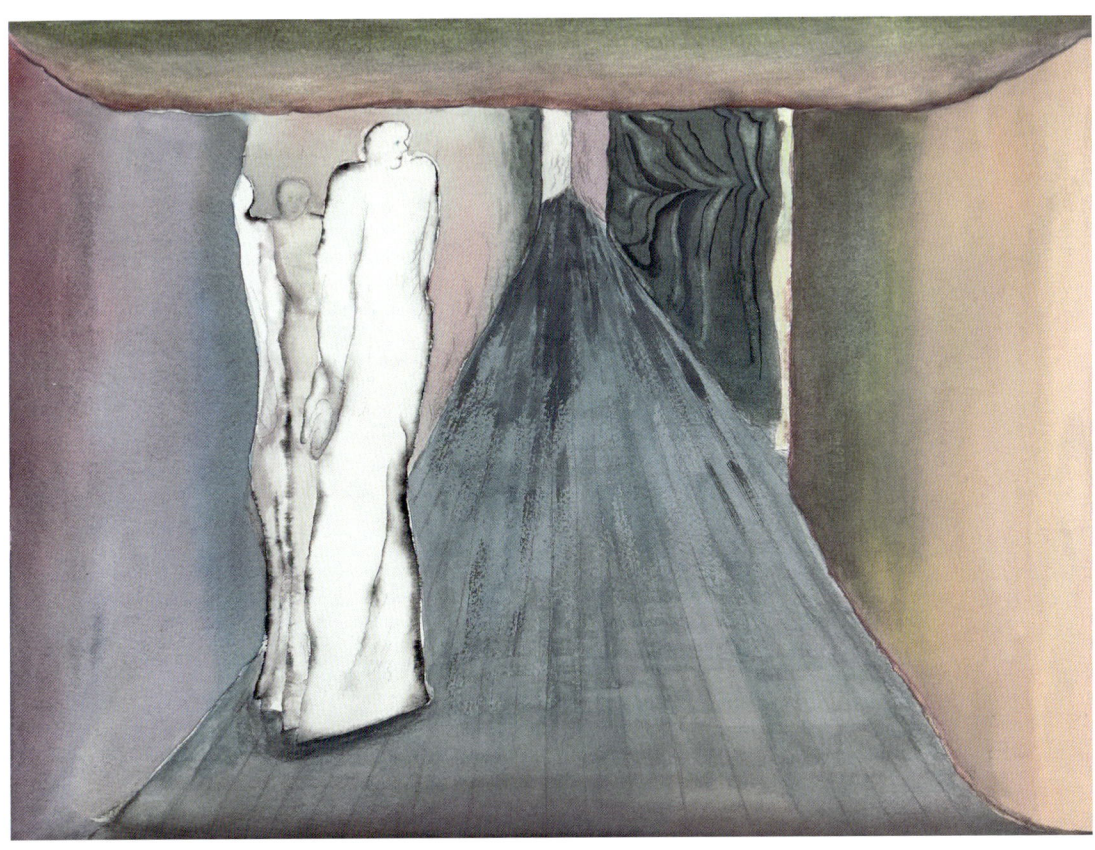

Union, 2022, watercolour and gouache on paper, 31 × 41 cm

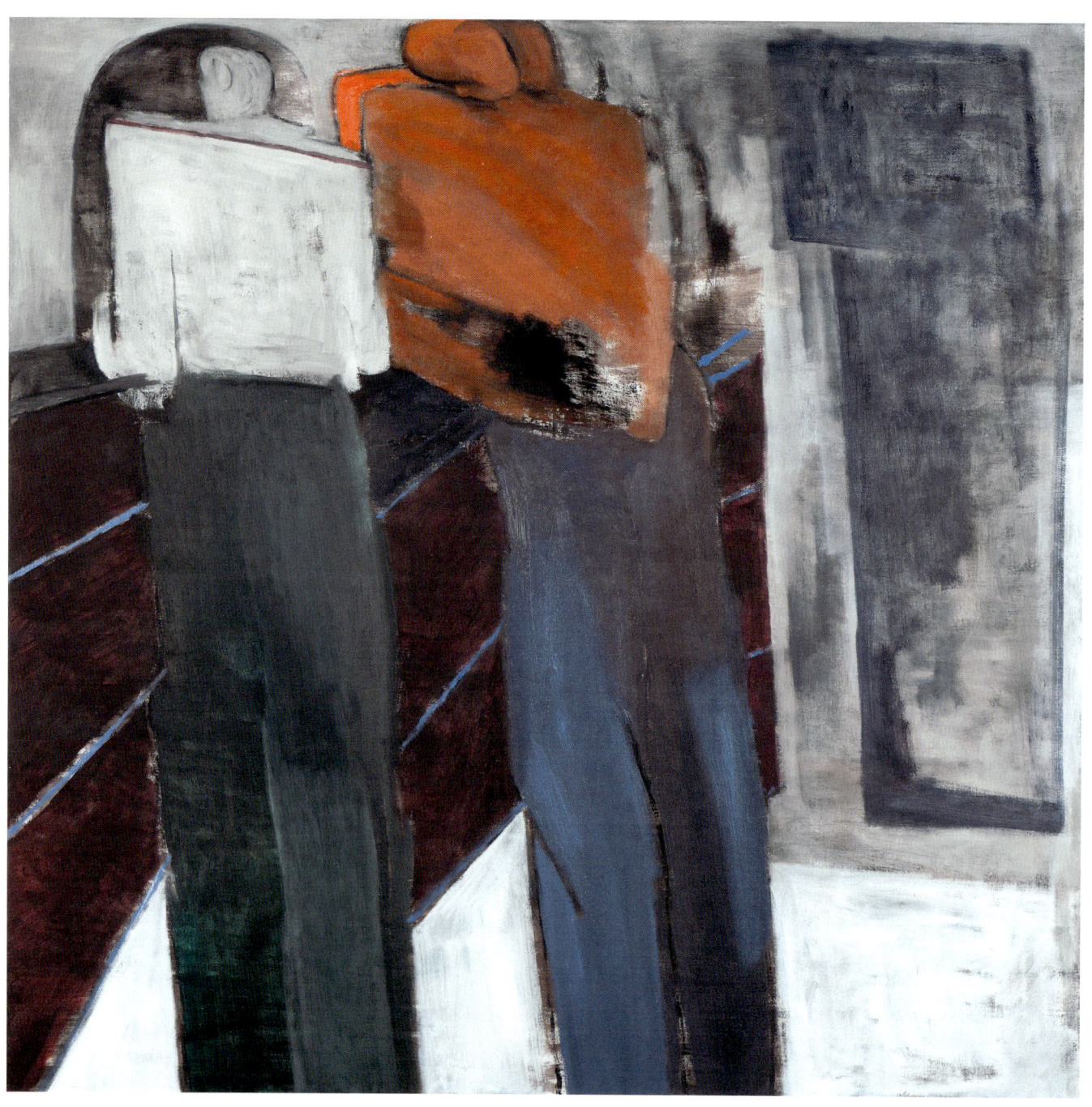
Information Center, 2018, oil on canvas, 110 × 110 cm

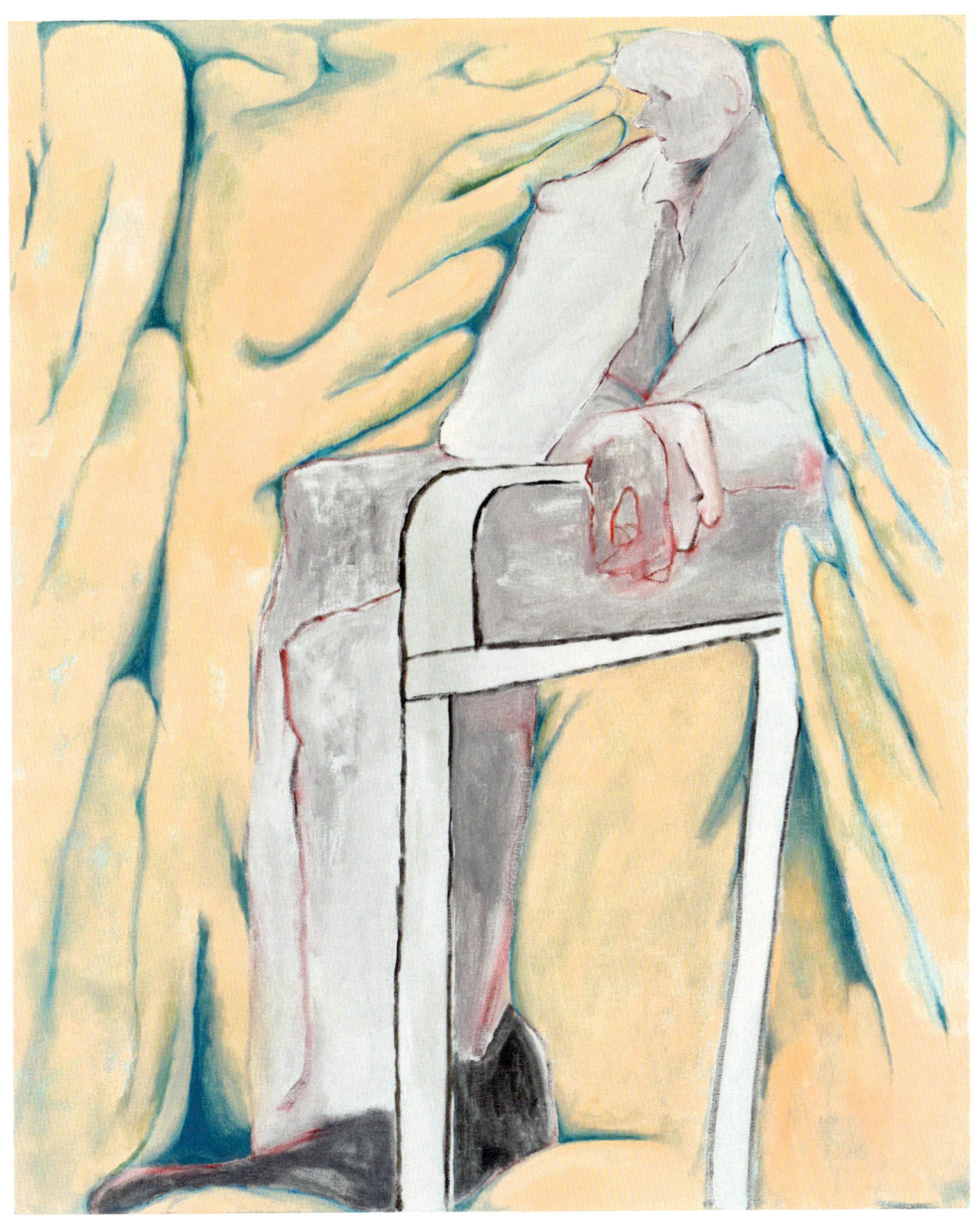

System #1, 2019, oil on canvas, 100 × 80 cm

Diego Marcon

Diego Marcon's work draws on analogue and digital film techniques. Combining theoretical and structural approaches, his films and installations often exaggerate features of a genre to the point of unfamiliarity. Their layering of traditional and contemporary formats blurs boundaries between art and cinema.

Monelle (2017) exists in two versions: a 13-minute looped film and a 16-minute theatrical release. The film is set in the Casa del Fascio in Como, a palazzo designed by architect Giuseppe Terragni (1904–43). The film begins in darkness. Moments of explosive sound and flashlight reveal an assortment of male and female figures within the interior of the Casa del Fascio. Except for these instants, the characters and modernist architecture are obscured by the dark. The only audible sounds are the rustling and movement of bodies. In one brief scene, a woman is shown being dragged across the floor and out of frame, seemingly caught in a state between sleep and death. Marcon's combination of 35mm film, real-life actors and CGI animation create the film's sense of unreality.

The projection of *Monelle* in cinemas and dark exhibition spaces enhances the immersive experience. As viewers, we feel as if we are stalking the inhabitants of the building. At the same time, the darkness of the film and presentation space feeds the suspicion that we too are being watched. As Marcon reflects: '… you have the distinct sensation of moving around a place of power, yet one manifested in a subtle and restless manner; it's a restlessness which is the reflection of a form of politics meant as an invisible, penetrating and all-enveloping force.' By using tropes of horror (suspense, darkness), *Monelle* explores tensions between seduction and fascination – in horror films and in relation to institutions of power.

The Casa del Fascio opened in 1936 as the local office for the National Fascist Party. After the end of the Second World War in 1945, it was forcibly occupied by the National Liberation Committee Parties. In 1957, the building became the headquarters of the Guardia di Finanza (local finance police) who still occupy it today. In the 1980s, The Ministry of Culture recognised the Casa del Fascio as a building of significant cultural heritage. By situating *Monelle* in this historic building, Marcon invites viewers to reflect on the relevance of Italian modernist architecture in contemporary society and culture.

LM

Born 1985, Busto Arsizio, Italy
Lives and works in Milan

Diego Marcon's films, videos and installations consider the relationship between reality and representation. They make connections between theoretical discourse on the ontology of the moving image and popular forms of genre cinema and television, such as horror. His film *Monelle* (2017) has been screened in public galleries and film programmes, including *Can a door be fascist?* (Institute of Contemporary Art, London, UK, 2021). His recent film, *The Parents' Room* (2021), was screened during Directors' Fortnight at the 74th Cannes Film Festival (2021) and presented in the 59th Venice Biennale, *The Milk of Dreams* (2022). Recent solo exhibitions include *The Parents' Room*, Madre Museum, Naples (2021); *Ludwig*, Institute of Contemporary Arts Singapore (2019), and *La miserabile*, La Triennale di Milan (2018).

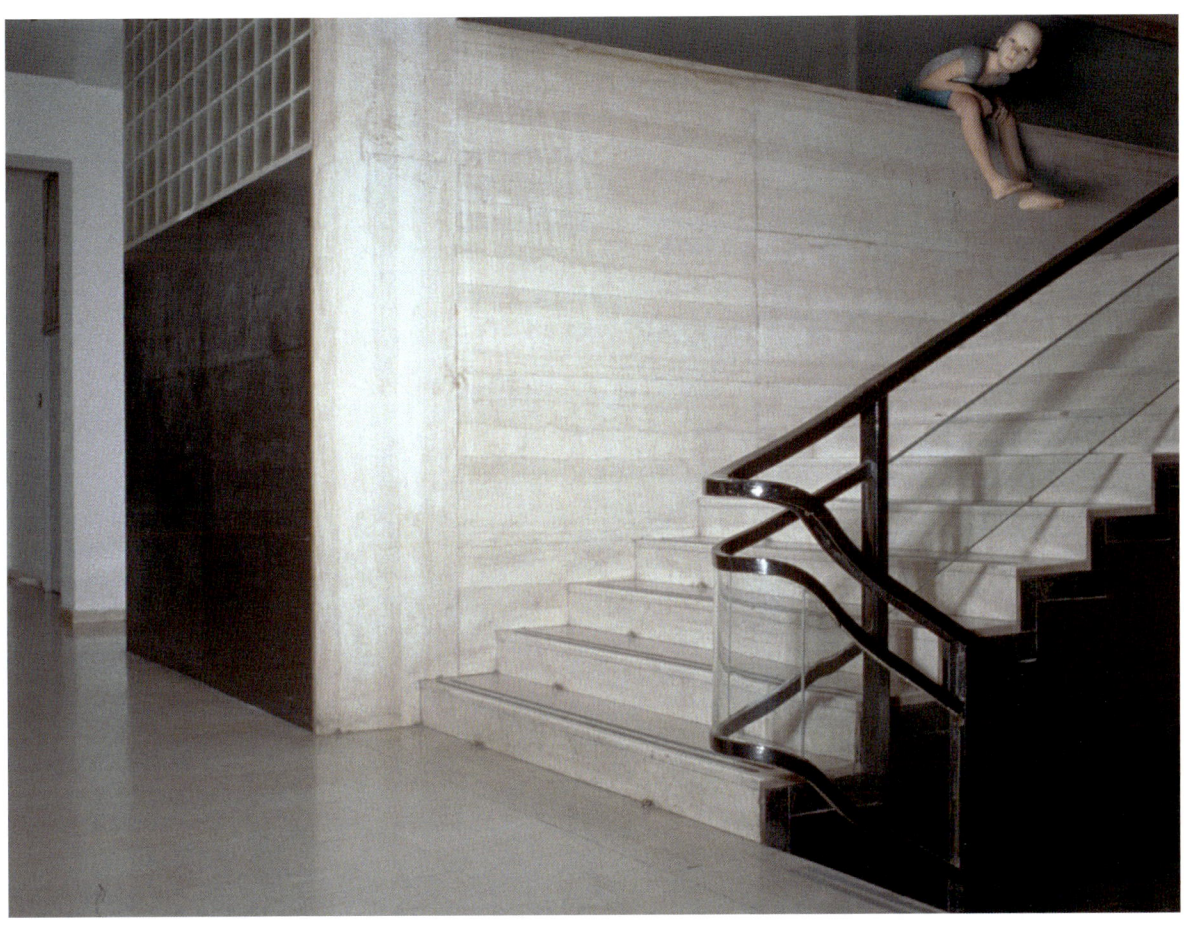

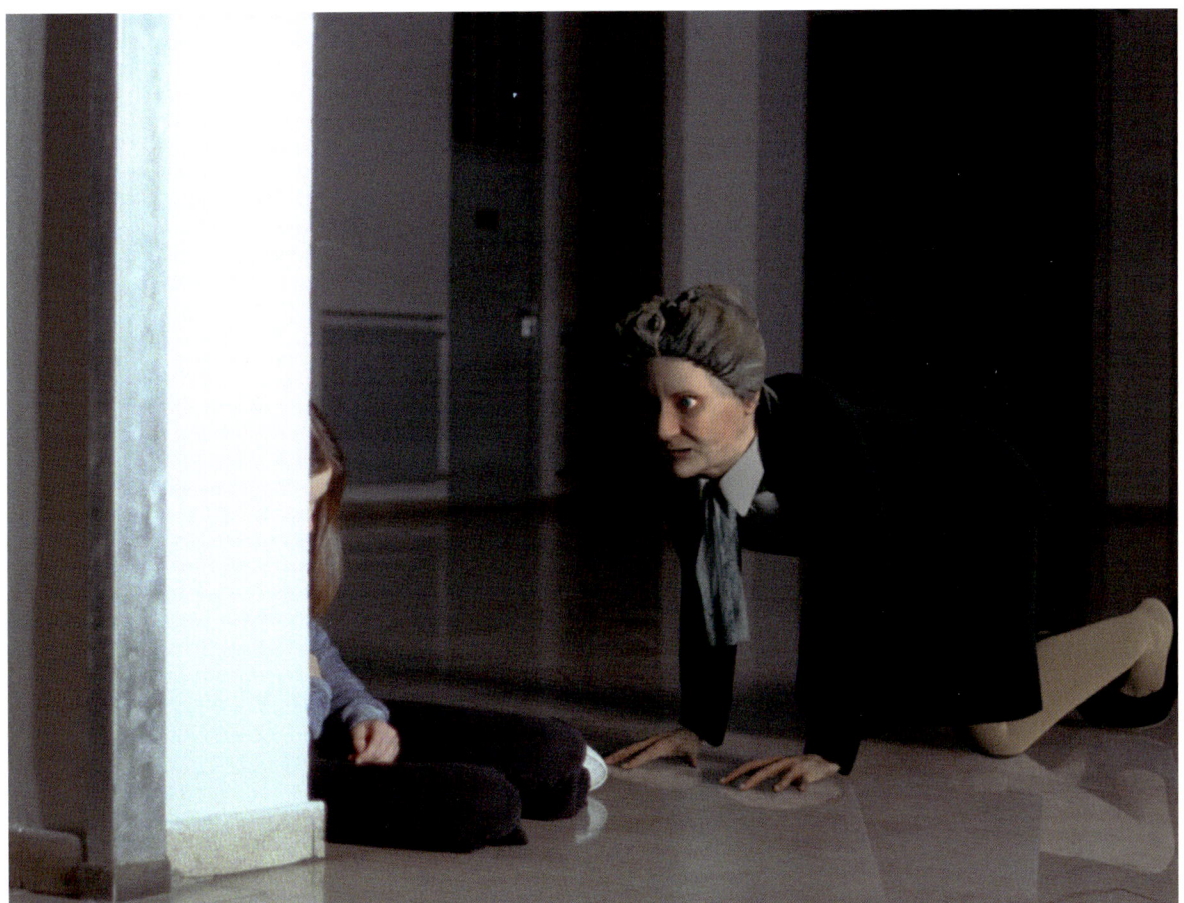

Monelle, 2017, 35 mm film, CGI animation, color, sound, 16:02 minutes, film stills

Ismael Monticelli

Brasília-based artist Ismael Monticelli is concerned with the intrinsic violence of utopian projects. In Brazil, the violence of erasure – integral to the establishment of utopias – follows a colonial logic and comes with both human and environmental costs. For the artist, the built environment of modernism – far from fulfilling the utopian promise for which it was designed – becomes a stage for political obscurantism and reactionism. Alluding to the resurgence of mysticism in contemporary Brazilian society and politics, Monticelli draws on ideas of bestiary that European settlers took with them to the New World, such as representations of monsters which were deemed to populate unknown regions. He also reflects on the legacy of Oscar Niemeyer's architecture for Brasília, including the Palácio da Alvorada (the President's official residence since 1958) and the city's Catholic cathedral, completed in 1970.

With his installation *Spaghetti Junction* (2022), Monticelli draws parallels between Birmingham and Brasília with a 'bestiary' of brutalism. He deliberately employs medieval allegories as a way of avoiding the use of hard-edged motifs and forms to represent modernism. The installation comprises a 12-metre-tall painted blue triangle, on to which paintings and sculptures are fixed in a totemic arrangement. Gravelly Hill Interchange in Birmingham – commonly known as 'Spaghetti Junction' – becomes a metaphor for entanglement in time and space, between the British city and Brasília, but also ancient Egypt, the Middle Ages, the mid-20th century and the present day. In Monticelli's paintings, the modernist buildings of Brasília take the form of black shadows and corpses, their remnants 'feasted' on by medieval and ancient beasts. Monticelli's systematic and methodological approach enables an examination of connections between the civic designs of Brasília and Birmingham, and of the relationship between architecture, politics and people. LM

Born 1987, Porto Alegre, Brazil
Lives and works in Brasília

Ismael Monticelli works with installation, photography, video and found objects. Based on meticulous research, his installations often reconfigure existing objects, creating new relationships between them and the spaces that they occupy. In 2019, he undertook a residency, supported by a grant from South American Artists [COINCIDENCIA Programme – Cultural Exchanges Switzerland / South America, ProHelvetia Foundation], held at La Becque Residence D'artistes – La Tour-de-Peilz / Switzerland. The same year, he also undertook a residency at the Institute of Contemporary Arts Singapore, developing an installation of sculptures by Brother Joseph McNally with a schematic rendering of Singapore's Housing Development Blocks and excerpts from Aldous Huxley's *Brave New World* (1932), whose dystopic vision was partly inspired by the British writer's travels to British Malaya.

Monticelli has a PhD in Contemporary Art and Culture from the State University of Rio de Janeiro. Solo exhibitions include *Overnone, overnone in chaos* (2022) at Portas Vilaseca Gallery, Rio De Janeiro; and *Futurology exercise* at Museu da Imagem e do Som (MIS), São Paulo (2018). He has received several art awards, including the 7th Marcantônio Vilaça Award (2019), PIPA 2018 Award, Foco Bradesco ArtRio Award (2017), and the Funarte Prize for Contemporary Art (2015).

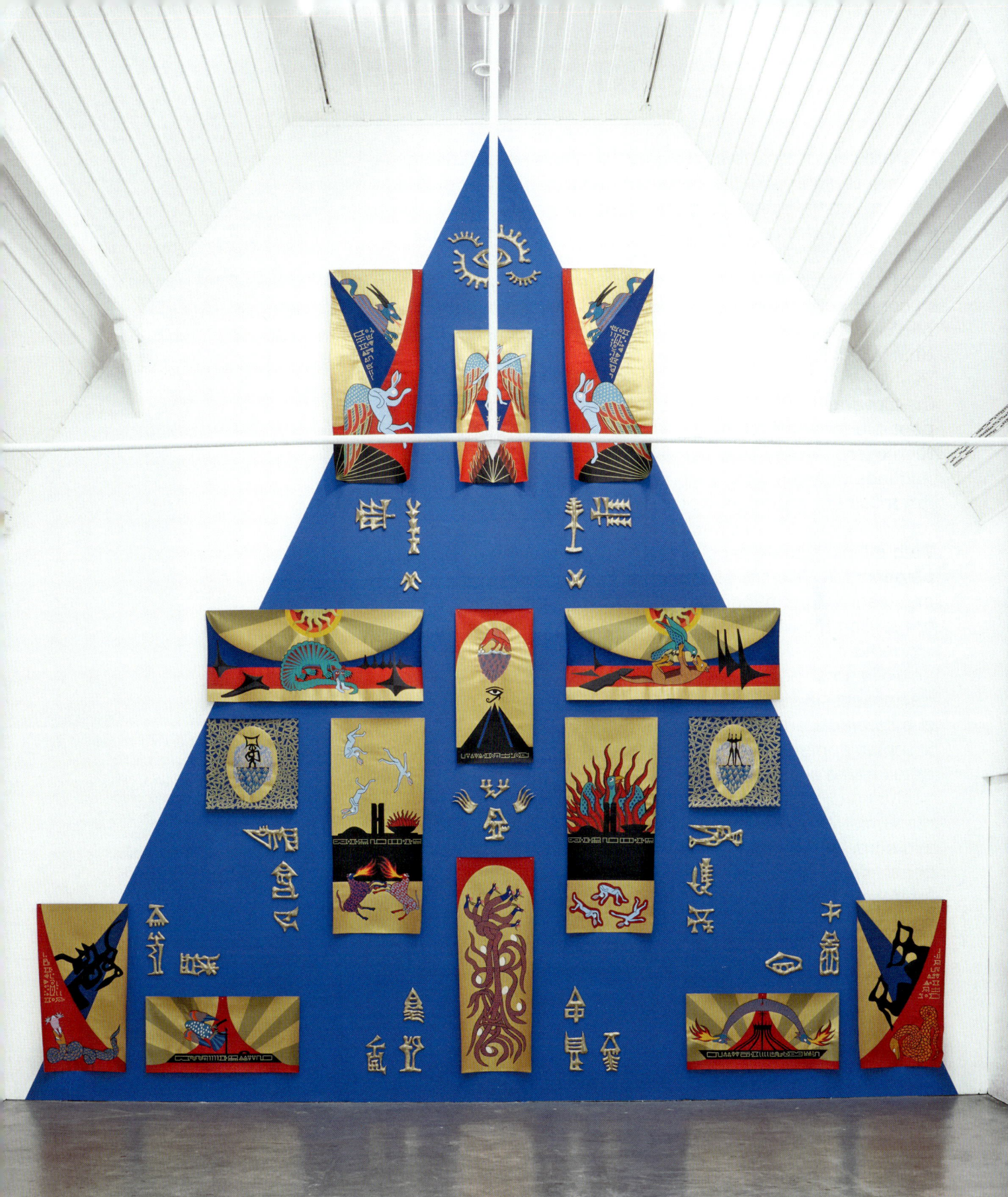

Spaghetti Junction, 2022, acrylic paint on wall, acrylic paint on canvas, wood, papier mâché objects, 637 × 605 cm, installation view from *Horror in the Modernist Block* at Ikon Gallery

NT

NT's previous films *Greta* (2020) and *Still Waters* (2013) use modernist landmarks the Barbican Centre in the City of London and Southmere Estate in Thamesmead as enigmatic backdrops for human portraits. *BRUTAL* (2022) – a new commission for *Horror in the Modernist Block* – expands on the artist's interests in the changing urban landscape and the impact of this change on communities, people and places in Birmingham. The 'portrait' and subject matter of *BRUTAL* are solely the buildings themselves.

The film draws attention to what NT describes as 'grey areas': the often overlooked modernist housing estates and homes of people who live and work in the city. By engaging with residential buildings in Aston New Town and Druids Heath, *BRUTAL* brings into focus the importance of these estates for their residents – not just their function as homes but communities. Filmed at night, the outlines of tower blocks and housing complexes blend into the darkness. Swelling sound and panning shots build a sense of anticipation around the static buildings. Towards the end of the film, a 'Home Sweet Home' sign can be seen hanging outside a resident's door like a celebration wreath, backlit by the warm glow of a porch light. However, the dark and brooding score gives the scene a sinister undertone. Initially, this might be interpreted as a comment on the buildings and their residents, but it soon becomes apparent that what is truly sinister is the way films and media frame such adverse perceptions.

For NT, horror is not inherent in modernist architecture. Rather, it forms the backdrop to horror that is structured by society itself. Horror is something that is inflicted upon these buildings, and not something that lies within them; it is propagated through mistrust and fear. In *BRUTAL*, NT powerfully creates an immersive experience of modernist housing estates that subtly reveals and breaks down this dominant and unequal cultural gaze, inviting the viewer to reflect on, and become aware of their own relationship to it.

LM

NT's practice incorporates sound, film and performance. NT investigates historiography through their work: how history is made, interpreted and revisited, and how these interpretations are altered and presented. Their films *Greta* (2020), *South More V2* (2014), and *Still Waters* (2013) use the architecture of post-war London as a way to explore social history, the changing urban landscape of the city, and the impact of this change on community, people and places.

They completed their MA at the Royal College of Art in 2013, where they were awarded the Augustus Martin Prize and the RCA Graduate Jealous Print Prize. Alongside their artistic practice, they are a lecturer in Fine Art at Central Saint Martins. Exhibitions and screenings include *Untitled: Art On The Conditions Of Our Time*, Kettle's Yard, Cambridge (2021), and New Art Exchange, Nottingham (2017); Encounters Film Festival, Bristol (2019); Deptford X, London (2018); British Film Institute, London (2018); The Showroom (2016); Institute of Contemporary Arts, London (2015); Sir John Soane's Museum, London (2014), and tank.tv (2013), among others.

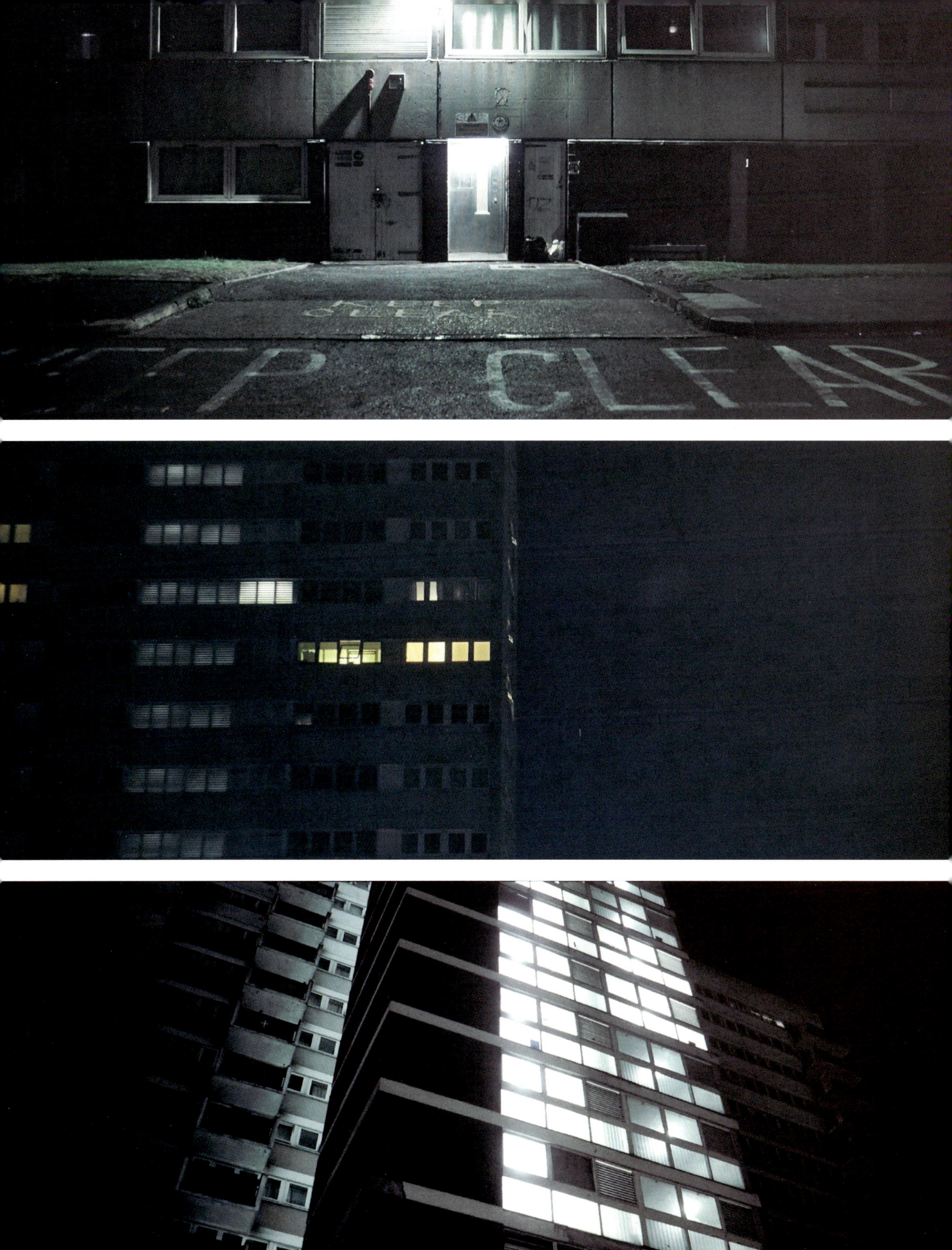

BRUTAL, 2022, HD video, colour, stereo sound, 10:42 minutes

Amba Sayal-Bennett

Amba Sayal-Bennett's sculptures stem from digital and physical manipulations of space and form. Made from solid materials such as steel, their form is cut by a CNC machine, which traces the lines of preparatory drawings created by the artist in Rhino, a commercial computer-aided design (CAD) software application. Sculptural and architectural in nature, these works explore the hybrid assemblage of human operator and inhuman instrument – where an instrument can be anything from an ordinary object such as a stencil to a computer programme or astrolabe (an ancient astronomical instrument used to calculate the position of stars and planets).

CAD software involves the digital suppression of space, or, in the words of Sayal-Bennett, a 'collapsed chronology'. The drawings *King Horn* (2019), *Soja* (2019), *Temp* (2020) and *Ex-run* (2020) appear architectural, yet also organic, their parameters and scale informed by the artist's body. The nature of certain tools and materials also determines the nature of the finished work, creating a synthesis of human and nonhuman agencies.

Sayal-Bennett's recent research undertaken during a residency at the British School in Rome focuses on the 'migration of rational forms' and their role within fascist and brutalist architecture. Her work explores the role of modernism in the expression of ideology in failed utopias. In such ideologies, abstraction is an act of imposition: geometric forms and schemas are translated and employed to create a new starting point, sweeping away or obscuring what was there before. LM

Born 1991, London
Lives and works in London

Amba Sayal-Bennett is a British-Indian artist working across drawing, projection and sculptural installation. Her practice explores how methods of abstraction are exclusionary and performative, crafting boundaries between what is present, manifestly absent, and othered. Her research focuses on the migration of rational forms and their role within fascist and brutalist architecture. Using translation as method, she explores the movement of bodies, knowledge and form across different sites, processes inherent to the diasporic experience.

Sayal-Bennett received her BFA from Oxford University, her MA in History of Art from The Courtauld Institute and was awarded her PhD in Art Practice and Learning from Goldsmiths. She is a cofounder of Cypher Billboard, an artist-run public programme of site-specific billboard artworks and off-site projects based in London. She is currently an associate lecturer in Visual Culture at UWE Bristol. Between January and March 2022, Sayal-Bennett was The Derek Hill Foundation scholar at the British School at Rome in Italy. Recent exhibitions include *Geometries of Difference*, Somerset House, London (2022); *A Track to Bare*, Carbon 12, Dubai (2021); AORA, London (2021), White Cube, London (2021); Indigo+Madder, London (2019), among others.

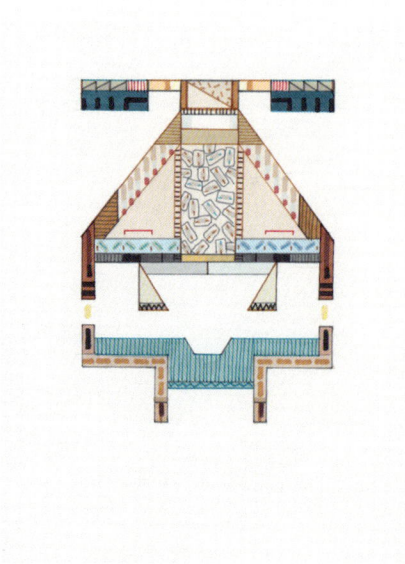

Soja, 2019, ink, pro-marker and graphite on paper, 21 × 14.8 cm

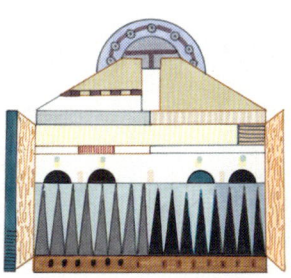

King Horn, 2019, ink, pro-marker and graphite on paper, 21 × 14.8 cm

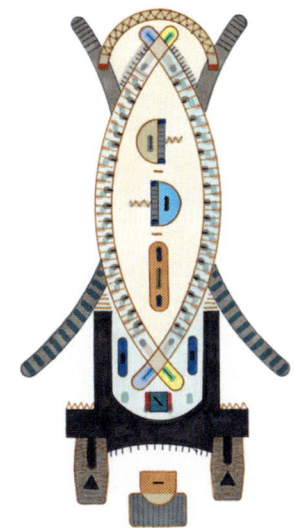

Ex-run, 2020, ink, pro-marker and graphite on paper, 21 × 29.7 cm

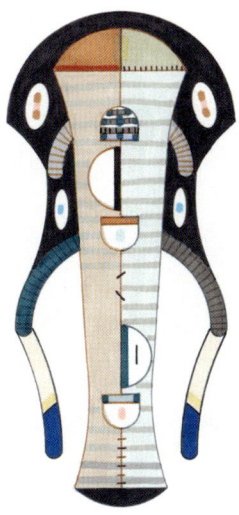

Temp, 2020, ink, pro-marker and graphite on paper, 21 × 29.7 cm

Carus, 2020, powder coated mild steel, chemiwood, MDF, resin, velvet, magnets, 133 × 43 × 64 cm

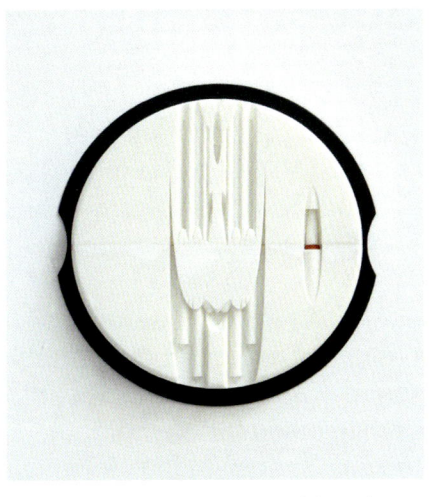

Daro, 2022, powder coated mild steel, fabric, PLA, 30 × 29 × 4 cm

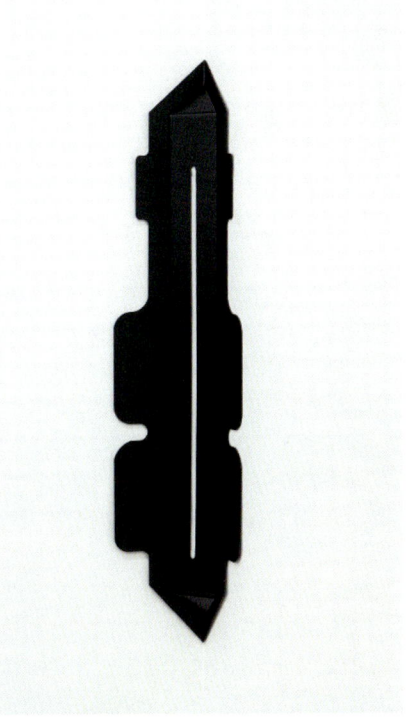

Aperture, 2020, powder coated mild steel, silk, 96 × 22 × 11 cm

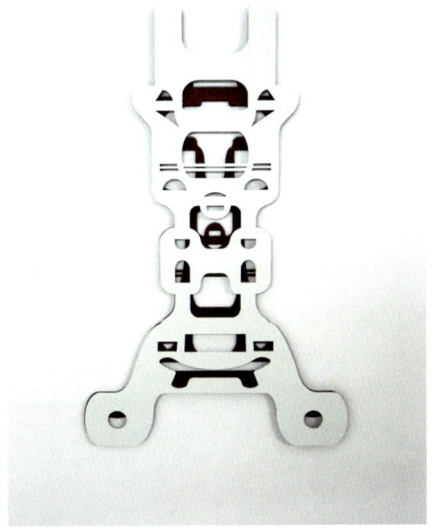

Fennec, 2020, powder coated mild steel, 33 × 19 × 0.6 cm

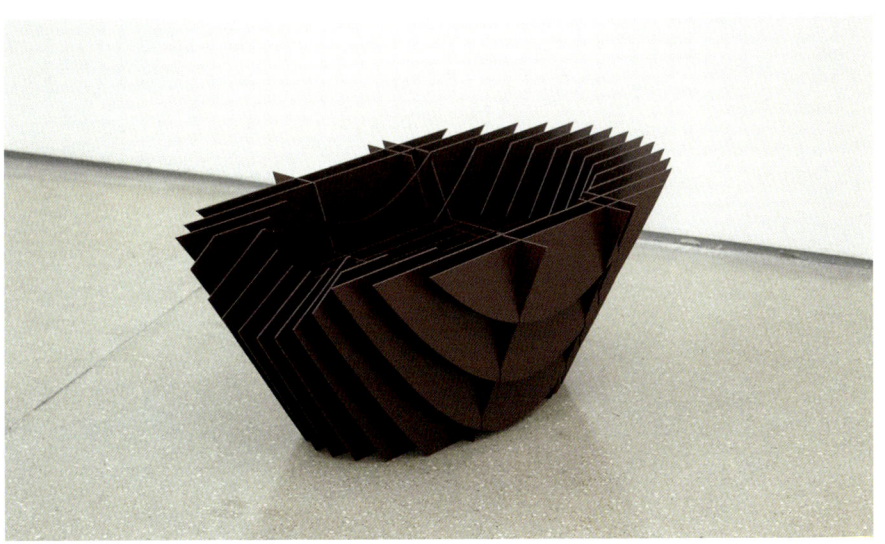

Ova, 2022, powder coated mild steel, 30 × 47 × 76 cm

Seher Shah

Seher Shah uses drawing and printmaking to represent the experiential nature of space. Over the past 10 years, the legacy of modernism in Europe, America and South Asia has informed her work exploring mass, permanence and erasure.

Shah's series of etchings *Unit Object* (2014) reference Unité d'Habitation, a typology of modern housing designed by French-Swiss architect Le Corbusier. Exposed white paper represents the structure of imagined facades, while inked areas indicate windows, panes and surrounding terrain. Spectral black forms in *Unit Object (sculpture garden)* and *Unit Object (landscape view)* suggest modernist sculpture and architectural doppelgangers.

Notes from a City Unknown (2021) is a series of screen-prints that Shah made whilst living in New Delhi, India. The 32 prints comprise a title page, introduction, and three sets of ten prints that pair abstract evocations of brutalist architecture with text. The enigmatic images reference the block-shaped forms of modernism and the textured and cracked surfaces of aged concrete. Black ink occupies a significant portion of the images – an allusion to the 'empty' space and shadows cast by architectural modernism.

The texts are drawn from memories recorded by Shah. Among the poignant reflections are instances of sectarian violence and individuals bearing the consequences of failed political and architectural idealism. In several texts, architecture forms a metaphor for misguided desires and the dangers of ethno-nationalism – an ongoing crisis in Indian politics. The last print in each set is composed entirely of text. In these prints, words taken from preceding notes become a form of architecture, their placement and gaps between them signifying divides between inside and outside.

MP

Born 1975, Karachi, Pakistan
Lives and works in Barcelona

Shah's practice is dedicated to drawing, printmaking and sculpture. The intimacy of the hand, through mark-making, has been a source of curiosity, research and experimentation in her practice. She has worked with drawing and printmaking to explore ideas in architecture and perspective drawing traditions; contested relationships between history, objects and time; and the relationship between poetry and abstraction.

Seher Shah received her BFA and BArch from the Rhode Island School of Design in 1998. Her work has recently been shown at the Lyon Biennale (2022); Jameel Arts Centre, Dubai (2019); Austrian Cultural Forum, New York (2018); Dhaka Art Summit (2018); Jawahar Kala Kendra, Jaipur (2018); *Mémoires des Futurs*, Centre Pompidou (2107); Nature Morte, New Delhi (2016); Green Art Gallery, Dubai (2012 & 2016); Kiran Nadar Museum of Art, New Delhi (2015); The Museum of Modern Art, New York (2015); the Samuel Dorsky Museum of Art, New York (2015); Glasgow Print Studio (2015); Experimenter, Kolkata (2014); Athr Gallery, Jeddah (2014), and Jhaveri Contemporary, Mumbai (2013). Shah's works can be found in the collections of the Metropolitan Museum of Art, New York; The Museum of Modern Art, New York; Queens Museum, New York; Brooklyn Museum, New York; Centre Pompidou; Tate, and Art Jameel Collection, Dubai. She is represented by Green Art Gallery, Dubai, and Nature Morte, New Delhi.

II

CITY OF THE DETERMINED

In the corners and edges of the city
A wall of executions
She rests her head on a pillow of iron

City of the Determined taken from *Notes from a City Unknown*, 2021,
portfolio of 32 screen-prints, each 23 × 30.5 cm

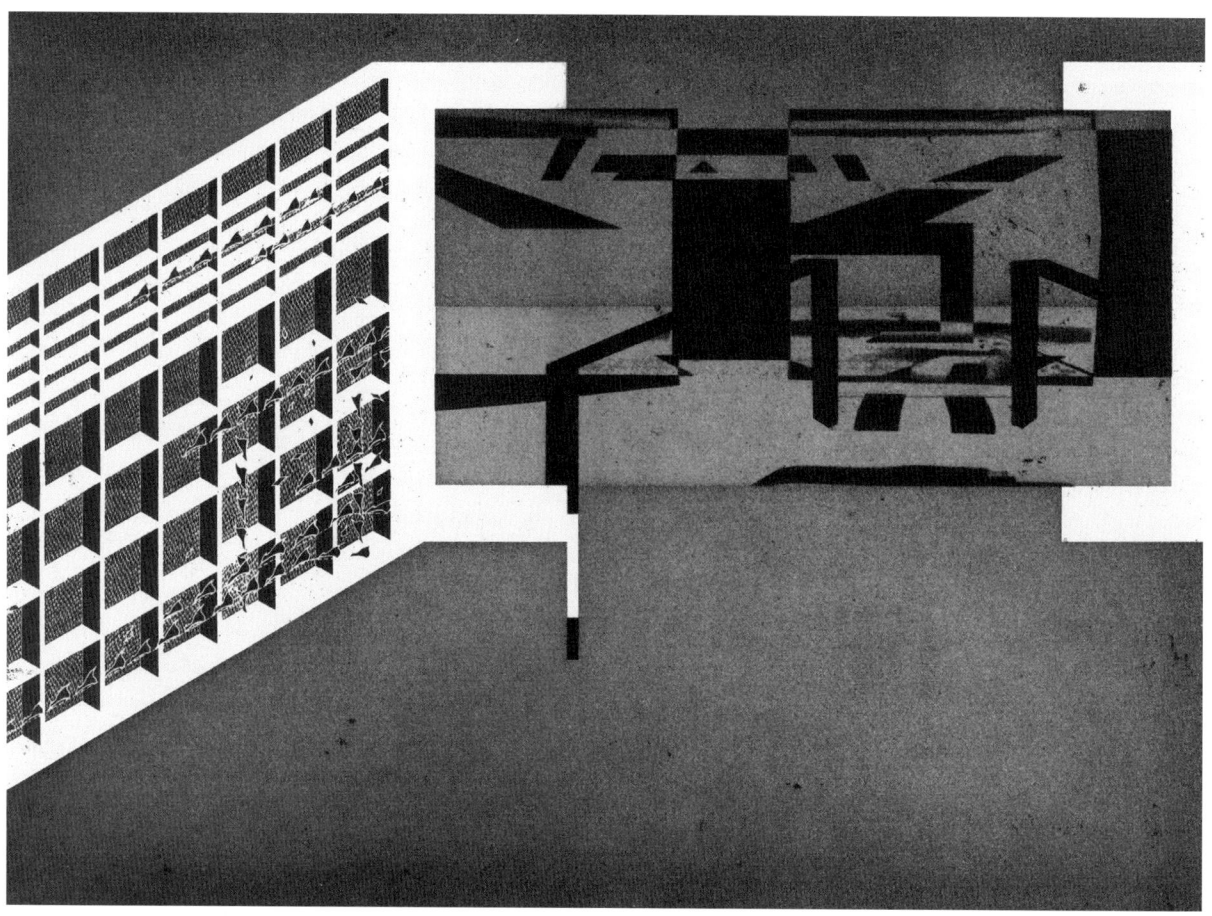

Unit Object (landscape view), 2014, etching, 53 × 62.5 cm, edition of 20

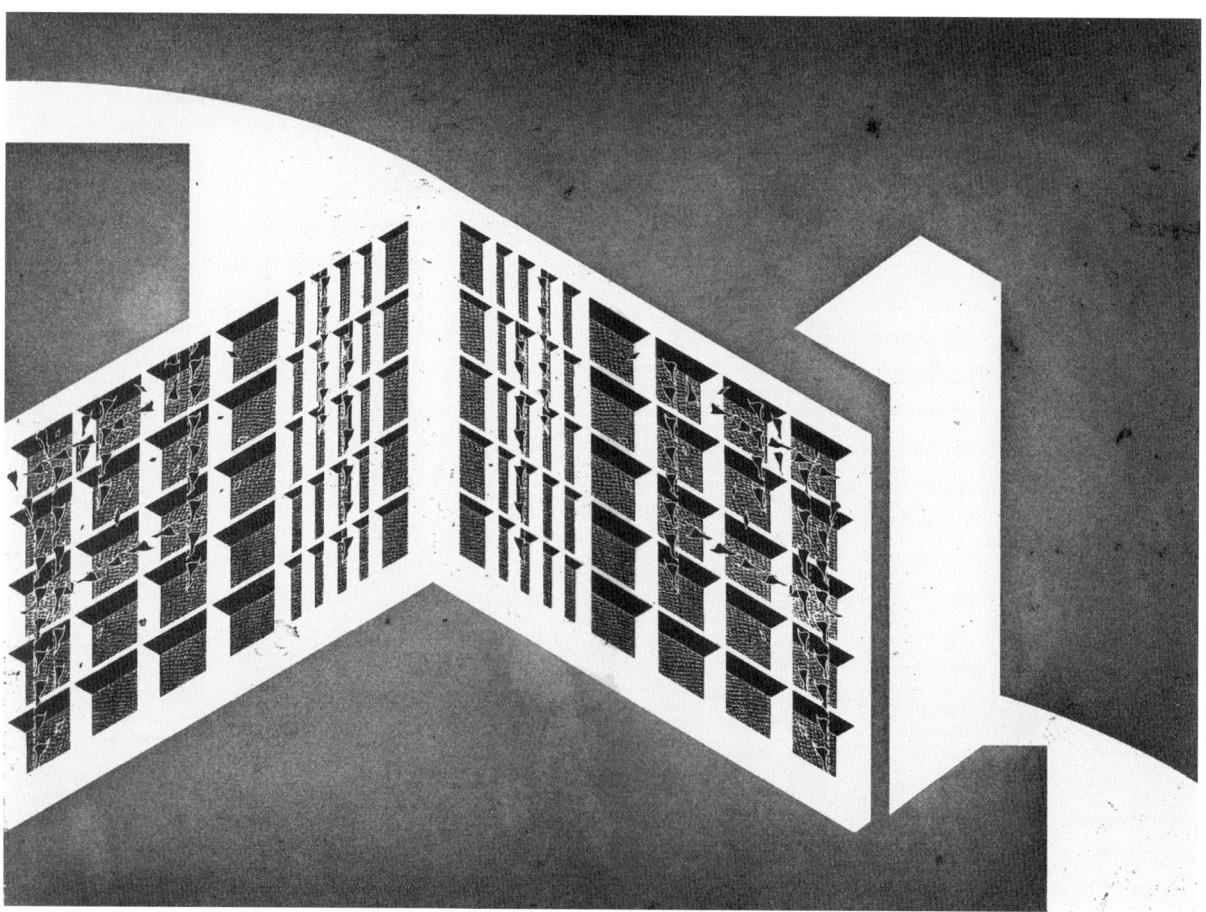

Unit Object (gate), 2014, etching, 53 × 62.5 cm, edition of 20

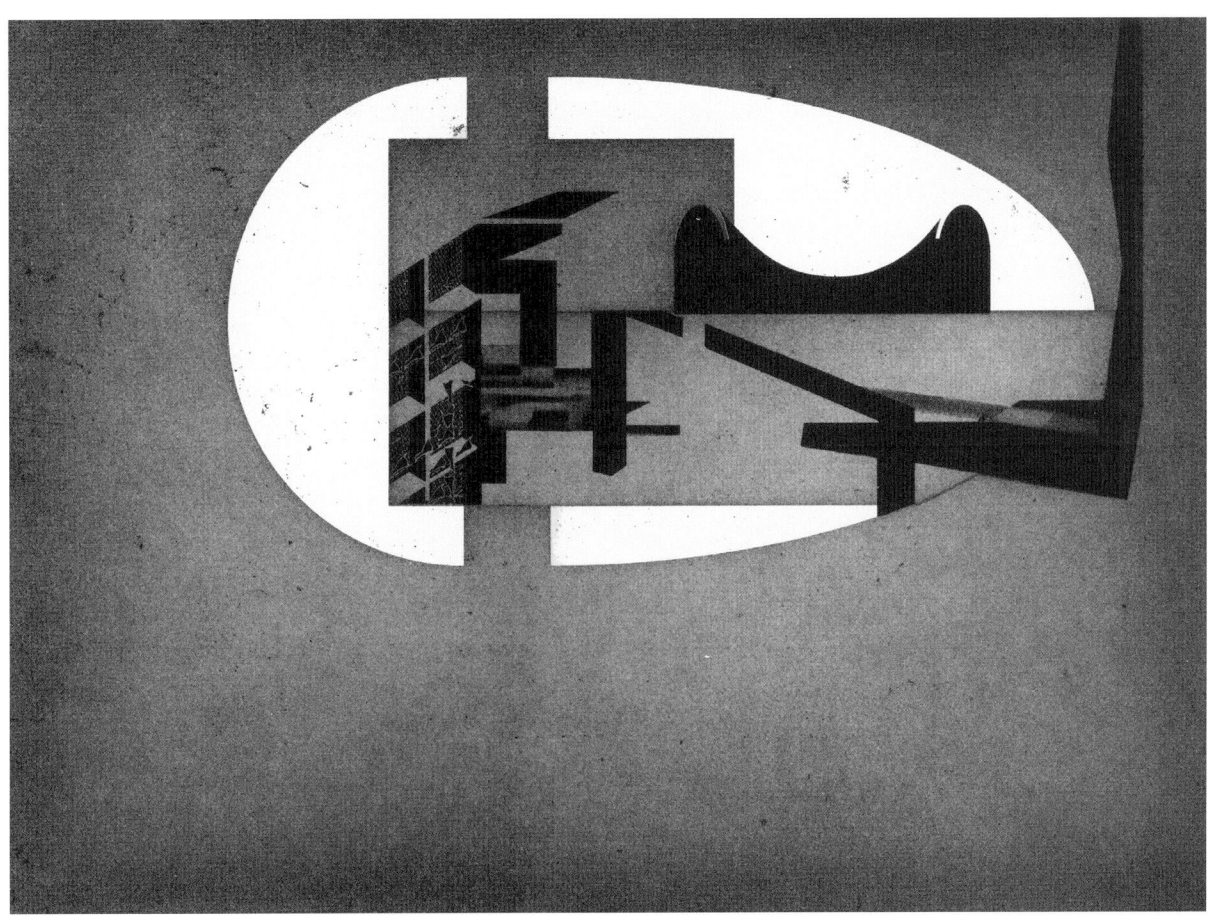

Unit Object (sculpture garden), 2014, etching, 53 × 62.5 cm, edition of 20

Monika Sosnowska

Trained as a painter, Monika Sosnowska started creating three-dimensional works as an extension of painting: she found that her paintings started to 'escape' the canvas. The artist's sculptures are imposing and robust, composed of heavy industrial materials. While she designs them alone, she collaborates with factories and engineers to create their vast scale. The people she works with are often older engineers who have experience of building commissions in post-war Poland, many of whom lost their industrial jobs after the fall of Communism in the country in 1989. By testing the limits of materials, Sosnowska's practice challenges the possibilities of production and design, and grapples with complex legacies of social memory through architectural quotation and industrial processes.

The intricate shuttlecock-like shape of Sosnowska's *Tower* (2019) belies the inherent strength of its steel material. The sculpture is part of a series of works that respond to the distinctive techniques and geometry of early Soviet radio towers designed by Vladimir Shukhov (1853–1939), the most famous of which is Shabolovka Tower (or Shukhov Tower) in Moscow. Assembled during the Russian Civil War, the Shukhov Tower comprises six stacked hyperboloid structures – an architectural form invented by Shukhov composed of inward curving metal cylinders. The design of the tower made efficient use of scarce materials and could be assembled without cranes. However, a tragedy occurred during its construction: on 29 June 1921, the metal cylinders which had been heated and loaded with weight to create their 'squashed' form buckled, causing the top segment of the tower to collapse. The incident resulted in the deaths of several workers, and the temporary demise of Shukhov's vanguard design. Many such towers were built across the Soviet Union, often falling into disrepair, and were stripped for materials. Completed in 1922, the Shukhov Tower was spared this fate through popular pressure, which saved the tower from demolition in 2014. LM

Born 1972, Ryki, Poland
Lives and works in Warsaw

Monika Sosnowska's sculptural language emerges from a process of experimentation with, and appropriation of, construction materials such as steel beams, concrete, reinforcing rods and pipes. These elements – the solid and rigid foundations of buildings – are manipulated and warped, taking on an independence in which their former functionality is implied yet defunct. The formal language of her works echoes different contradictory modernisms: that of the Polish constructivism of the 1930s; the minimal and conceptual tendencies of the international art of the 1960s and 1970s; and modernist architecture as experienced in Eastern Europe. In her recent works, Sosnowska conveys both political and psychological tones by incorporating elements of modernist architecture to create unexpected encounters that reflect on buildings as sites of memory. Sosnowska achieved international renown with her work *The Corridor* (2003), which formed part of the Arsenale exhibition of the 50th Venice Biennale.

Exhibitions include Zachęta – National Gallery of Art, Warsaw (2020); Muzeum Susch, Engadin, Switzerland (2017); Indianapolis Museum of Art, Indiana, USA (2016); Serralves Foundation, Porto (2015); Pérez Art Museum Miami (2013); Contemporary Art Gallery, Vancouver (2013); The Polish Pavilion, 52nd Venice Biennale (2007); The Museum of Modern Art, New York (2006); The Sigmund Freud Museum, Vienna (2005), and the Serpentine Gallery, London (2004), among others. Her work is represented by The Modern Institute, Glasgow, and Hauser & Wirth.

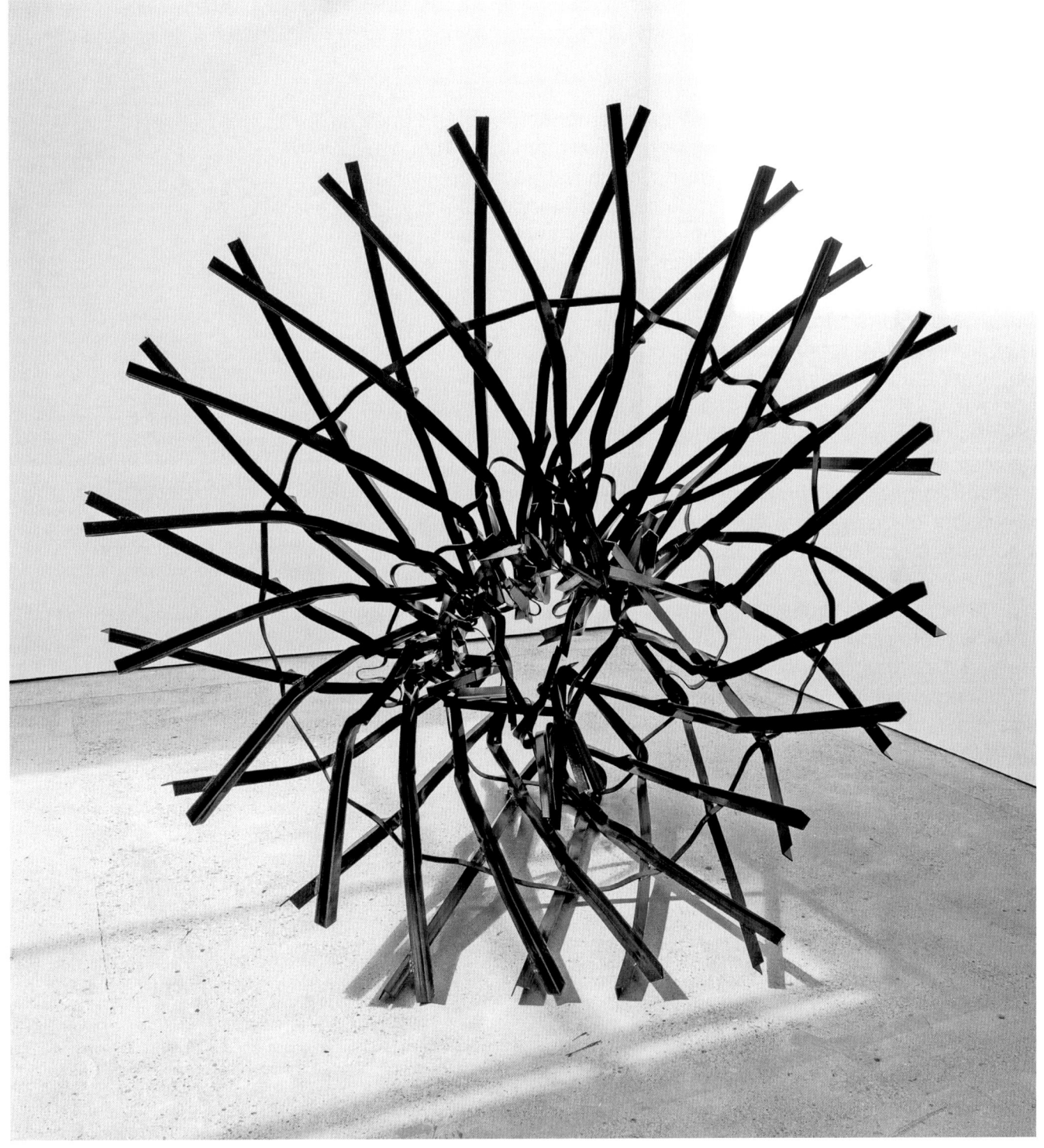

Tower, 2019, steel, paint, 168 × 220 × 215 cm

Maria Taniguchi

Legacies of modernism and their relationship to art and architecture in the Philippines are recurring themes of Taniguchi's art. Many of her works combine the rationalism of rectilinear modernism with the fluidity of myth and perception. Her ongoing series of 'brick' paintings depict grids of individually painted 2 × 6-centimetre black rectangles, the different densities of which create surface illusions through the reflection of light. Often displayed propped against walls, the large paintings have the quality of totems, with their ritualistic sense of repetition and architectural motif.

Mies 421 (2010) is a four-minute video composed of black-and-white photographs taken by Taniguchi of German-American architect Ludwig Mies van der Rohe's reconstructed pavilion in Barcelona. The artist's images reflect the primary medium through which many people experienced the pavilion, which was disassembled one year after its construction. Originally an ephemeral structure built for the International Exhibition in 1929, Mies' steel, glass and marble cantilevered design earnt mythical status through widespread circulation of its documentation, leading to the pavilion's reconstruction in 1986.

Mies 421 presents different perspectives of the pavilion with forensic precision. Some images capture visitors walking through its cavernous interior, their bodies masked by shadows. A number of images show the pavilion's internal courtyard and pool, which contains *Der Morgen* (Morning) (1925), a sculpture of a woman dancing by the German artist Georg Kolbe. Framed by the pavilion's architecture, the woman's arms are raised, as if shielding her face from the Mediterranean sun. The transition between each photograph is marked by the sound of a click, the speed of which increases until the last image disappears. The film's bullet-like soundtrack, stark imagery and ambiguous narrative inadvertently create a work of cinematic horror, in which Mies' pavilion becomes the stage set for an invisible threat.

MP

Born 1981, Dumaguete City, Philippines
Lives and works in Manila

Maria Taniguchi works across a diverse range of media which includes painting, video, sculpture, pottery, printmaking, drawing and writing. Her work focuses on concepts of composing, constructing and framing, whilst referring to the craftsmanship and history of the Philippines. She works with a variety of approaches towards processing the legacies of modernism within an ambiguous cross-cultural context.

Selected solo and group exhibitions include *Art Histories of a Forever War: Modernism Between Space and Home*, Taipei Fine Arts Museum (2021); 5th Dhaka Art Summit (2020); Museum of Contemporary Art and Design (MCAD), Manila (2020); Bangkok Art and Culture Centre (BACC) (2019); Contemporary Art Centre (CAC), Vilnius, Lithuania (2019); M+ Pavilion (2018); 12th Gwangju Biennale (2018); 21st Biennale of Sydney (2018); Centre Pompidou (2017); Institute of Contemporary Arts (ICA) Singapore (2016); Para Site, Hong Kong (2016); Rockbund Art Museum, Shanghai (2015); Museum of Contemporary Art (M HKA), Antwerp (2014); Metropolitan Museum of Manila (2013); Ateneo Art Gallery, Manila (2012); Artspace Aotearoa, Auckland (2012); Jorge B. Vargas Museum & Filipiniana Research Center, University of the Philippines, Manila (2011); Cell Project Space, London (2010), and Tate Modern (2010), among others. Her work is represented by carlier | gebauer, Silverlens, and Taka Ishii.

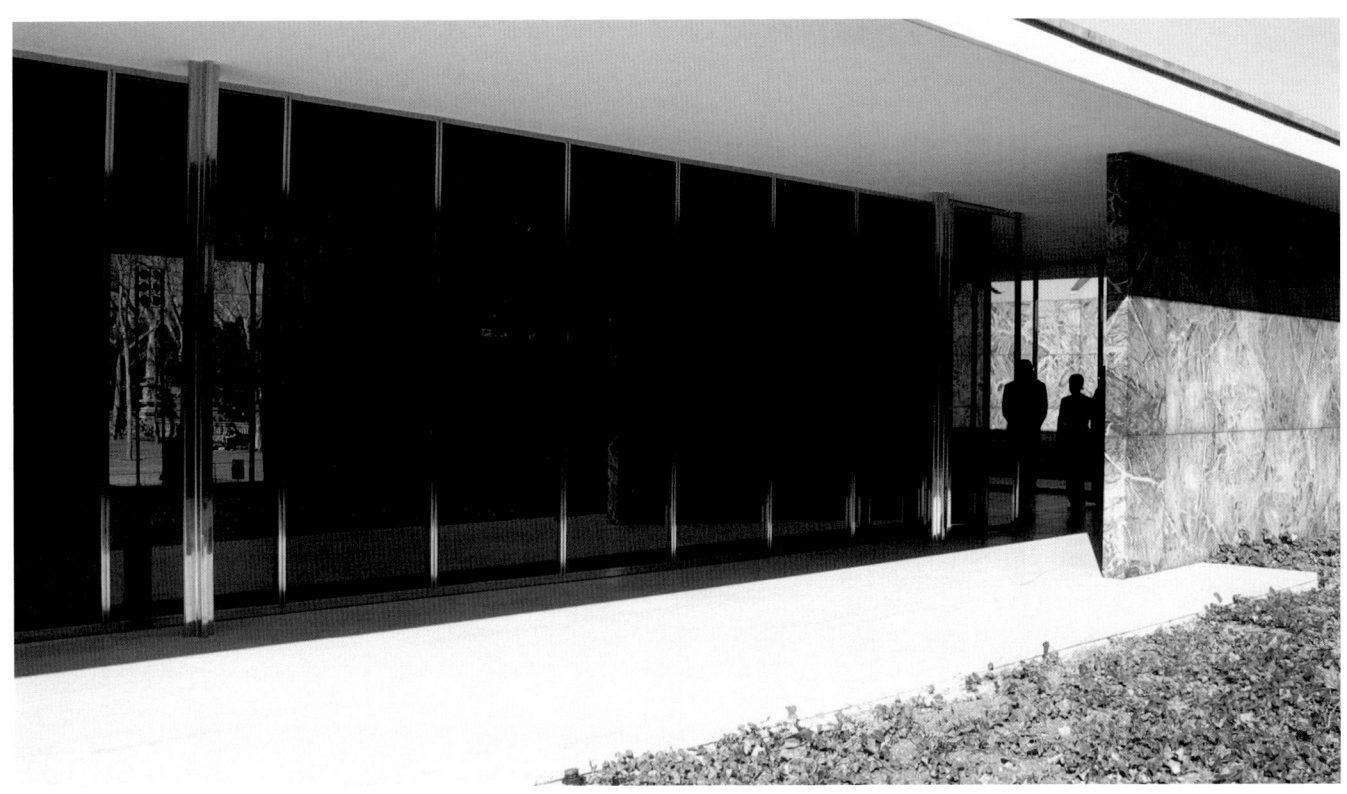
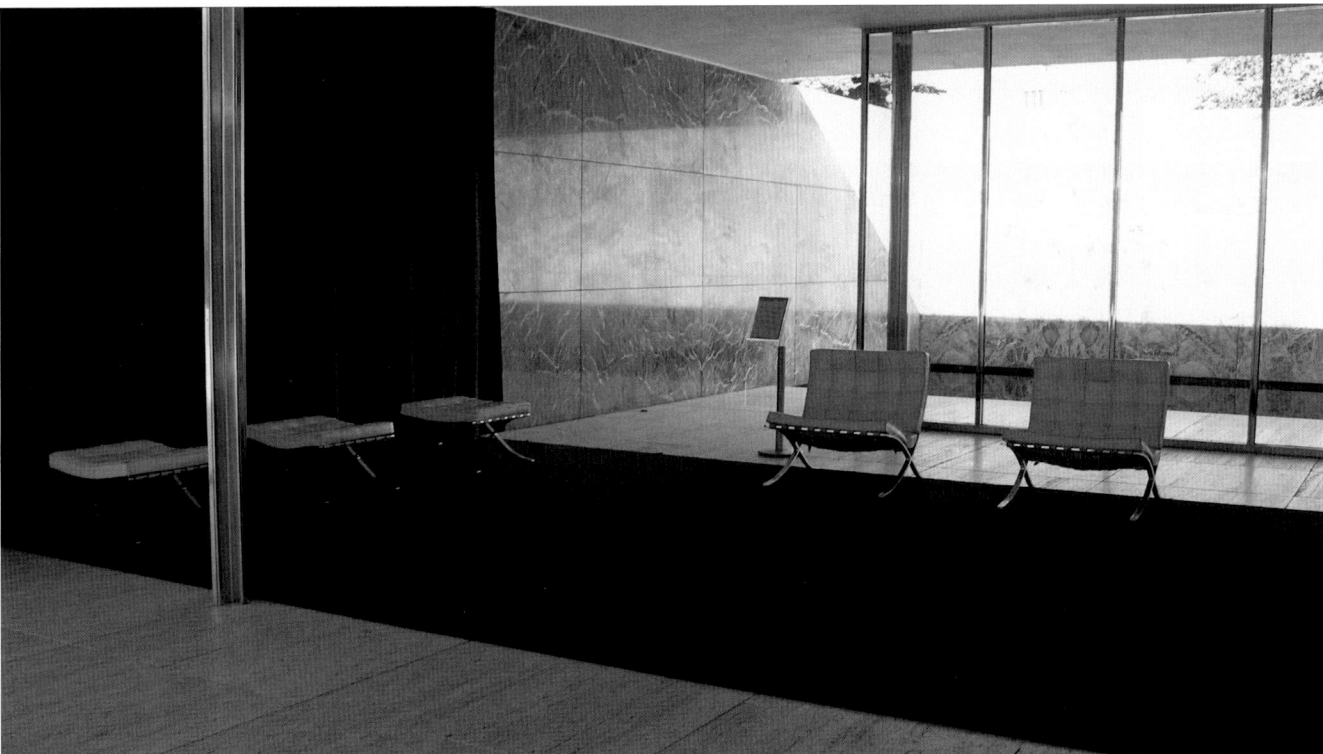

Mies 421, 2010, single-channel video, black and white, sound, 4:06 minutes, film stills

Abbas Zahedi

Abbas Zahedi's multi-disciplinary practice explores the interrelation of personal and collective histories. Through interventions into existing situations and architecture, he highlights the psychological disconnect between societal structures and individual and communal experience.

At first glance, *Exit Sign* (2021) resembles the kind of exit signage designed to signal safe routes out of buildings. On closer inspection, the illuminated sign features figures running upside down towards an arrow pointing upwards. Steel chains reference rituals of lamentation and mourning and allude to the association of the exit sign's green colour with paradise in Islam. For Zahedi, the work is a poignant personal reflection on the fire that took place at Grenfell Tower in London in 2017, killing 72 people including Zahedi's friend and fellow artist, Khadija Saye.

Zahedi's intervention into health and safety signage is a direct response to British MP Jacob Rees-Mogg's callous claim that, if he had been a resident at Grenfell Tower, he would have simply used 'common-sense' to exit the building, contradicting the stay-put policy that was in place. Replacing the exit sign above the doorway to Ikon's First Floor galleries, Zahedi's *Exit Sign* draws attention to the gallery's existing architecture, making audiences aware of how their movement through it is mediated by externally imposed regulations.

Tensions between the human body and the built environment are also apparent in *Artist with Pipe* (2015–22). The photograph shows Zahedi blowing a cloud of shisha smoke, surrounded by found objects. Performing the function of a roof is a makeshift thatch – a visual identifier of the English countryside, ominous for its dislocation from the structure of a cottage. The low saturation of the photograph is in direct contrast to the picture-postcard bucolic scenes in which one might expect to find thatched roofs. This contrast is reinforced by the photograph's setting in the backyard of a housing estate in London. The overall incongruity of the scene is in keeping with Zahedi's interest in difference: the 'othering' effect that our surroundings can have on us.   LM

Born 1984, London
Lives and works in London

Abbas Zahedi's interdisciplinary practice blends contemporary philosophy, poetics and social dynamics with sound, sculpture and other performative media. With an emphasis on how personal and collective histories interweave, Zahedi makes connections with the people around, in proximity to, or involved with the situations upon which he focuses.

Zahedi studied medicine at University College London, before completing his MA in Contemporary Photography: Practices and Philosophies at Central Saint Martins in 2019. Solo exhibitions include *Metatopia 10013*, Anonymous Gallery, New York (2022); *11 & 1*, Belmacz, London (2021); *Ouranophobia SW3*, Chelsea Sorting Office, London (2020), and *How to Make a How From a Why?*, South London Gallery (2020). He has participated in group exhibitions at the Barbican (2022); Whitechapel Gallery (2022); Goldsmiths Centre for Contemporary Art (2022); Somerset House (2021); FUTURA, Prague (2021); Wolverhampton Art Gallery (2018) and the Diaspora Pavilion, Venice (2017), among others. Zahedi has been the recipient of numerous awards including the Frieze Artist Award (2022); the Paul Hamlyn Foundation Awards for Artists (2021); the Serpentine Galleries' Support Structures for Support Structures (2021); Artangel, Thinking Time (2020); Jerwood Arts Bursary (2019); Aziz Foundation Academic Scholarship (2018); and Khadija Saye Memorial Fund Scholarship (2017). He is represented by Belmacz, London.

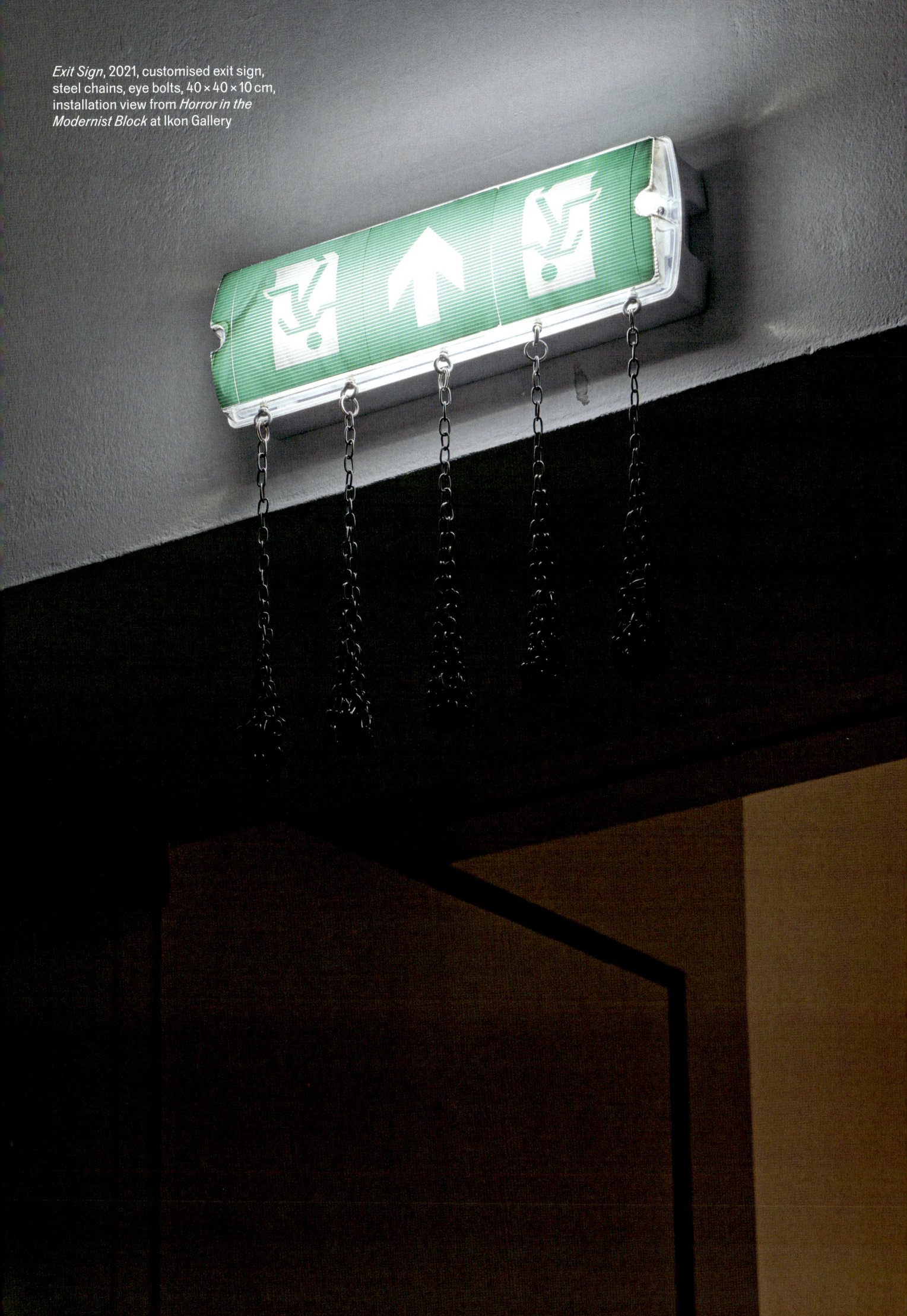

Exit Sign, 2021, customised exit sign, steel chains, eye bolts, 40 × 40 × 10 cm, installation view from *Horror in the Modernist Block* at Ikon Gallery

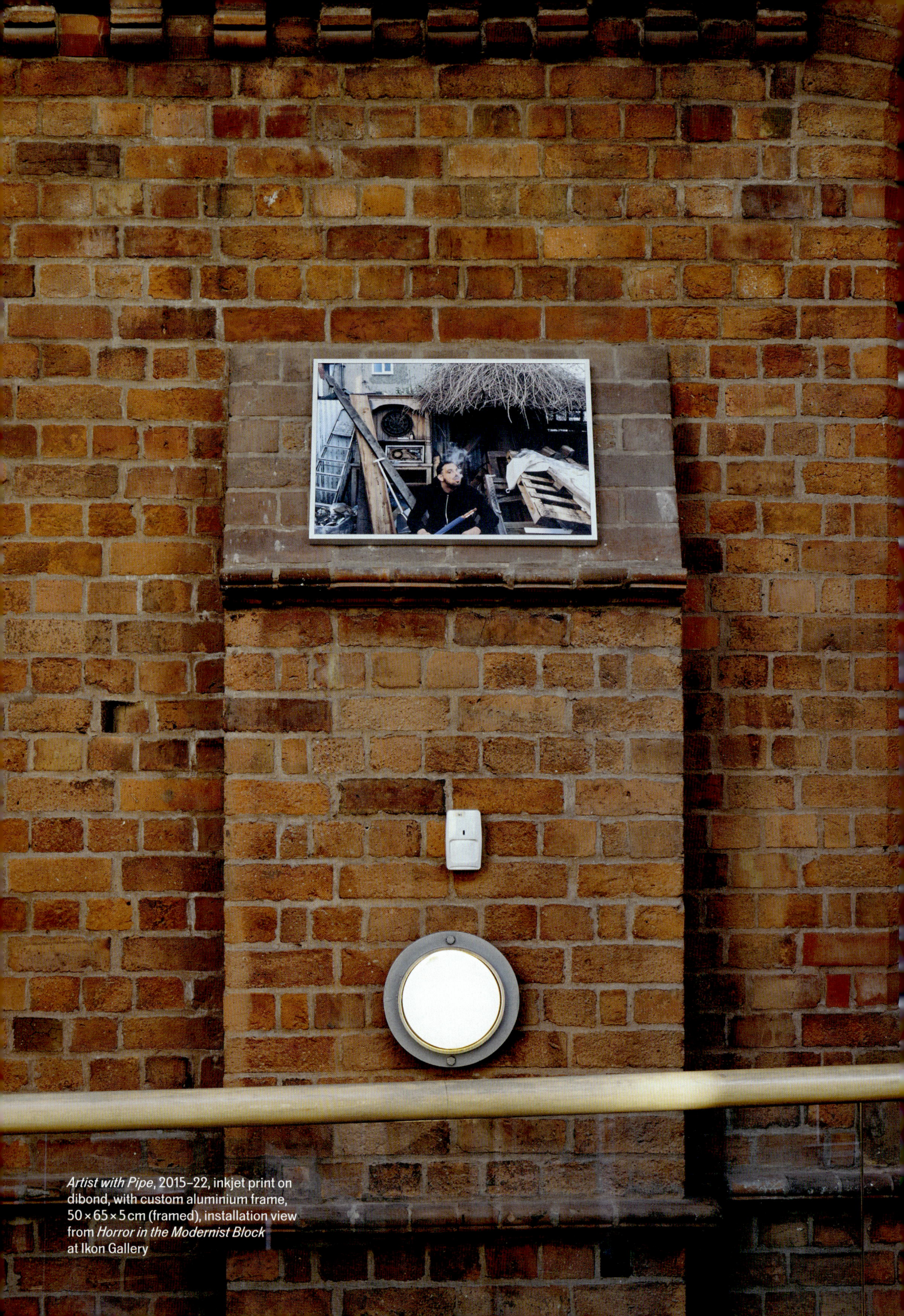

Artist with Pipe, 2015–22, inkjet print on dibond, with custom aluminium frame, 50 × 65 × 5 cm (framed), installation view from *Horror in the Modernist Block* at Ikon Gallery

Plum Pudding: Boot House

Stuart Whipps

Preface

This text began – like so many things in 2020 – with a long walk at a slightly awkward distance. Curator Melanie Pocock was in the early stages of developing an exhibition around horror and modernist architecture and was interested in how it might relate to things I was working on. I had an idea kicking around about links between the new town of Stevenage in Hertfordshire and Pyongyang in North Korea, yearning for the return of international travel, even if that travel was to a totalitarian dictatorship. However, as we walked through the near empty city centre, I began talking about Birmingham, pointing out small architectural traces that triggered long forgotten memories and also talking a lot about the way Birmingham had impacted (perhaps more accurately, infected) the way I read and experienced different cities. In the weeks that followed I reflected on our conversation a lot and began to think about other, perhaps smaller ideas of 'horror'.

In 'Plum Pudding: Boot House' I'll be writing about several buildings that have been or are important to me. I'm starting however with a story of a building I've never been to and have no personal connection with. It's a ghost story of sorts…

The Great Spiritual Tower

On June 15 1883, a correspondent for *The Medium and Daybreak* – a weekly journal devoted to the history, phenomena, philosophy and teachings of spiritualism – provided an account of his visit to Andrew Peterson in the Hampshire village of Sway during the construction of what remains the largest structure of unreinforced concrete in the country (fig.1).

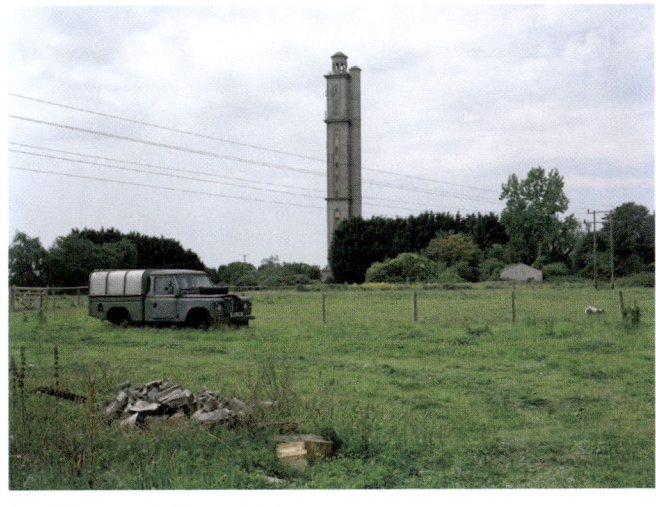

Fig. 1. Peterson's Tower, 2011

In retirement, Peterson became an advocate and patron of the spiritualist movement in the UK and claimed to be building his tower under the instruction of the ghost of Sir Christopher Wren. In *The Medium and Daybeak* we can read the prosaic manifestation of this:

> 'What breadth are you going to make your foundation?' asked the spirit. 'Well I was thinking of making it 20 feet – a tenth part of the contemplated height, that is, 200 feet.'
> 'Had you not better make it 24 feet?' added the spirit, at the same time giving reasons for the recommendation.[1]

The chosen material for these foundations – concrete – is central to the stories that follow, as is a broader exploration of haunting, horror and trauma. We'll leave Peterson's tower to consider (figs. 2, 3, 4, 5):

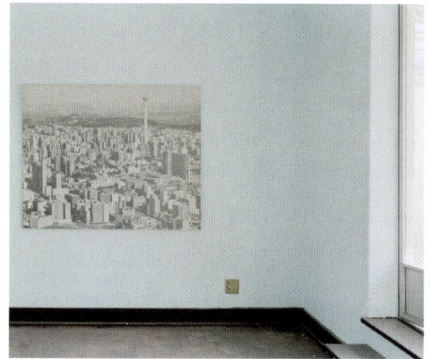

Fig. 2. Concrete buildings of the Central Business District in Johannesburg, South Africa, 2007

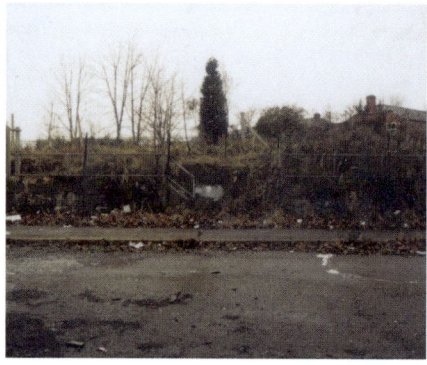

Fig. 3. The now demolished Boot houses of Perry Common, Enderby Road, 2006

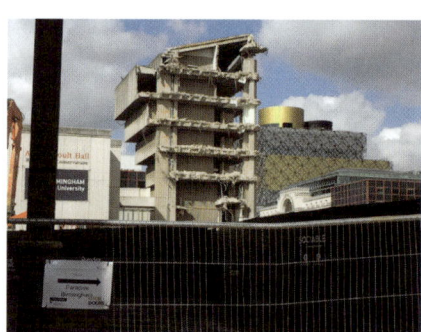

Fig. 4. Birmingham Central Library and The Library of Birmingham, 2016

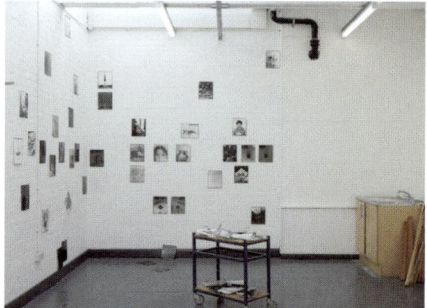

Fig. 5. View of installation by Margaret Salmon, *British Art Show 9*, Wolverhampton School of Art (2022)

The article in *The Medium and Daybreak* has itself something to say about concrete:

> But what is concrete? the reader may ask. The word signifies a compound or combination. A plum pudding is undoubtably 'concrete'. And indeed the material of which we write bears not a little resemblance to that well known and highly relished Viand.[2]

1. Anonymous, 'A Visit to A.T.T.P's Country Seat: The Great Spiritual Tower', *The Medium and Daybreak* 14, no. 689 (London: James Burns 1883).

2. Ibid.

Johannesburg

In the three years I spent studying photography I almost exclusively photographed buildings and places. It wasn't that I didn't wish to tell human stories; the opposite was true. I just couldn't see a way to fix the deep unease I felt at the way people were represented, especially working-class people, who were generally photographed by sneering, middle class photographers.

My own early experiences had also shown me that buildings have real impacts on lives and communities.

In 2007, for my first significant commission after leaving art school, I spent three months on a residency in Johannesburg photographing the disused buildings of the Central Business District. I made 127 large format negatives over the three months, but with each new photograph, the realisation that I couldn't duck the ethical issues of representation by not photographing people became more apparent (figs. 6, 7, 8, 9).

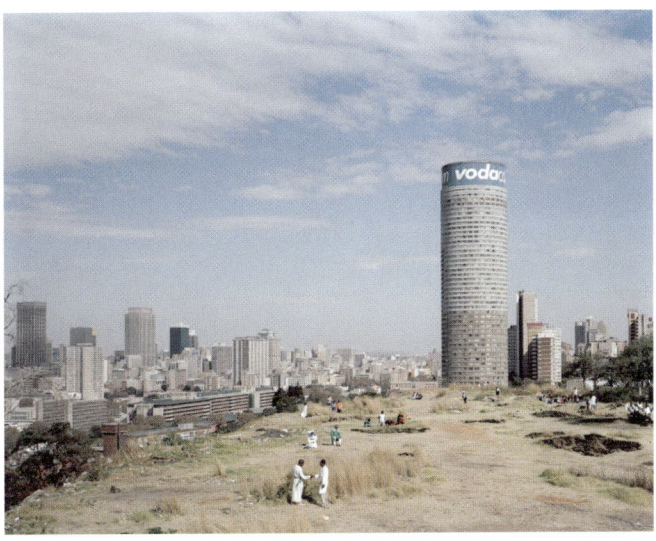

Fig. 6. Ponti, 2007

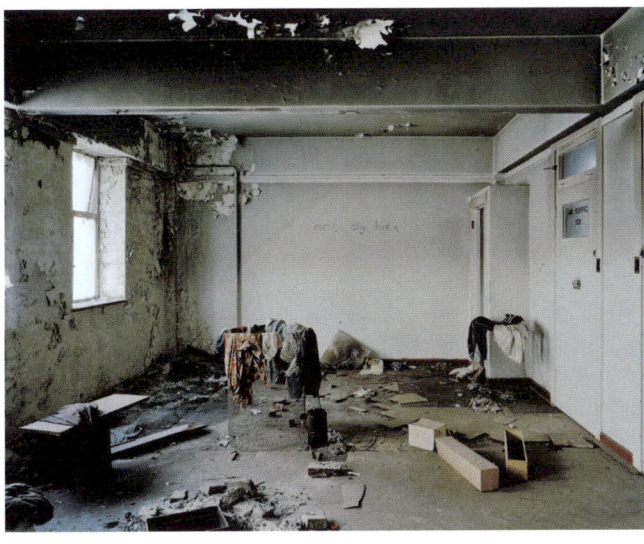

Fig. 7. C & A, Johannesburg, 2007

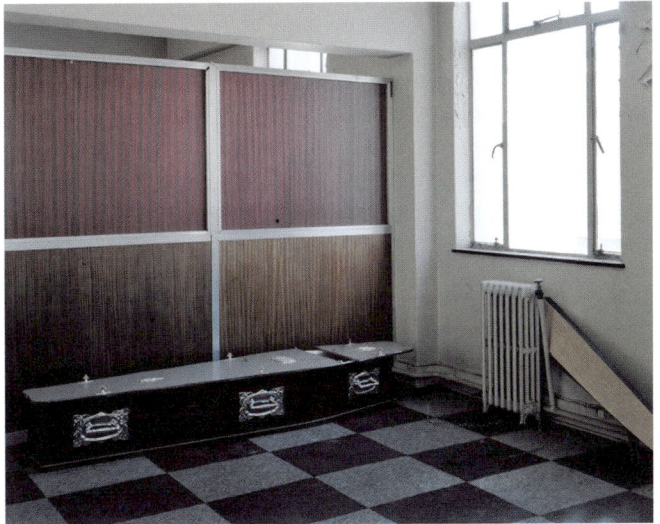

Fig. 8. Shakespeare House, Johannesburg, 2007

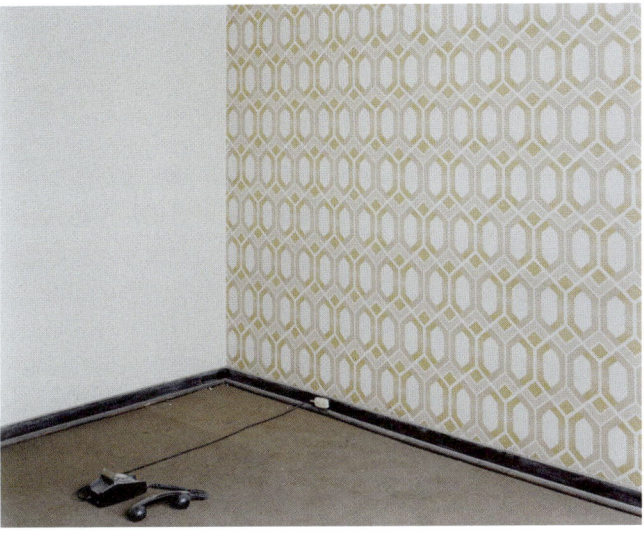

Fig. 9. Provincial Building, Johannesburg, 2007

On the surface, these places chimed with my own experiences of displacement, and the constant building and rebuilding of Birmingham. But of course, the traumatic and complex history of Johannesburg is very different to what I knew from home. In the last week of my residency, I encountered the empty offices of Photo Colour Services (PCS); a photography lab that serviced the needs of commercial clients in Johannesburg (figs. 10, 11). It looked as if all employees left in a hurry, leaving behind thousands of prints and negatives that were due to be incinerated later that week. Without any thought of what I might do with them, I boxed them up and had them shipped to my studio in Birmingham.

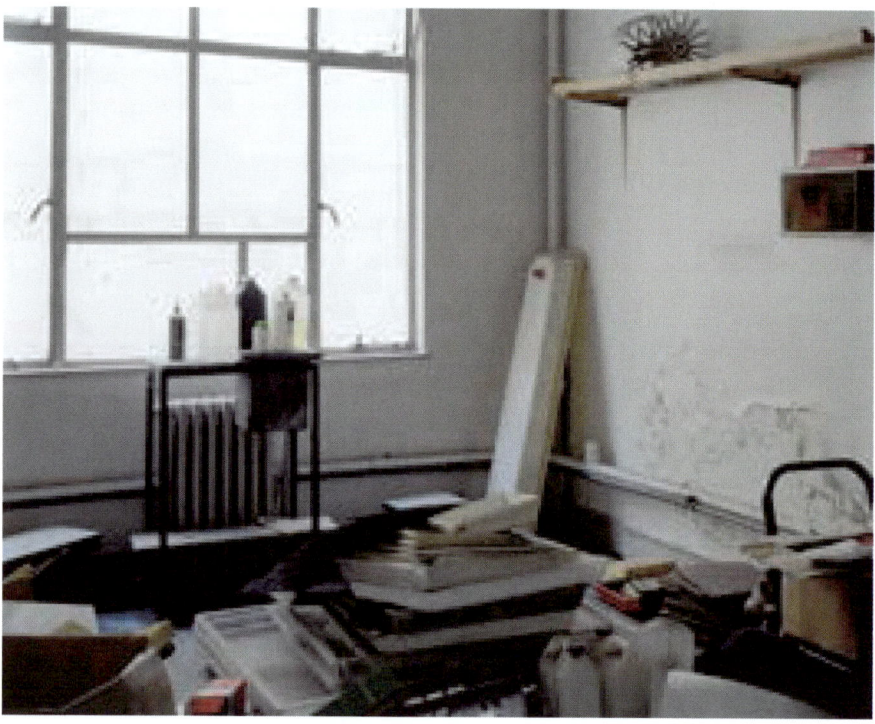

Fig. 10. Photo Colour Services (PCS), 2007

Over the years I worked to make spreads for books or ideas for exhibitions but the unease I felt around the photographs I'd made in Johannesburg was nothing to the ethical quagmire I was now in as I contemplated this material that I'd taken. In 2015 I had the chance to return to Johannesburg and set about printing every negative I'd recovered from PCS. I took this material back with me and worked to find a place for it in South Africa and to learn from and prioritise the experiences and voices of people in Johannesburg. The effort to find a home for the photographs was ultimately futile, but the time spent working with people to interrogate the material opened new ways of understanding the photographs and the city itself (figs. 12, 13).

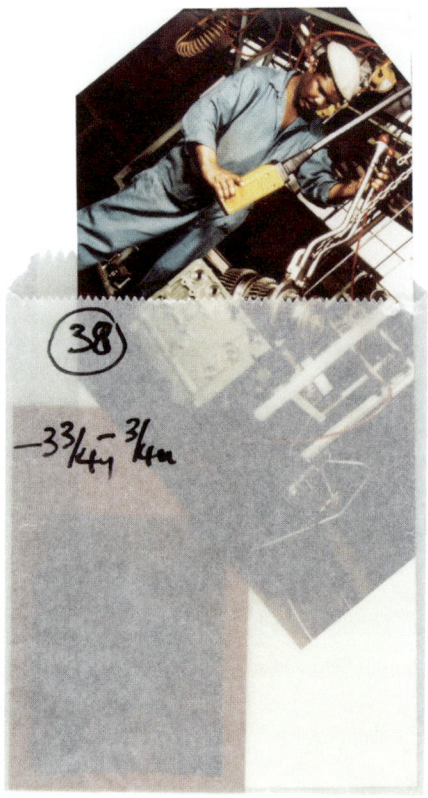

Fig. 11. Found negative and print from PCS, 2009

If you take a measurement from the bottom of its deepest mine to the top of its tallest building, Johannesburg is the tallest city in the world. With legacies of its mining history everywhere it's no surprise that in a creative writing workshop at the University of the Witwatersrand the writer Sheena Magenya wrote about this photograph of three miners (fig. 14). This is her short story, *Breathe Deeply* (2016):

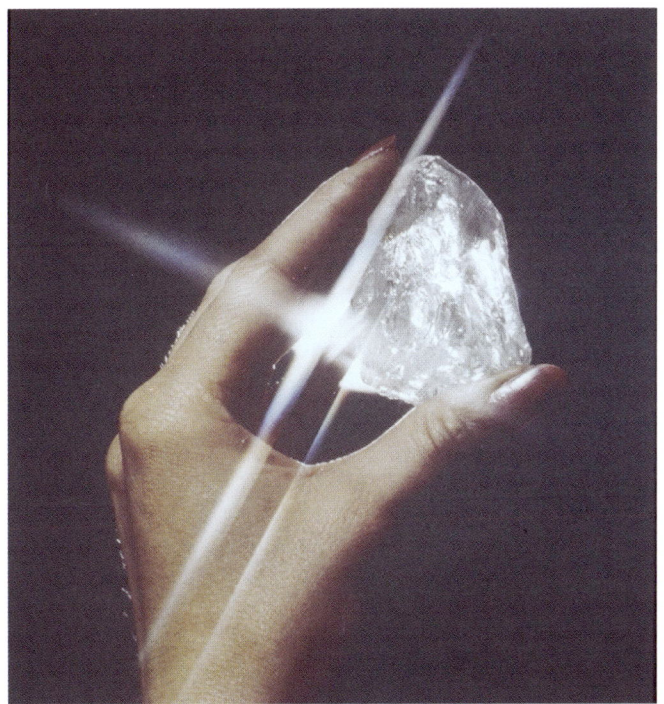

Fig. 12. PCS_0220, 2009

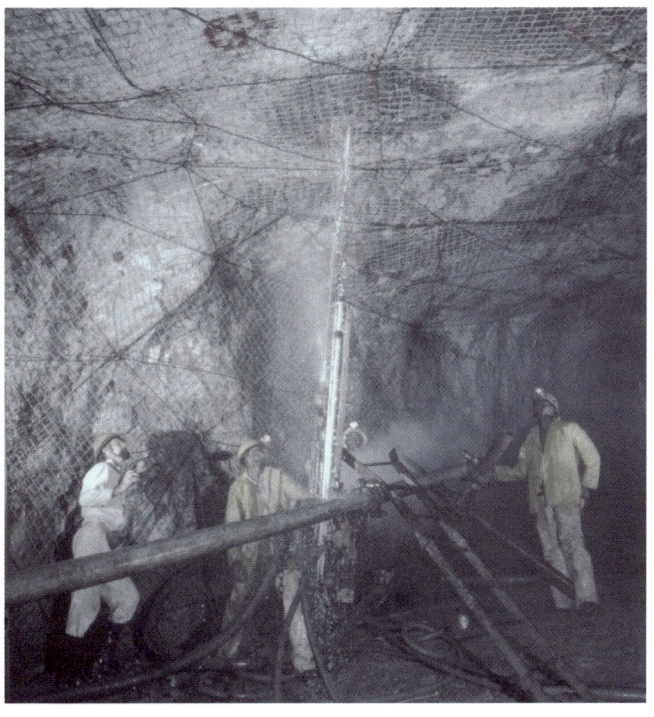

Fig. 13. PCS_0075, 2009

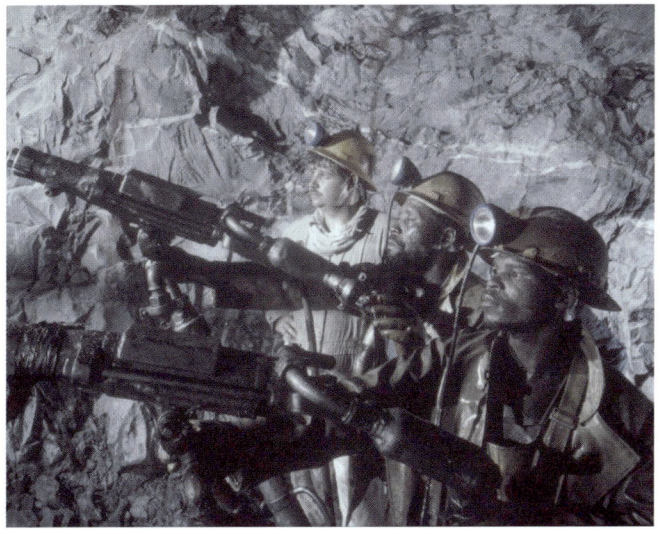

Fig. 14. PCS_0067, 2009

Even with the loud drilling and the endless vibrating I can still feel the letter, in the trousers under my overalls, sharp edges scratching my dry thighs. I'm sick, the letter says, and I have to go home. I don't know this, Musa read the letter for me. I asked the *bass* why. *Bass* said I have sickness in my lungs, and I can't work in the pits anymore. Musa says I will get lots of money, and I can finally go home. To Refilwe and my children, whose names don't come so easily to me anymore. I drill harder, and hope that the letters in my pocket will fall off, or rearrange themselves into meaning something else. If I have to die, I'd like to die here. I have to stay down here as long as I possibly can. Because you see, I inhale it. I take deep breaths of it while I drill away. Sometimes it swirls in my mouth like mud and I swallow it all. Someone said, and I believe them. Someone said that if you stay here long enough, and you inhale enough of it, when you die, they will find it. In your kidneys and your lungs, and maybe your liver if you don't drink too much. They can't send me back alive. I'm no good to Refilwe and my children alive. But my body, they can have. And they can take it to the *inyanga* that will know where to find the little pieces of gold sitting in my body, that I have been inhaling for the last twenty years.[3]

3. Sheena Magenya, 'Breathe Deeply', *Source* 87 (Autumn 2016): 36.

Boot House

At the same time Johannesburg's concrete skyscrapers were being built, a very different form of modernism was taking shape in the English provinces at Perry Common in north Birmingham, the council estate I lived on for the first 14 years of my life (fig. 15). The houses were built by the Henry Boot construction firm with homes coming to be known affectionately as 'boot houses'. The affection, like the houses, would soon begin to crack.

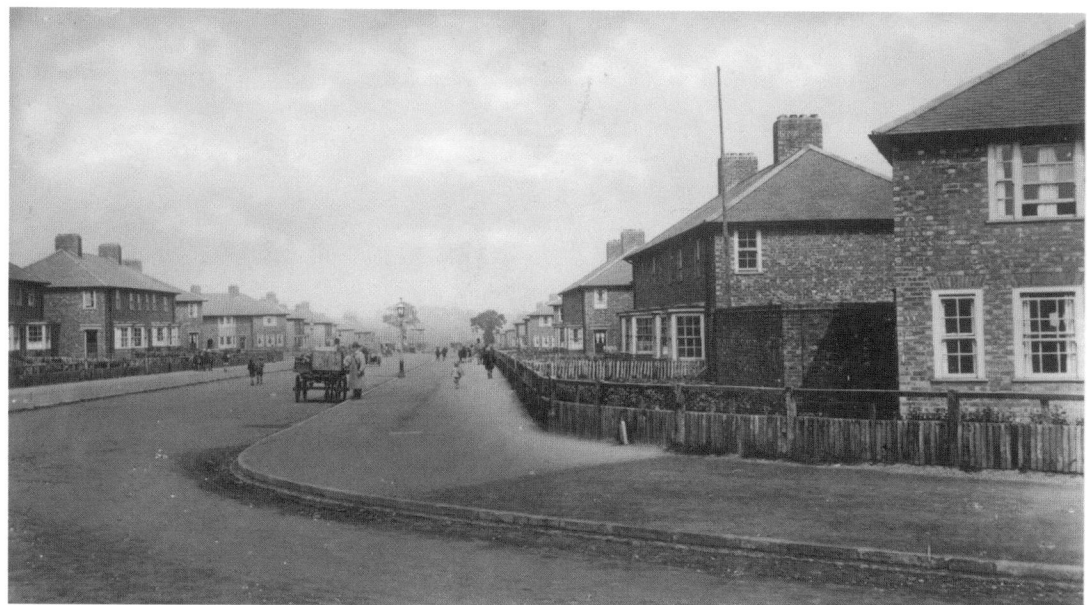

Fig. 15. Witton Lodge Road, Perry Common, date unknown, postcard

It is said that the walls most likely to constrain us are the walls we build inside our heads. The walls that constrained me as a child can be traced on my skin in a literal sense. On the back of my head is a cluster of small scars (fig. 16). I don't know if I remember the incident and the injury itself or the retelling of it. A family story that gets told and embellished year after year.

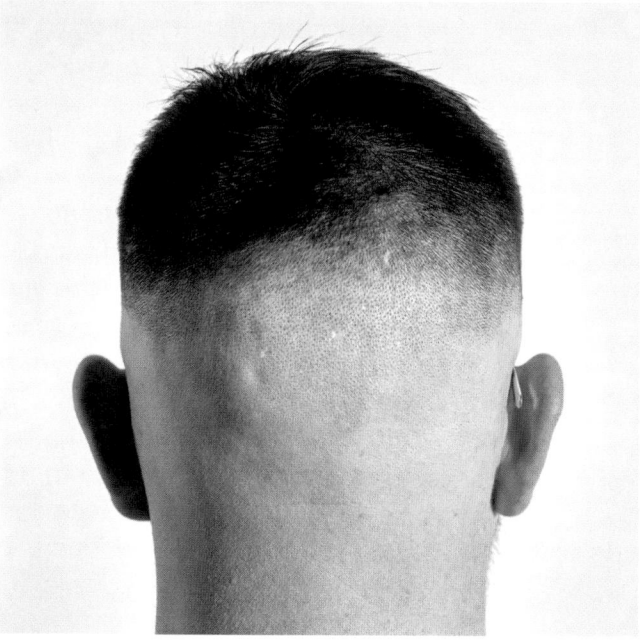

Fig. 16. The back of my head, 2022

Me and my brother Ian, five years older than me, were playing army in the back garden of our house in Perry Common in Birmingham (fig.17). The play acting had moved on from the rattle of twig and stick machine guns to an interrogation against the exterior wall of the house. With one firm crack against the pebbledash (that apparently reverberated through the concrete structure) I was given a lasting imprint of the house I grew up in. If I'd have had the information he was looking for I'd have given it up gladly.

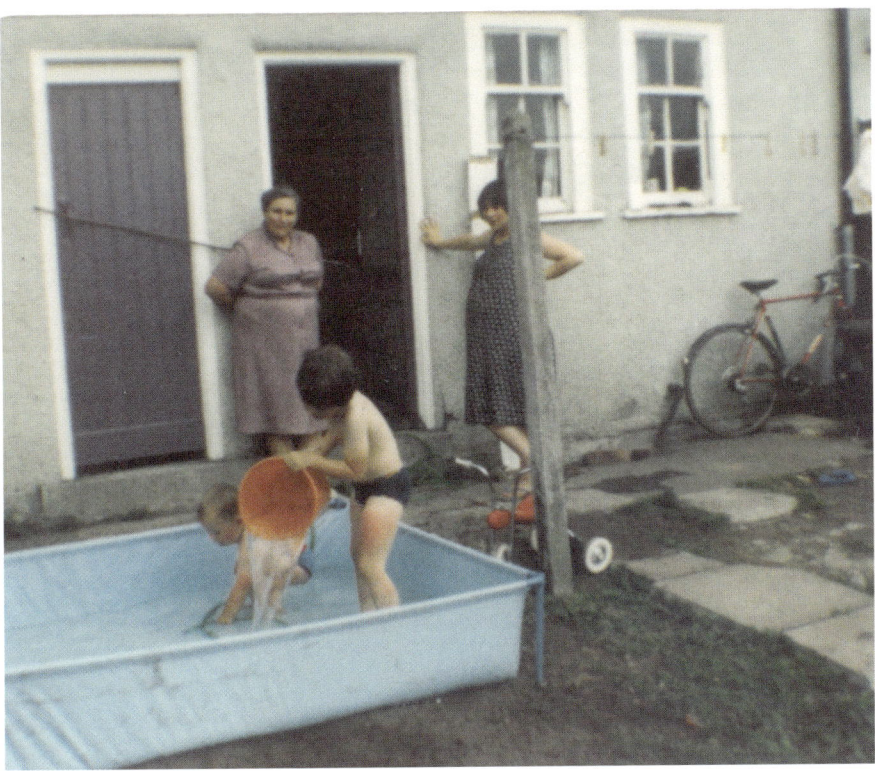

Fig. 17. Me, my brother, my mom and my nan in the back garden of Enderby Road, Perry Common, 1981

I had an acute understanding of where I lived that transcended the knocking of my head into the exterior walls. I know I lived in a boot house from the times spent at community meetings, at MP surgeries and through overheard chats over the garden fence.

I knew this because the 'boot houses' were fucked.

It is no surprise that the sound of my head being smashed against the wall could be heard throughout the house. The pressing of a light switch was enough to start a cascade of loose concrete behind the woodchip. My mom used to joke that if anybody ever tried to sell the house the listing would say 'close to the shops. Getting closer every day...'

We arrived in 1981 from a maisonette on a much worse estate called Topcroft, so the house was a big step up for us, but by the end of the decade, Perry Common, and its sister estate Pipe Hayes (which coincidentally, my auntie Josie, my mom's sister, lived in)[4] had been condemned. We would live at 10 Enderby Rd until 1992. Plenty of time to acquire further scars.

4. It is worth noting that my mom and Josie were no strangers to upheaval. They had grown up in Aston, just outside of the city centre in the shadows of the HP sauce factory in a 'back to back' house. If you want to see a traditional 'back to back' then you can visit the National Trust reconstruction in Birmingham city centre but my mom says that it's a 'posh version'. All of Birmingham's 'back to backs' were demolished as part of the slum clearances of the 1960s. The site of my mom's old house is now the A38M, the Aston Expressway.

This from an attempt to navigate the giant roundabout, known as 'the ring' on a skateboard, on my stomach, using my hands to stop (fig. 18)

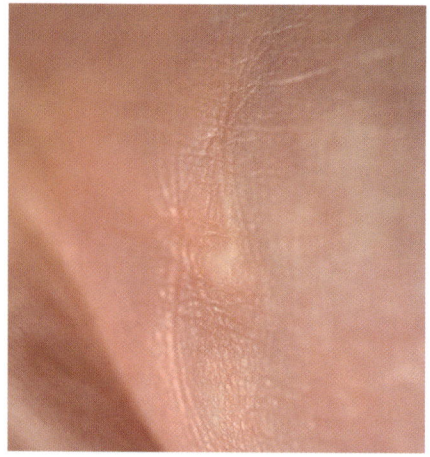 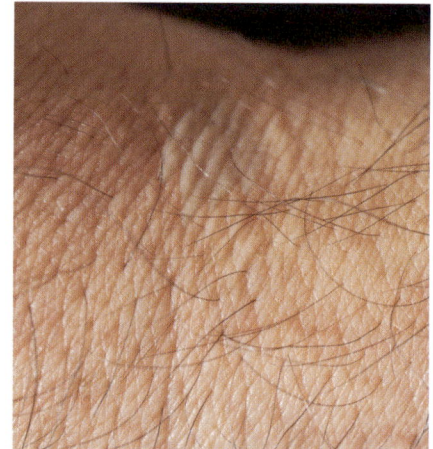

Fig. 18. Scar on my right palm, 2022   Fig. 19. Scar on my left wrist

This from a tumble off the one piece of play equipment in our junior school playground; a giant concrete saddle (fig. 19)

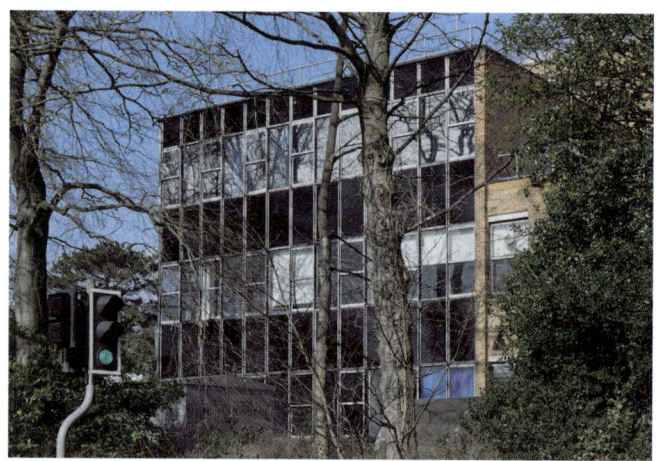

Fig. 20. Good Hope hospital, 2022

All of these injuries would precipitate a visit to A&E which would bring its own silent traumas. The nearest hospital was Good Hope in Sutton Coldfield which was (and perhaps still is) known as 'No Hope' (fig 20). Another example of mid-century provincial modernism, it is where me and my brother were born. It is also where my mom lost a daughter during childbirth in 1981.

In an act of callous indifference, she was placed on a ward with the sound of crying babies of the maternity department to one side, and a view of the neighbouring cemetery to the other. I was oblivious at the time, worried only by my own brakes and scrapes, but each visit to that hospital must have been a harrowing ordeal for my mom and dad.

All of this was playing out in a city that felt very much past its prime. The hospital, along with great swathes of Birmingham, was heavily redeveloped in the 1960s and 70s but by the early 90s, it was all fading. The city centre was a broken mess.

Central Library

Birmingham Central Library sat on a natural ridge in the civic heart of the city. An imposing, concrete structure that offered an austere counterpoint to the whimsy of the neighbouring Town Hall, built in the style of a Corinthian temple. Demolition of the library would begin in 2013. Less than forty years after it opened to the public in 1974 and one year after the death of its architect, John Madin.

In what would have been the loading bay for Birmingham Central Library all that remains is a constellation of concrete stalactites. Formed over the lifetime of the library by the slow seepage and percolation of water through the concrete, they cling to the remains of the old structure as it is swallowed by the new 'Paradise' redevelopment.[5] What was once civic land is now private property.

I knocked about around Birmingham Central Library for years before I ever remember going inside.

The library had been planned as part of a much larger civic centre so its footprint was expansive and empty. Flanked by the 1980s infill of the Copthorne Hotel on one side and a sweeping bank of steps on the other, the inverted concrete ziggurat form of the library itself was also hollow. It is suggested there would have been a spectacular installation of plants, trees and falling water if the initial budgets had been maintained. A hanging garden of Birmingham...

However, by the time I first experienced it the ground floor had instead been sectioned into commercial units. I only remember McDonalds at the Chamberlain Square side, and Raphael's, a Roman/Greco themed wine bar at the Centenary Square side. Later there was a branch of Hooters and later still, a J.D. Wetherspoons.

Going 'up town' as a child and teenager was a big deal. Birmingham may be the UK's second largest city but its size manifests as a horizontal sprawl. 'Town', the city centre, was and is comparably small but brings with that a sense of drama when travelling to it from the suburban edges of the city. Always travelling by bus, we would cash in on the discounted extra

5. From the Paradise website: 'Bringing a new urban neighbourhood to life in the heart of Birmingham by creating a thriving hub of favourite events, spaces, squares, restaurants and cafés; a place to work and where you can be, and be seen; a place to visit, spend a day with the family and enjoy.' An insight into the aspirations for Paradise. www.paradisebirmingham.co.uk.

value meals that the West Midlands Travel ticket provided. On the steps in front of the library we would eat our McChicken sandwiches (no mayo) sat next to a statue of Thomas Attwood – Birmingham's first MP – who was positioned, like us, slumped as if he too had just taken a break from mooching through the racks of Alive T-Shirts and HMV (fig. 21).

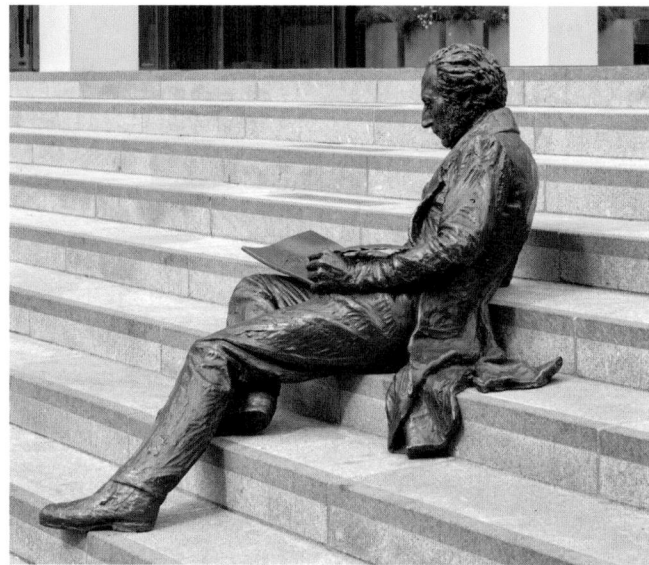

Fig. 21. Thomas Attwood, 2022

Fast forward to spring 2005 I was in the last months of a photography degree and was lucky to have a tutorial with Deb Robinson, Head of Exhibitions at the New Art Gallery Walsall. It was Deb who suggested I get in touch with Pete James, Head of Photography at Birmingham Central Library which I duly did and was invited to come in and meet with him. At this first meeting with Pete I nervously showed him the new work I had just started at the Longbridge factory in Birmingham. The meeting lasted for hours as Pete talked with knowledge and passion about photography, industry, Birmingham and stuff I had never come across before. Lots of it was work I would later encounter and learn from in the library collection. Pete also gave me some money to buy film and pay for developing costs. It was a modest amount, but at that time it represented a belief in me and my work and was everything. The meeting would change my life, and the library – this place that had been a backdrop – became central to my work.[6]

There was no denying that by 2005 the building looked about as bad as it ever had with netting installed across the structure to protect pedestrians from falling concrete. It was severely underfunded, but it did work and was always busy. Perhaps because of this neglect, Pete was able to carve out enough autonomy to grow the photography collection and to showcase it extensively across the world. It became one of the national collections of photography and despite the neglect, the library felt like an essential civic space (figs. 22, 23). Working both formally and informally with Pete I got to continue my education through the incredible collection that he had built.

6. Some things I worked on with Pete James: *Bill Brandt in Bournville* (International Project Space, 2006); *Ming Jue: Photographs of Longbridge and Nanjing* (New Art Gallery Walsall, 2008); *Rea* (a series of postcards to commemorate ten years of Birmingham having a Poet Laureate, 2008); *Birmingham Seen* (Birmingham Museum & Art Gallery, 2009); *Why Contribute to The Spread of Ugliness?* (Ikon Gallery, 2011); *Reference Works* (Library of Birmingham, 2013); *Reference Works China* (Nanjing Library, 2015).

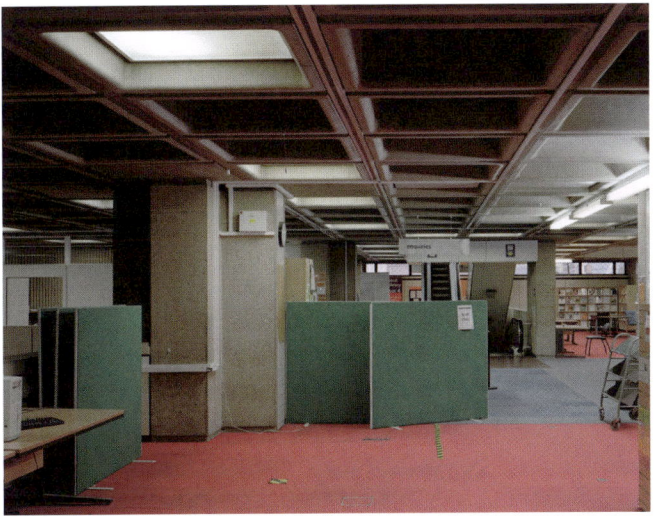

Fig. 22. Birmingham Central Library, 2011

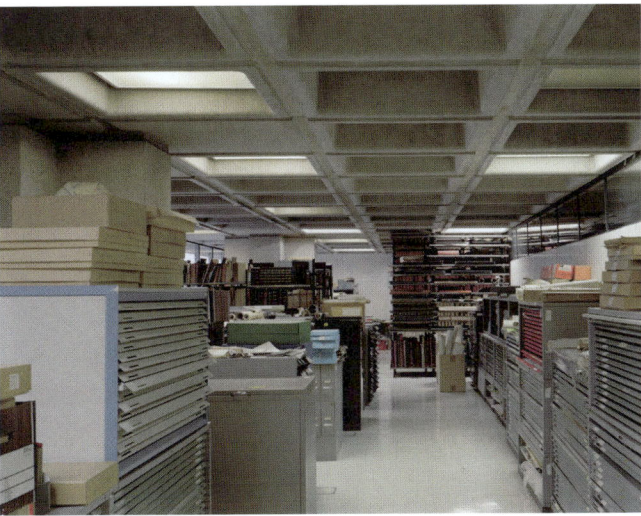

Fig. 23. Birmingham Central Library, 2012

Two hundred metres from the site of the old library is the new one (fig. 24). The Library of Birmingham, which opened in 2013, is also a ziggurat, the second volume of which is clad in gold and is where Birmingham's archives and special collections are stored. There is a photography collection of deep international significance in the library's 'golden box' but you would never know. Access is limited and controlled, and the collection sits in a form of stasis.

The reasons that led to the demolition of Birmingham Central Library are complicated but are mostly about money, although discussions of aesthetics and it being an 'ugly' building have never been far from the conversation. These perceived horrors of its brutalist design have been replaced by a new brutality of underinvestment in a library that is too small to contain the books from the building it replaced. Too expensive to retain the specialist staff who make the library work.

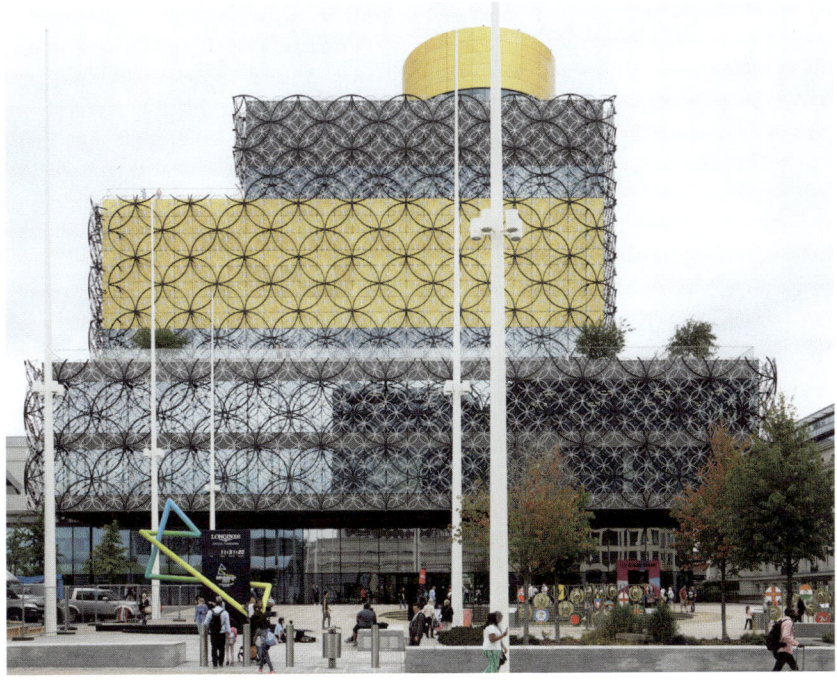

Fig. 24. Library of Birmingham, 2022

Wolverhampton School of Art

From the stalactite concrete forms of Birmingham Central Library to the stalagmite shapes of ariels and phone masts on the roof of the Wolverhampton School of Art, I would like to end this text by briefly focusing on my time studying for my degree in Photography between 2001 and 2005.

I remember starting art school with a clarity borne from the unlikeliness that I would ever be there. I left college at eighteen with a barely respectable BTEC qualification in Media Studies and worked full time in retail for some years before starting my degree a little before my twenty-third birthday. On my first day there I walked apprehensively, passed the big Asda and towards the school from Molineux Street, named after the neighbouring 'Wolves' ground.[7] Molineux Street is a hill, the school sits at the top of it, and appears at the last moment. A bold and heroic structure that is known affectionately as the 'Milk Crate' (fig. 25).

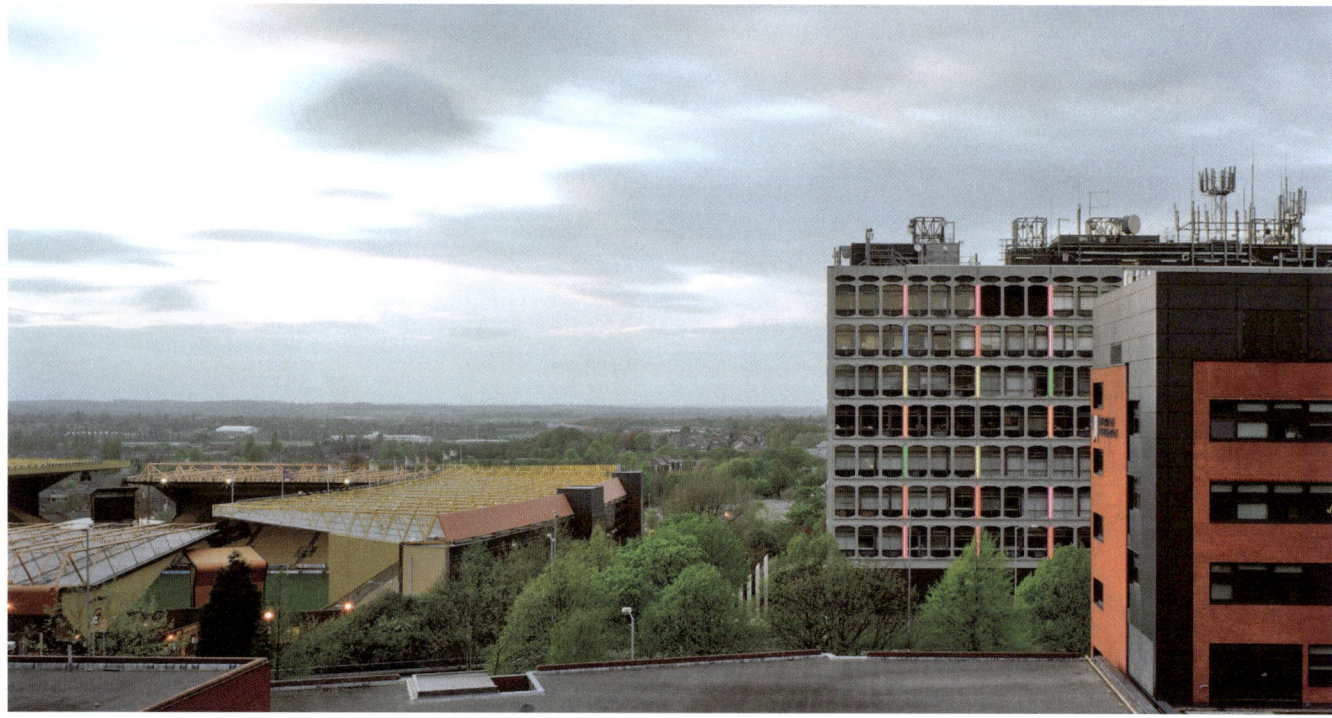

Fig. 25. Milk Crate & Molineux Street, 2005

It felt to me like a special place, and I couldn't have been happier to be there. The drudgery of my years working in shops were not completely behind me. I had to work through the course and beyond, but I was on a different path and in those first days I knew that it was the right one.

7. The Wolverhampton Wanderers football team are known as the Wolves and occasionally we would have lectures in the stadium. One of my most vivid memories was when Rut Blees Luxemburg had to show slides of her nighttime photographs in a corporate hospitality suite that had no blinds on the windows.

Our lectures and tutorials in the second year took place in a much less impressive portacabin that had been dropped in the car park at the back of the school. It was in this shabby, makeshift classroom that a couple of conversations with visiting artists galvanised my approach to my work and my belief in the importance of art schools outside of the recognised centres of the art world.

In the first tutorial, with the photographer Simon Norfolk, I was told that my suburban landscapes were boring (they were boring but that was the point) and I should instead take the same sort of photographs in North Korea. Maybe it's why I'm still looking to get to Pyongyang after all these years, but at the time the suggestion was ludicrous and dispiriting. The second tutorial was with Rut Blees Luxemburg who immediately connected these same landscapes to the much wider context of working-class creativity that is forged in the boredom and frustrations of the suburbs and the estates.

My friends at Wolverhampton were all from working-class backgrounds. From different versions of the 'boot houses'. In the poured concrete and glass of the art school we had found a place where our lives and experiences were not just accommodated but given value as the material that would shape our ideas, our work and our identities. However clichéd it may sound, it was life changing.

As I write this the Wolverhampton School of Art is subject to unprecedented cuts that will see all MA and most BA courses withdrawn. 138 creative courses across the university will be scrapped.

I began this story with a haunting as a form of modernist creation at Andrew Peterson's concrete tower in the New Forest. I end here, in the concrete 'milk crate' of the Wolverhampton School of Art, and an act of wilful cultural vandalism that will haunt generations to come, depriving working-class people of the very opportunities that enabled me to write this text.

Dedicated to Pete James

Contributors

Joshua Comaroff

Joshua Comaroff is Assistant Professor at Yale-NUS College, Singapore. He regularly writes about architecture, urbanism, and politics, with a focus on the subject of haunted landscapes and urban memory in Singapore. Alongside his partner, Ong Ker-Shing, Comaroff oversees Lekker Architects, a multidisciplinary design practice. Together they cowrote *Horror in Architecture* (Oro Editions, 2013).

Comaroff is the recipient of Singapore's President's Design Award, and Harvard's Wheelwright Traveling Fellowship. Prior to completing his PhD in cultural geography at University of California Los Angeles (UCLA) in 2009, Comaroff studied on the Master of Architecture and Master of Landscape Architecture programmes at Harvard University Graduate School of Design working as part of Rem Koolhaas' Harvard Design School Project on the City.

Lucy Mounfield

Lucy Mounfield is Assistant Curator at Ikon. She was awarded her PhD in History of Art from the University of Nottingham in August 2022. Her thesis provides a recontextualisation of the ideological, spatial and material conditions to which women photographers were subject in the United States after the Second World War.

Mounfield held the position of Kluge Fellow in 2020, undertaking a three-month research fellowship at the Library of Congress in Washington D.C. Whilst presenting her research at academic conferences within the UK and abroad, she has also published widely on the history and theory of photography. Her peer-reviewed article – 'Little Gems of Color: Kodak, Camera Design as Fashion, and the Gendering of Photography' – was published in the leading photography journal, *Transbordeur* (Éditions Macula, 2021). Prior to her doctorate, she gained her BA and MA – both in art history – from the University of Birmingham.

Melanie Pocock

Melanie Pocock is Acting Artistic Director, Exhibitions at Ikon, where she leads the gallery's exhibition programme, publications, and, with the wider team, off-site projects. Appointed Curator in 2020, she has curated solo exhibitions by Mit Jai Inn, Krištof Kintera, James T. Hong, Betsy Bradley, Abdulrazaq Awofeso and Yhonnie Scarce. In 2022 she curated *Foreign Exchange*, a reimagining of Birmingham's city-centre statue of Queen Victoria by Guyanese-British artist Hew Locke RA for the Birmingham 2022 Festival.

Pocock previously held curatorial roles at Modern Art Oxford and Art Scene China. From 2014–2019 she was Assistant Curator at the Institute of Contemporary Arts Singapore, where she curated more than 60 exhibitions with Southeast Asian and international artists. As an editor and writer Pocock contributes to exhibition catalogues and artists' monographs, and has written essays, articles and reviews for *ArtAsiaPacific, Art Monthly, Frieze, Kaleidoscope, LEAP, Ocula, Phaidon, The Financial Times, Journal of Curatorial Studies, Di'van / A Journal of Accounts* and *Third Text*. In 2014, she edited and co-wrote the first monograph on Malaysian artist Shooshie Sulaiman, published by Kerber Verlag. A member of the International Association of Art Critics (AICA), she holds an MA with distinction in Curating Contemporary Art, Royal College of Art, London. Pocock's areas of expertise are international contemporary art, the representation of global majority artists in public institutions, and mentorship for artists and emerging curators.

Stuart Whipps

Stuart Whipps is an artist and Senior Lecturer in Fine Art at Birmingham School of Art. Multidisciplinary and interdisciplinary in approach, Whipps works predominantly with photography and video, incorporating text, archival material and found objects into his practice as a way of highlighting stories that have been marginalised in public discourse. His recent film, *Homes for the People* (2020), is the product of his ongoing research into the architectural and social histories of post-war British new towns. Whipps has previously exhibited at Ikon, most notably *Why Contribute to the Spread of Ugliness?* (2011), and his most recent solo exhibition was held at Dundee Contemporary Arts (*If Wishes Were Thrushes, Beggars Would Eat Birds*, 2020). His work has been included in a number of prestigious group exhibitions, including *The Lie of The Land* at MK Gallery, Milton Keynes, UK (2019).

List of Works

Laëtitia Badaut Haussmann

Espace vaincu, Énergie contrôlée (Vanquished space, Controlled energy), 2022, vinyl, paint, screen-print, lacquered and painted wood, carpet, glasses, water, gin, metal, mirror, light, photography, sound, 35 minutes (looped), 6071 × 474 × 268 cm, courtesy of the artist

Simon & Tom Bloor

How to live in a city, 2022, concrete, polystyrene, wood, paint, fixings, 4 parts, each approximately 46 × 180 × 66 cm, courtesy of the artists

Ruth Claxton

Here I am, waiting, 2014–22, plaster, foil, rebar, retroreflective pigment, courtesy of the artist

Shezad Dawood

The Directorate, 2019, tapestry in teak artist's frame, wallpaper, 159 × 116 cm (framed), courtesy of the artist, Jhaveri Contemporary, Mumbai and Timothy Taylor, London

Ola Hassanain

An Early Road Before a Modern One, 2022, beech wood embroidery hoop with black-and-white print on fabric, 150 × 200 cm, courtesy of the artist

The Line That Follows, 2022, 4K video with archival footage montage, 11:52 minutes, courtesy of the artist

Ho Tzu Nyen

The Cloud of Unknowing, 2011, HD video projection, colour, lights, 5:1 sound, synchronised smoke machine, 28:28 minutes, courtesy of the artist and Kiang Malingue Gallery, Hong Kong

Richard Hughes

If Socks Aren't Pulled Up Heads Will Roll, 2009, glass reinforced polyester, iron powder, polyurethane and acrylic, 301 × 62.5 × 28 cm, courtesy of the artist and The Modern Institute / Toby Webster Ltd., Glasgow

Lithobolia Happy Meal, 2022, cast polyester resin and fibreglass, steel rod, acrylic and enamel paint, trampoline parts, 540 × 300 × 254 cm, courtesy of the artist and The Modern Institute / Toby Webster Ltd., Glasgow

Karim Kal

Entourage 1, Lyon / La Guillotière, 2017, inkjet print on baryta paper, laminated on dibond, 150 × 225 cm, courtesy of the artist

Entourage 7, Rillieux-la-pape, 2017, inkjet print on baryta paper, laminated on dibond, 150 × 225 cm, courtesy of the artist

Sol 2, Noisy-le-sec, 2021, inkjet print on baryta paper, laminated on dibond, 120 × 80 cm, courtesy of the artist

Kihlberg & Henry

Slow Violence, 2018–22, HD video, colour, stereo sound, 16:10 minutes, courtesy of the artists

Firenze Lai

Alignment (Pattern), 2017, charcoal on paper, 23.8 × 31.7 cm (image), courtesy of the artist and Vitamin Creative Space

Information Center, 2018, oil on canvas, 110 × 110 cm, private collection

System #1, 2019, oil on canvas, 100 × 80 cm, courtesy of the artist and Vitamin Creative Space

Living and Living Room, 2020, watercolour and ink on paper, 31 × 41 cm (image), private collection

Union, 2022, watercolour and gouache on paper, 31 × 41 cm (image), courtesy of the artist and Vitamin Creative Space

Diego Marcon

Monelle, 2017, 35mm film, CGI animation, colour, sound, 16:02 minutes, courtesy of the artist and Sadie Coles HQ, London

Ismael Monticelli

Spaghetti Junction, 2022, acrylic painted on wall, acrylic paint on canvas, wood papier mâché objects, 637 × 605 cm, courtesy of the artist

NT

BRUTAL, 2022, HD video, stereo, 10:42 minutes, courtesy of the artist

Amba Sayal-Bennett

King Horn, 2019, ink, pro-marker and graphite on paper, 21 × 14.8 cm (image), courtesy of the artist

Soja, 2019, ink, pro-marker and graphite on paper, 21 × 14.8 cm (image), courtesy of the artist

Aperture, 2020, powder coated mild steel, silk, 96 × 22 × 11 cm, courtesy of the artist

Carus, 2020, powder coated mild steel, chemiwood, MDF, resin, velvet, magnets, 133 × 43 × 64 cm, courtesy of the artist

Ex-run, 2020, ink, pro-marker and graphite on paper, 21 × 29.7 cm (image), courtesy of the artist

Fennec, 2020, powder coated mild steel, 33 × 19 × 0.6 cm, courtesy of the artist

Temp, 2020, ink, pro-marker and graphite on paper, 21 × 29.7 cm (image), courtesy of the artist

Daro, 2022, powder coated mild steel, fabric, PLA, 30 × 29 × 4 cm, courtesy of the artist

Ova, 2022, powder coated mild steel, 30 × 47 × 76 cm, courtesy of the artist

Seher Shah

Unit Object (landscape view), 2014, etching, edition of 20, 53 × 62.5 cm (image), courtesy of the artist and Glasgow Print Studio

Unit Object (gate), 2014, etching, edition of 20, 53 × 62.5 cm (image), courtesy of the artist and Glasgow Print Studio

Unit Object (sculpture garden), 2014, etching, edition of 20, 53 × 62.5 cm (image), courtesy of the artist and Glasgow Print Studio

Notes from a City Unknown, 2021, portfolio of 32 screen-prints on paper in custom box, 23 × 30.5 cm (image), courtesy of the artist

Monika Sosnowska

Tower, 2019, steel, paint, 168 × 220 × 215 cm, courtesy of the artist and The Modern Institute / Toby Webster Ltd., Glasgow

Maria Taniguchi

Mies 421, 2010, single-channel video, black and white, sound, 4:06 minutes, courtesy of the artist and carlier | gebauer

Abbas Zahedi

Exit Sign, 2021, customised exit sign, steel chains and eye bolts, 40 × 40 × 10 cm, courtesy of the artist and Belmacz

Artist with Pipe, 2015–22, inkjet print on dibond, with custom aluminium frame, 50 × 65 × 5 cm (framed), courtesy of the artist and Belmacz

Horror in the Modernist Block

Ikon Gallery, Birmingham
25 November 2022 – 1 May 2023

Curated by Melanie Pocock
with Lucy Mounfield

© The authors and Ikon Gallery

All rights reserved. No part of this book may be used or reproduced in any manner without written permission from the publisher, except in the context of reviews. The publisher has made every effort to contact all copyright holders. If proper acknowledgement has not been made, we ask copyright holders to contact the publisher.

ISBN: 978-1-911155-37-9

IKON

Ikon Gallery
1 Oozells Square, Brindleyplace,
Birmingham, B1 2HS, UK
T: +44 (0) 121 248 0708
www.ikon-gallery.org

Ikon Gallery Limited trading as Ikon
Registered charity no: 528892

Editors: Melanie Pocock
and Lucy Mounfield

Texts: Melanie Pocock, Joshua Comaroff, Lucy Mounfield and Stuart Whipps

Design: Fraser Muggeridge studio

Distributed by Cornerhouse Publications
2 Tony Wilson Place
Manchester, M15 4FN, UK
publications@cornerhouse.org
T: +44 (0)161 200 1503
F: +44 (0)161 200 1504

Ikon is supported using public funding by Arts Council England and Birmingham City Council

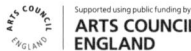 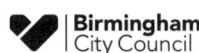

Horror in the Modernist Block is supported by Fluxus Arts Projects, Embassy of the Netherlands, Freelands Foundation, Italian Cultural Institute and The Modern Institute.

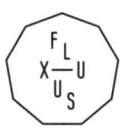 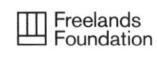
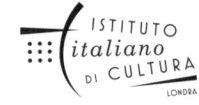
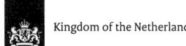

Image Credits

Front cover: Still from Maria Taniguchi's *Mies 421*, 2010, overlaid with a still from Ho Tzu Nyen's *The Cloud of Unknowing*, 2011. Maria Taniguchi: courtesy of the artist and carlier | gebauer. Ho Tzu Nyen: courtesy of the artist and Kiang Malingue Gallery, Hong Kong.

Inside front cover: Detail of Ismael Monticelli's *Spaghetti Junction*, 2022, overlaid with a detail from Laëtitia Badaut Haussmann's *Espace vaincu, Énergie contrôlée* (Vanquished space, Controlled energy), 2022. Ismael Monticelli: courtesy of the artist. Laëtitia Badaut Haussmann: Stuart Whipps.

Inside back cover: Detail of Abbas Zahedi's *Artist with Pipe*, 2015–2022, overlaid with a detail from Monika Sosnowska's *Tower*, 2019. Abbas Zahedi: courtesy of the artist and Belmacz. Monika Sosnowska: Patrick Jameson.

Back cover: Detail from Firenze Lai's *Living and Living Room*, 2020 overlaid with a still from Diego Marcon's *Monelle*, 2017. Diego Marcon: courtesy the artist and Sadie Coles HQ, London. Firenze Lai: courtesy of the artist and Vitamin Creative Space.

Front and back cover varnish: Detail from Seher Shah's *Unit Object (gate)*, 2014. Image courtesy of the artist and published by Glasgow Print Studio.

Introduction: fig. 1: © 1975 by J.G. Ballard. Reprinted by permission of The Random House Group Limited; fig. 2: © Marcus Lontra Costa; fig. 3: © Roberto Conte; fig. 4: Photo credit: Amiraram via Wikimedia Commons; fig. 5: © Shezad Dawood; fig. 6 © Courtesy of Diego Marcon and Sadie Coles HQ, London. Photo credit: Marco Cappelletti with DSL studio; fig. 7: Photo credit: Michael Francis McCarthy via Creative Commons; fig. 8: Photo credit: Pio Abad; fig. 9: Photo via Alamy Stock Photo; fig. 10: © Isabel Infantes / EMPICS Entertainment; fig. 11: © Andy Howlett; fig. 12: © Geoffrey Taunton / Alamy Stock Photo; fig. 13: © Pete Ashton; fig. 14: Out of copyright and in public domain; fig. 15: Photo credit: Tegen Kimbley; fig. 16: Photo credit: Stuart Whipps

Horrid Objectivity: fig. 1: © STUDIOCANAL

Artists: Laëtitia Badaut Haussmann: Stuart Whipps (p. 34); Simon & Tom Bloor: Stuart Whipps (p. 36); Ruth Claxton: Stuart Whipps (p. 39); Shezad Dawood: Sharjah Art Foundation (p. 41); Ola Hassanain: top, Stuart Whipps; bottom, Tegen Kimbley (p. 42); Ho Tzu Nyen: courtesy of the artist and Kiang Malingue Gallery, Hong Kong (p. 45); Richard Hughes: Nils Stærk (p. 47) and Stuart Whipps (p. 48–49); Karim Kal: courtesy of the artist (pp. 51–53); Kihlberg & Henry: courtesy of the artists (p. 55); Firenze Lai: courtesy of the artist and Vitamin Creative Space (pp. 56–59); Diego Marcon: courtesy the artist and Sadie Coles HQ, London (p. 61); Ismael Monticelli: Stuart Whipps (p. 63); NT: Stuart Whipps (p. 65); Amba Sayal-Bennett: courtesy of the artist (pp. 66–69); Seher Shah: courtesy of the artist (p. 71) and courtesy of the artist and published by Glasgow Print Studio (pp. 72–73); Monika Sosnowska: Patrick Jameson (p. 75); Maria Taniguchi: courtesy of the artist and carlier | gebauer (p. 77); Abbas Zahedi: Stuart Whipps (pp. 79–80).

Plum Pudding: Boot House: figs. 1–24: © Stuart Whipps; fig. 25: © John Fallon and Stuart Whipps

Installation Photography: Stuart Whipps (pp. 19–27, 33, 97–112)

Ikon Staff

Rosie Abbey, Ikon Youth Programme Coordinator; Alan Armstrong, Senior Technical Manager; Guy Blundall, Technician; Czarena Brown, Social Media Coordinator; Kerry Hawkes, Learning Manager; Matthew Hogan, Head of Operations; Ian Hyde, Acting Chief Executive Officer; Tegen Kimbley, Communications Assistant; James Latunji-Cockbill, Public Programmes Manager & Producer – Art at HMP Grendon; Megan Linekar-Wright, Front of House & Events Coordinator; Mengxia Liu, Ikon Shop Assistant; Emily Luxford, Digital Manager; Rachel Matthews, PA / Office Manager; Lucy Mounfield, Assistant Curator; Jack Nelson, Digital Producer; Julie Nicholls, Head of Finance; Dharmendra Parmar, Slow Boat Coordinator; Melanie Pocock, Acting Artistic Director, Exhibitions; Richard Short, Facilities Coordinator; Rebecca Small, Head of Communications; Philippa Somervell, Commercial & Visitor Services Manager; Linzi Stauvers, Acting Artistic Director, Education; Katharine Wade, Ikon Shop Assistant

Ikon Board

Lee Brocklehurst, Rachel Chiu, John Claughton, Councillor Jayne Francis, Professor Helen Higson OBE DL (Chair), Soweto Kinch, Harminder Randhawa, Dee Sekar, Nick Smith, Liam Smyth

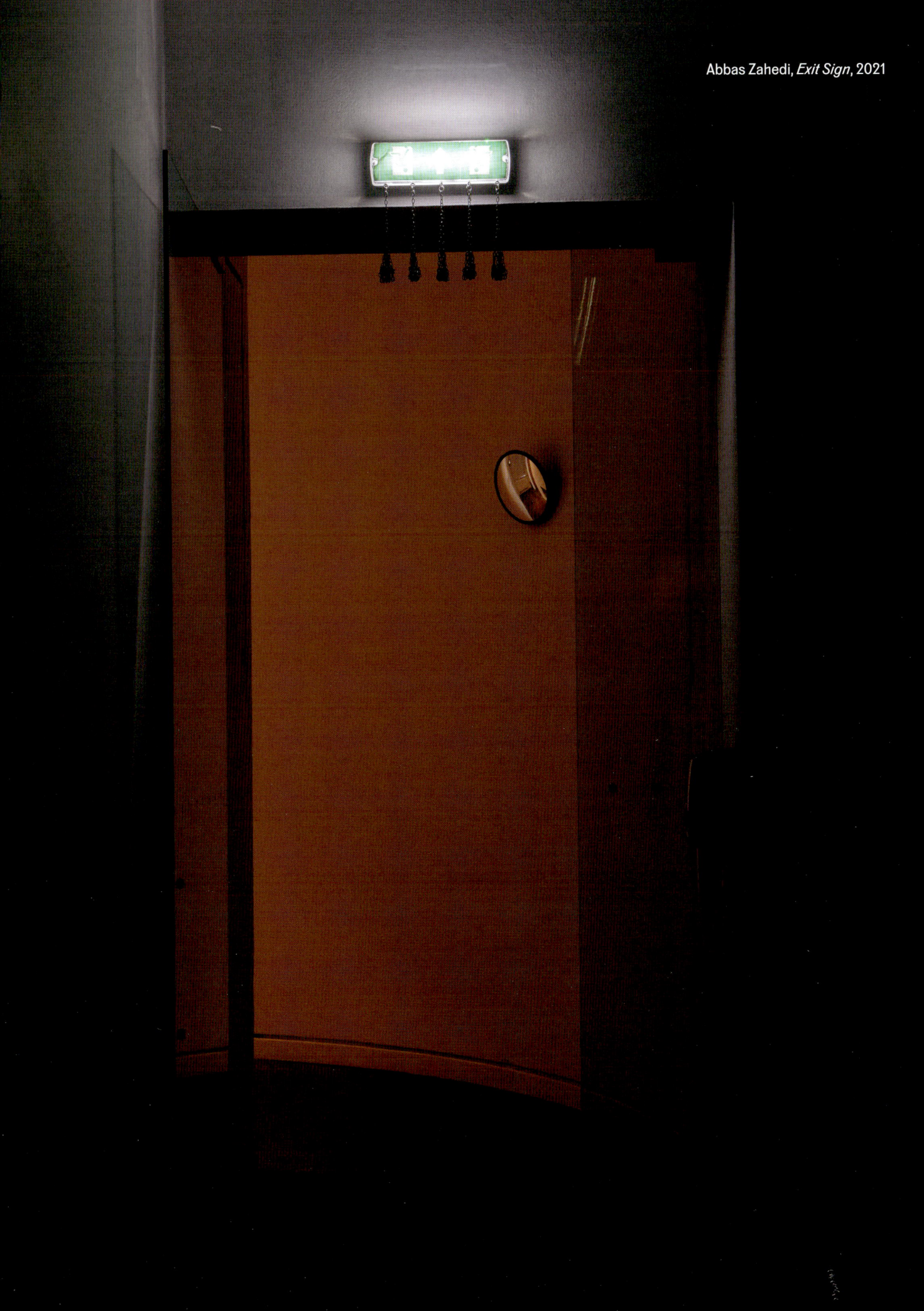

Abbas Zahedi, *Exit Sign*, 2021

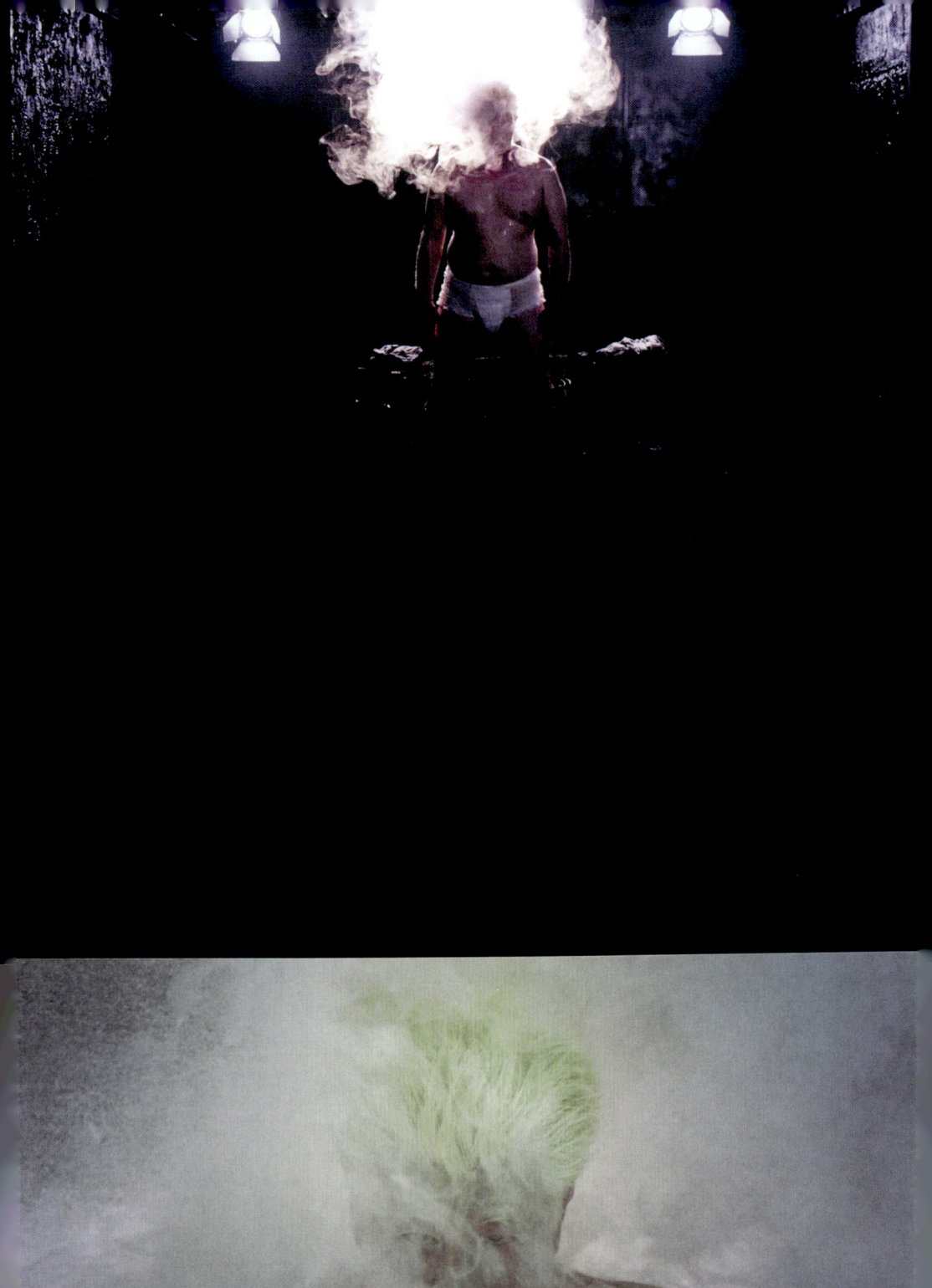

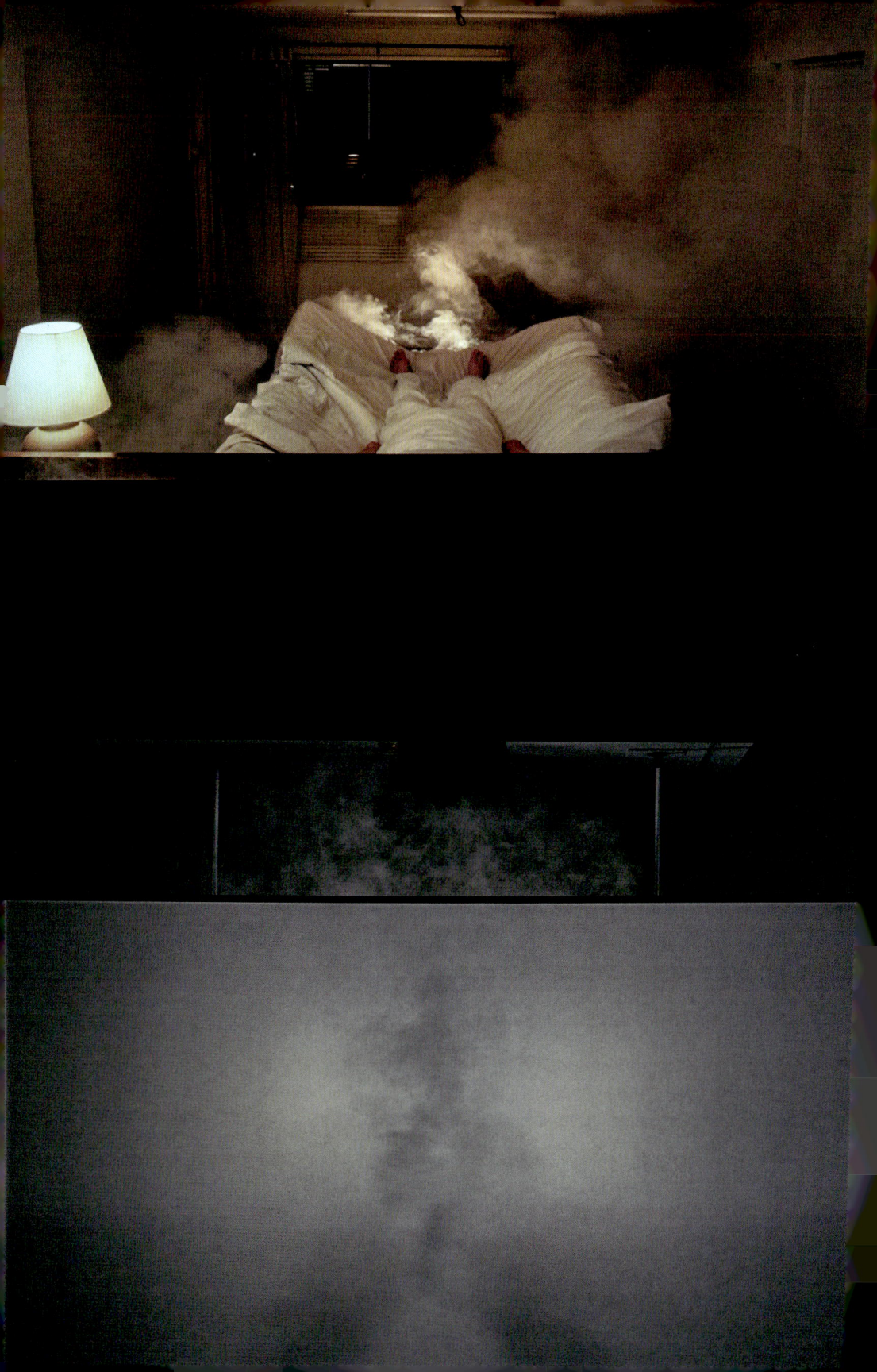

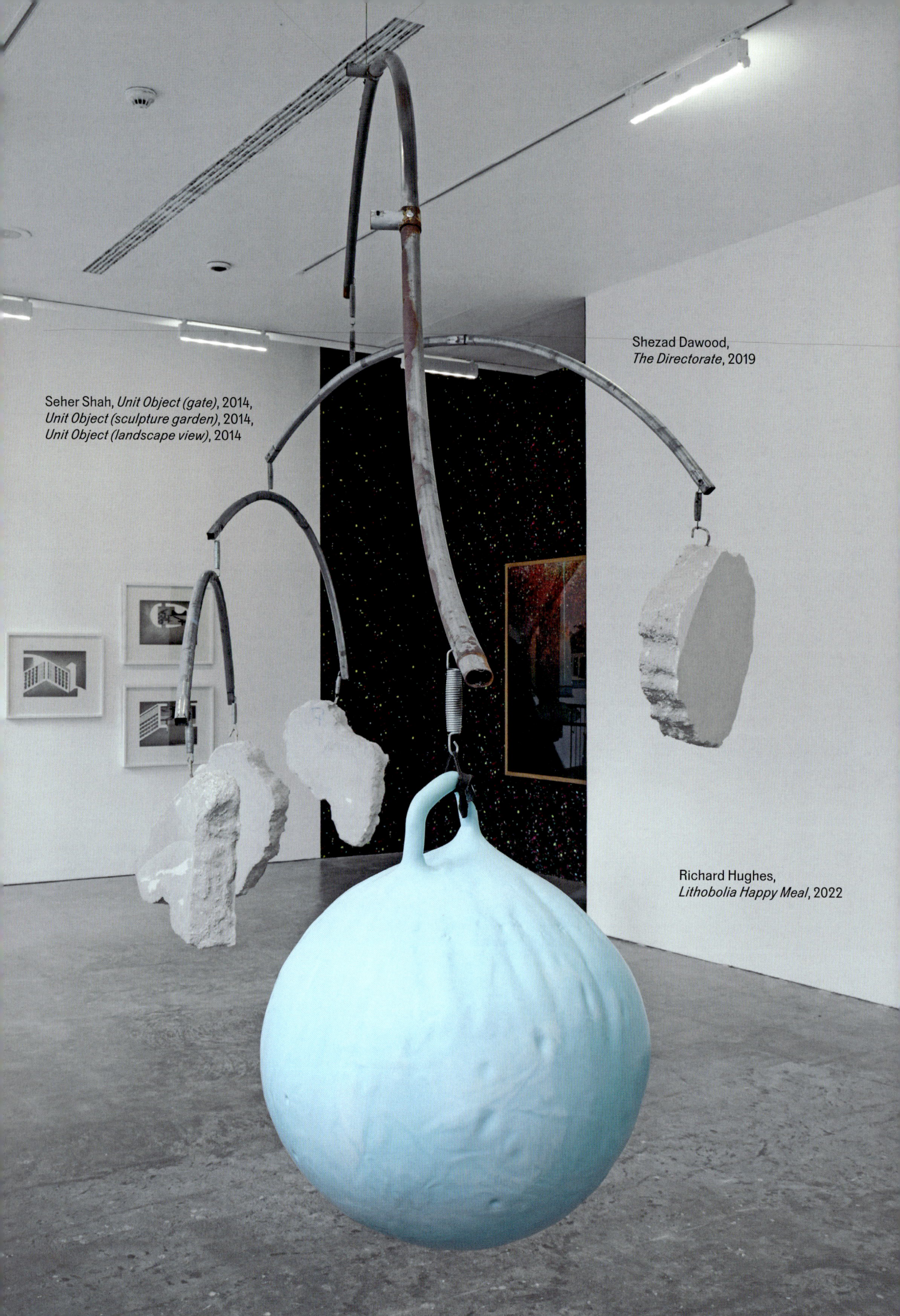

Seher Shah, *Unit Object (gate)*, 2014, *Unit Object (sculpture garden)*, 2014, *Unit Object (landscape view)*, 2014

Shezad Dawood, *The Directorate*, 2019

Richard Hughes, *Lithobolia Happy Meal*, 2022

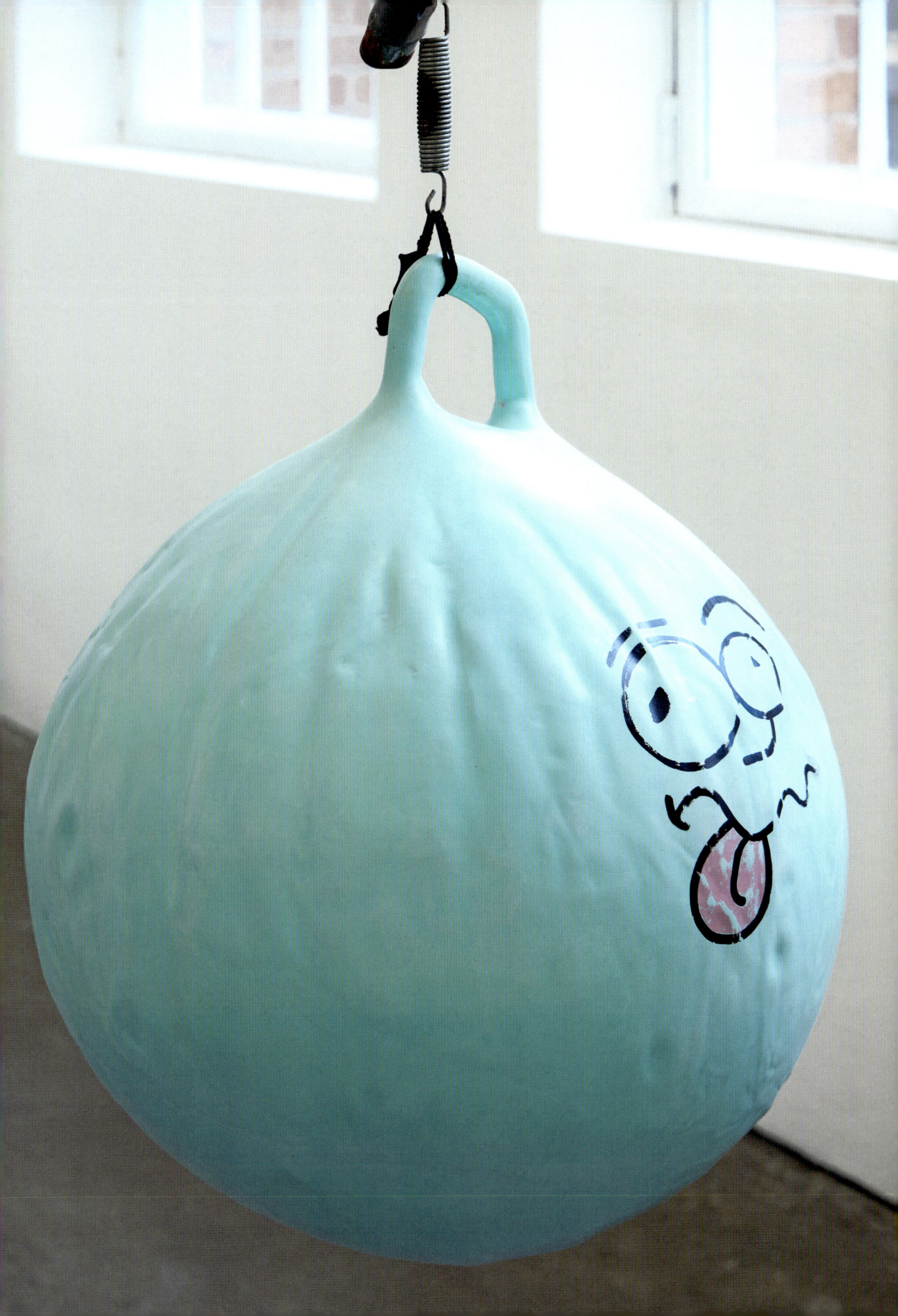

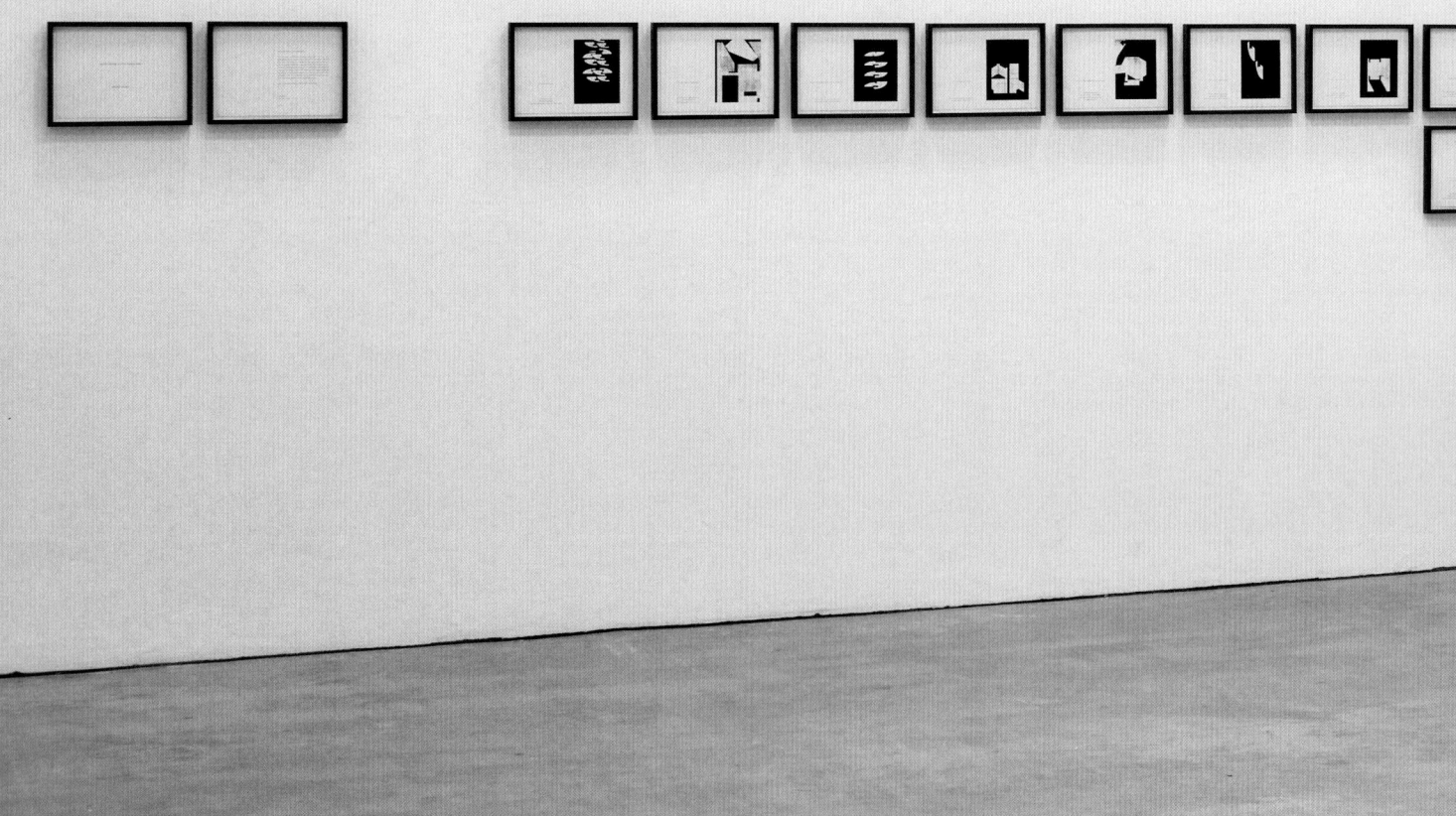

Seher Shah, *Notes from a City Unknown*, 2021

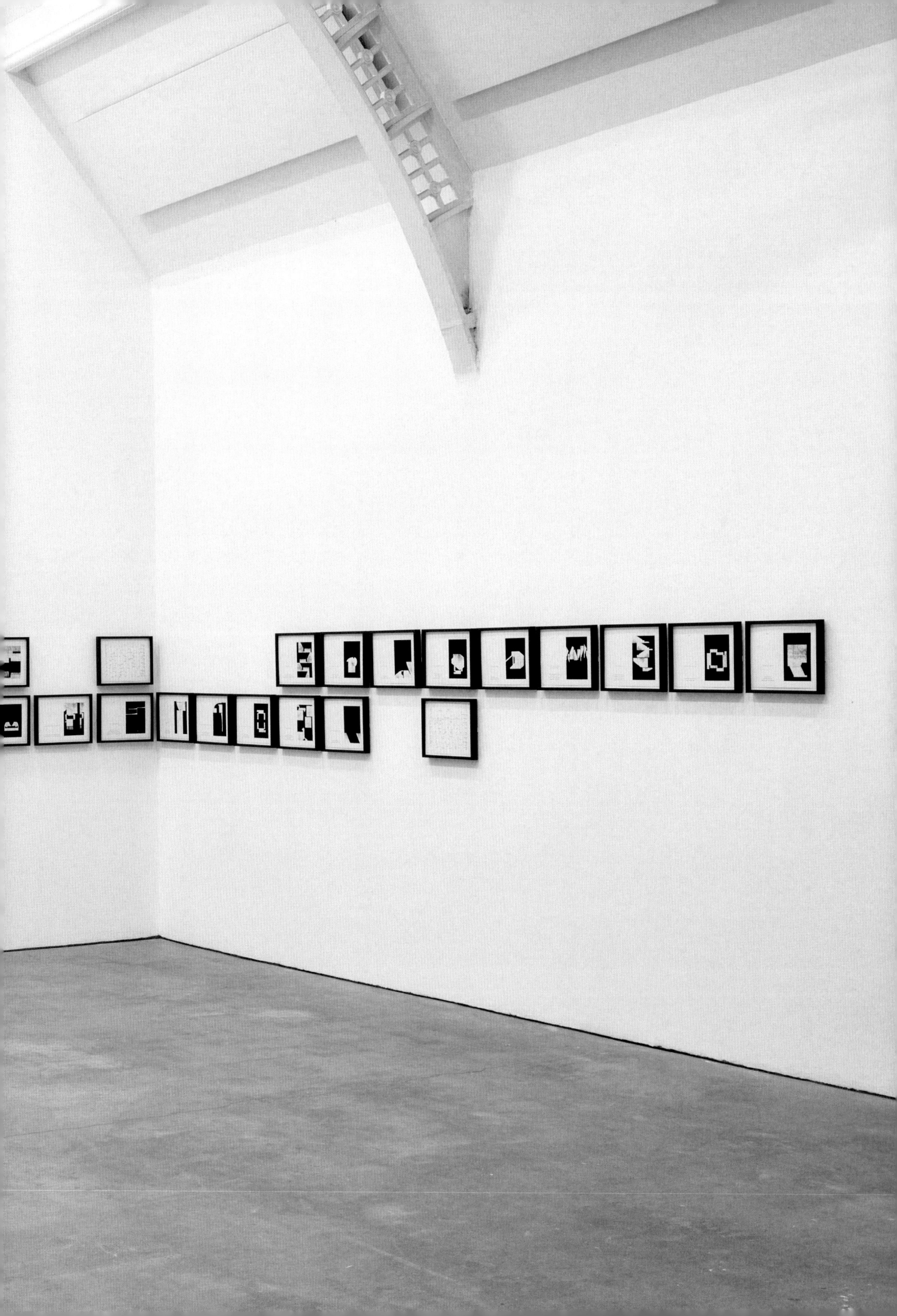

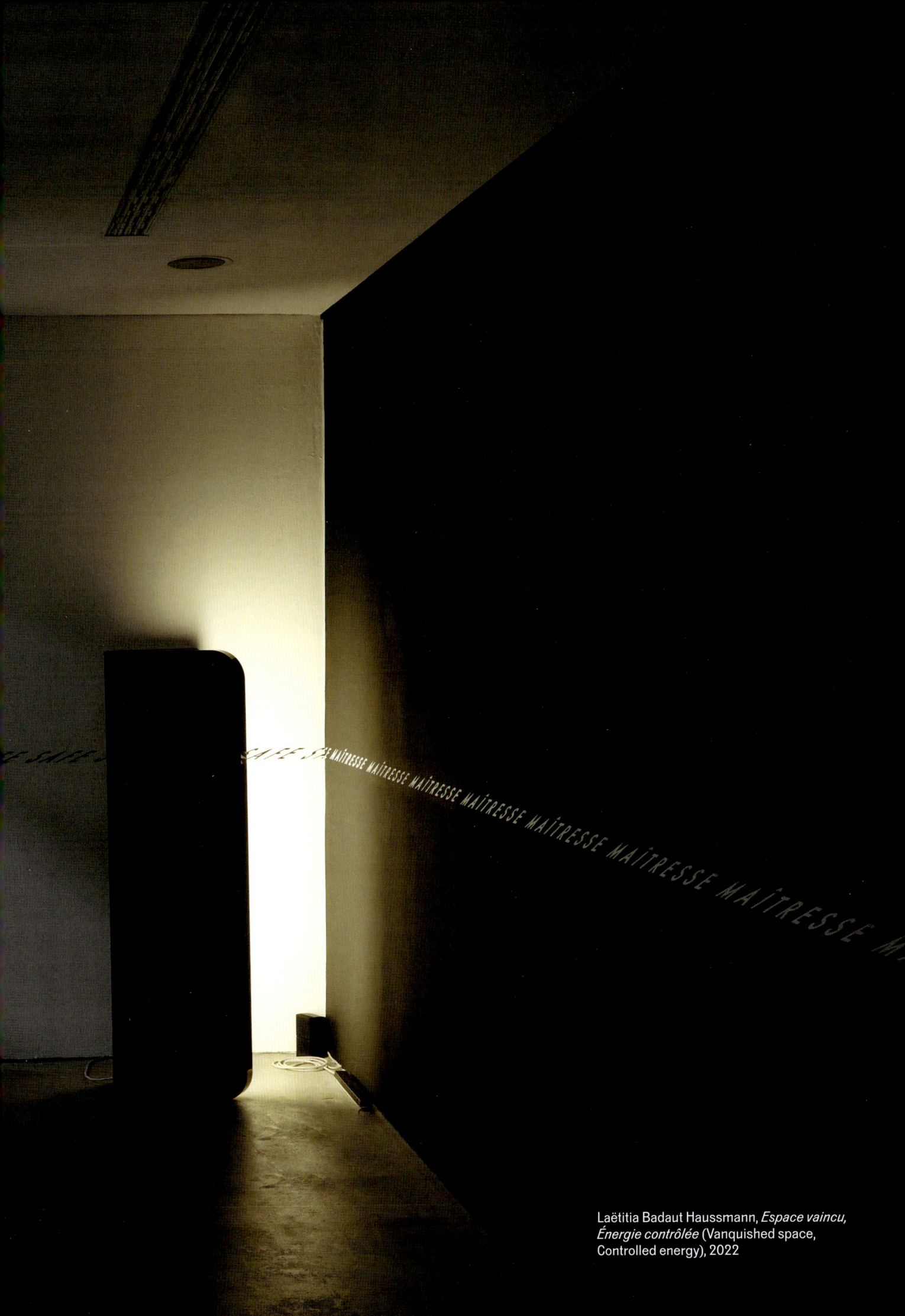

Laëtitia Badaut Haussmann, *Espace vaincu, Énergie contrôlée* (Vanquished space, Controlled energy), 2022

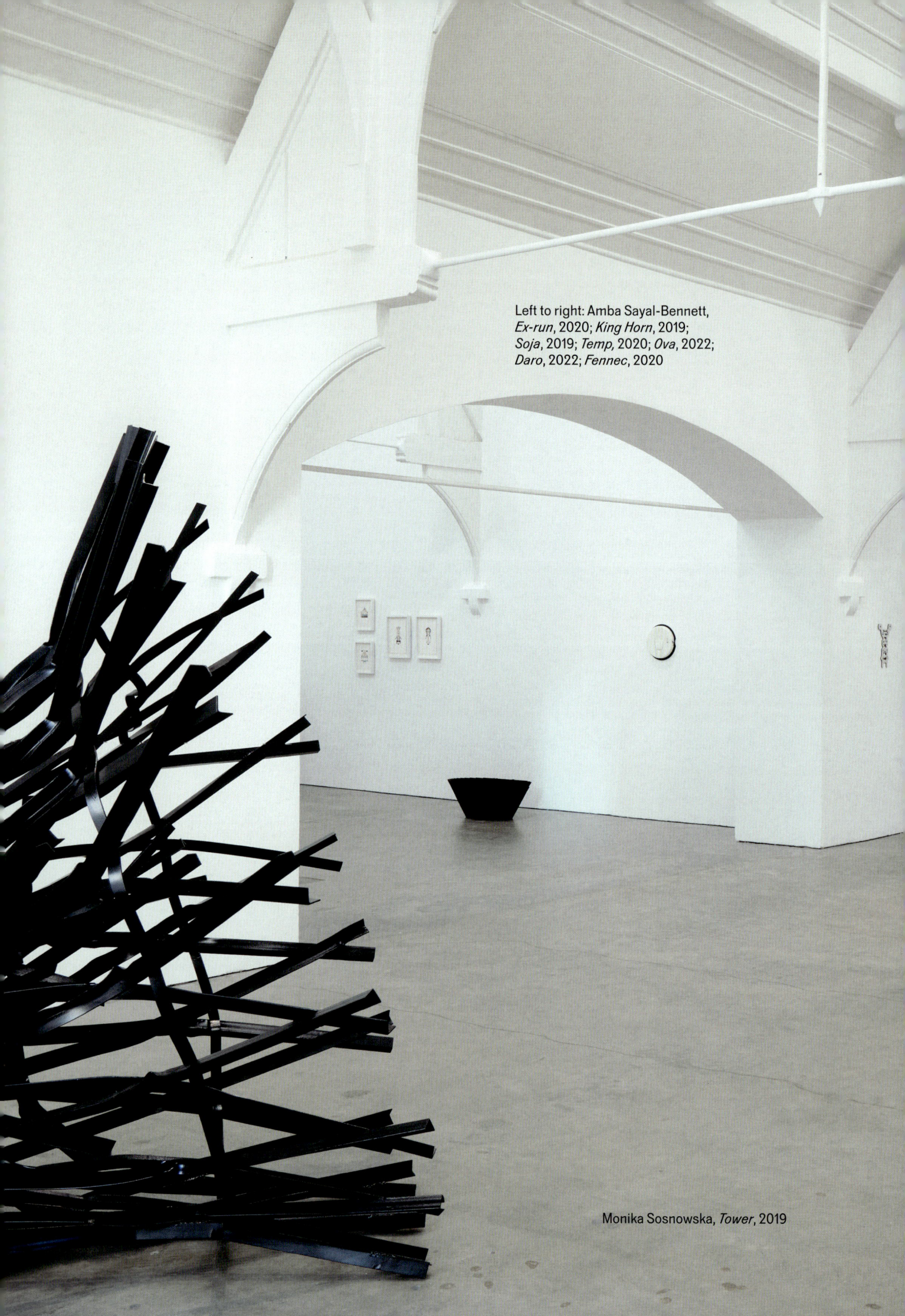

Left to right: Amba Sayal-Bennett, *Ex-run*, 2020; *King Horn*, 2019; *Soja*, 2019; *Temp*, 2020; *Ova*, 2022; *Daro*, 2022; *Fennec*, 2020

Monika Sosnowska, *Tower*, 2019

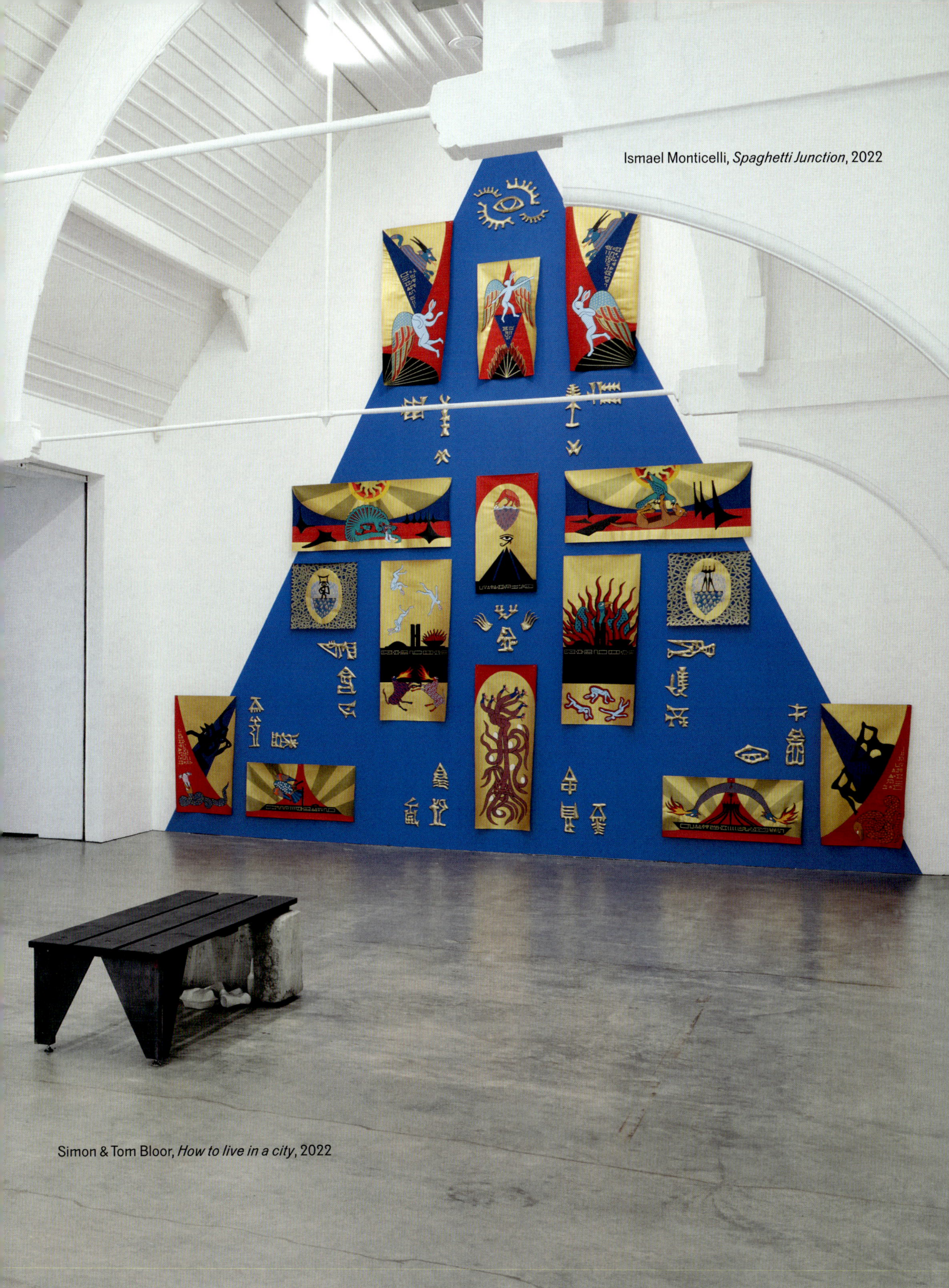

Ismael Monticelli, *Spaghetti Junction*, 2022

Simon & Tom Bloor, *How to live in a city*, 2022

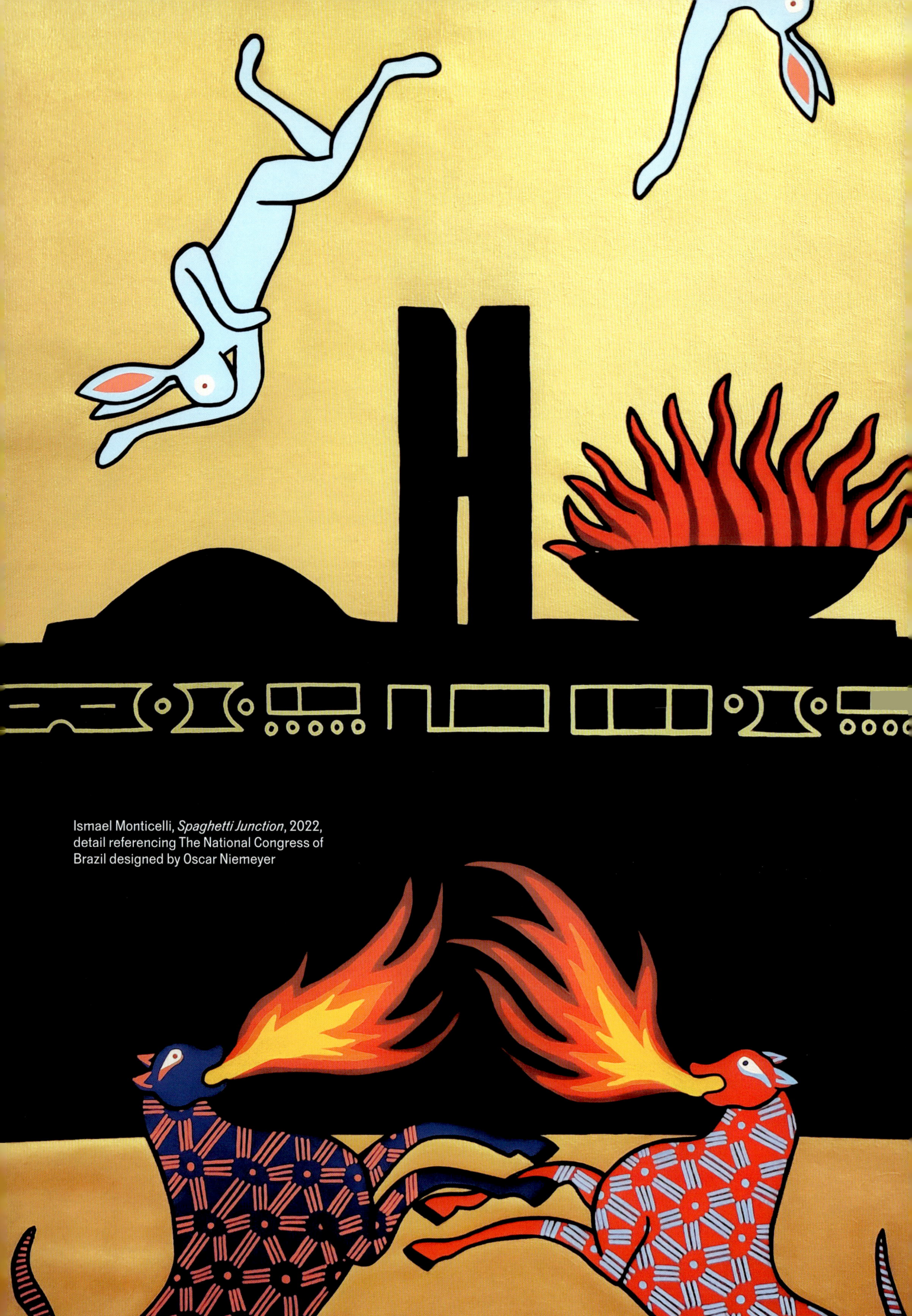

Ismael Monticelli, *Spaghetti Junction*, 2022, detail referencing The National Congress of Brazil designed by Oscar Niemeyer

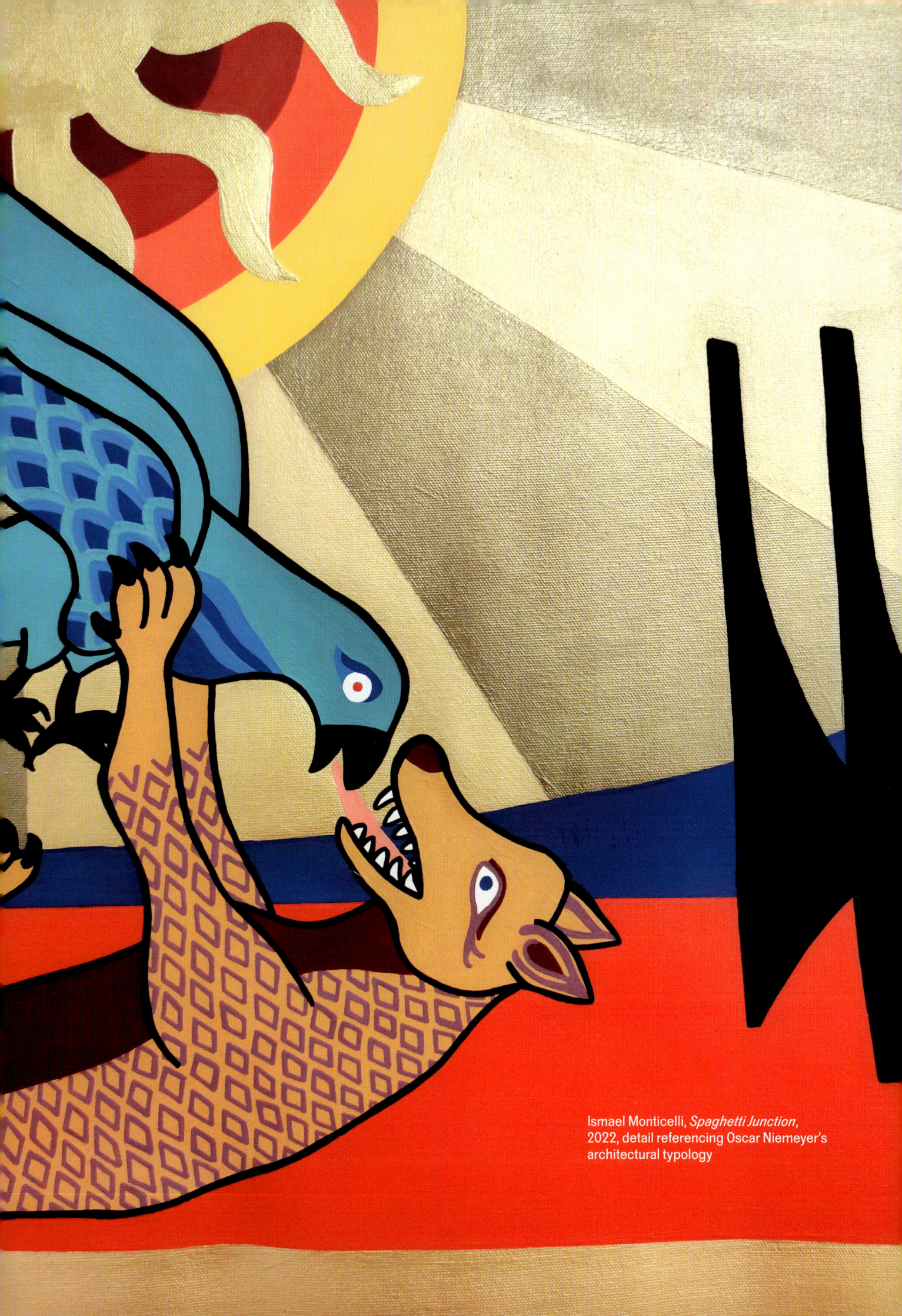

Ismael Monticelli, *Spaghetti Junction*, 2022, detail referencing Oscar Niemeyer's architectural typology

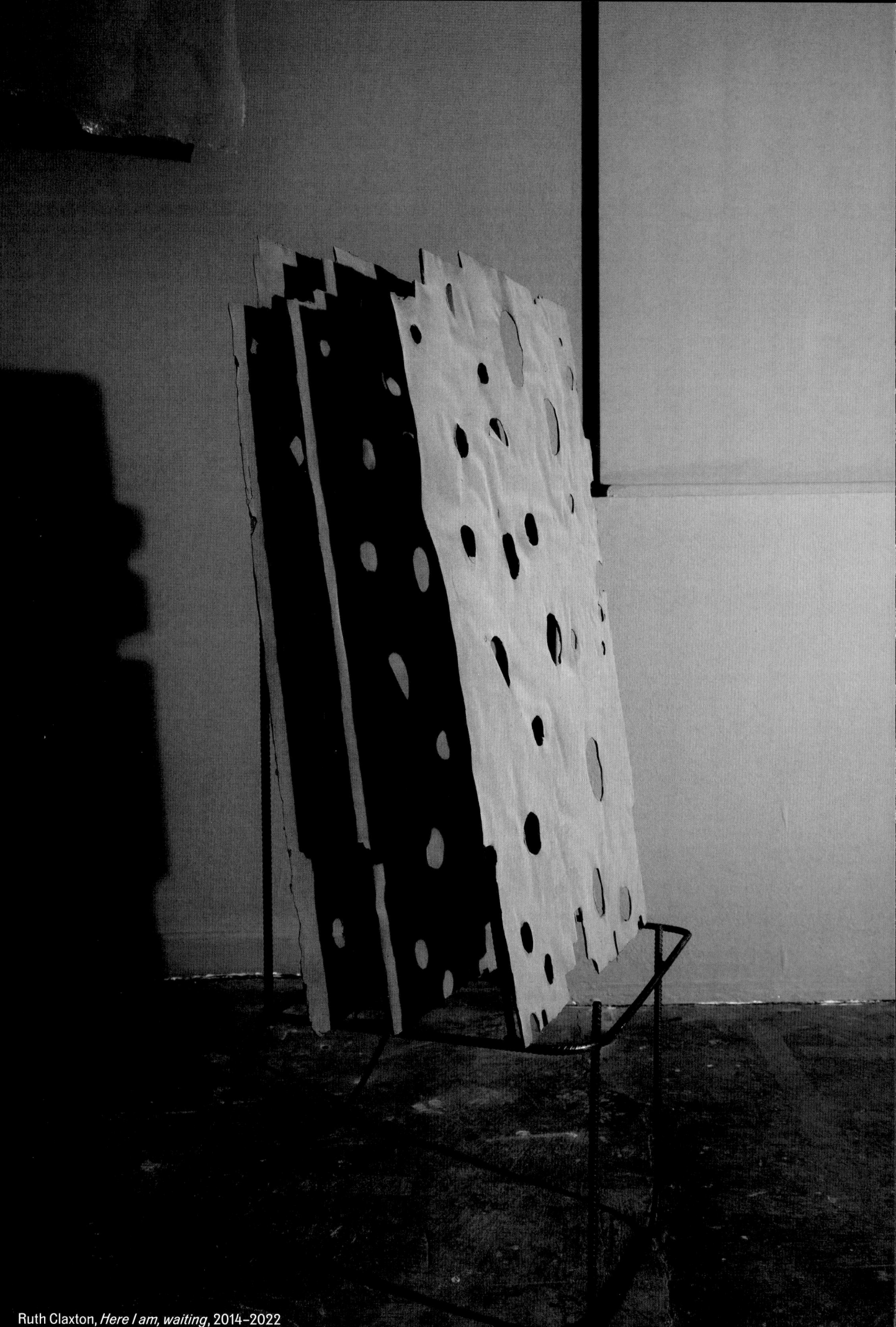
Ruth Claxton, *Here I am, waiting*, 2014–2022

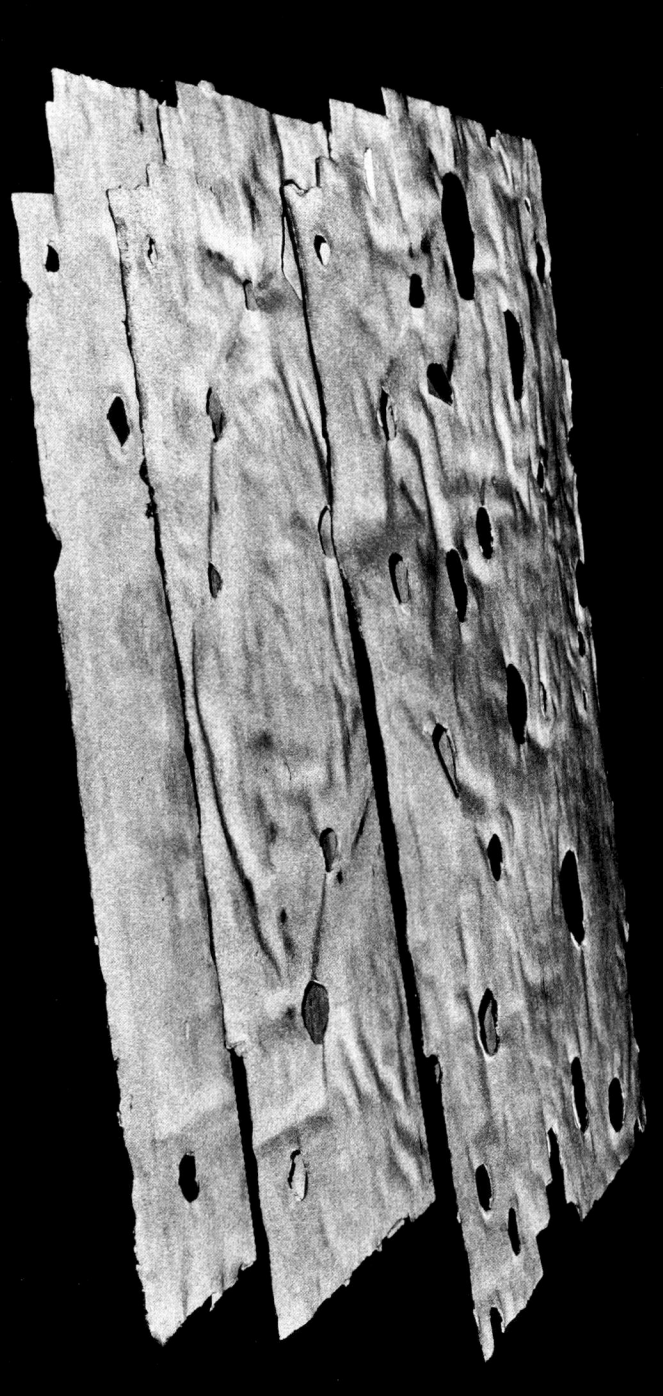

Richard Hughes, *If Socks Aren't Pulled Up Heads Will Roll* (detail), 2009